D0462362

Citizenship rites

(

F

Ilene Rose Feinman

CITIZENSHIP
RITES

FEMINIST SOLDIERS

AND FEMINIST

ANTIMILITARISTS

New York University Press

New York and London

NEW YORK UNIVERSITY PRESS
New York and London

Library of Congress Cataloging-in-Publication Data
Feinman, Ilene Rose, 1959–
Citizenship rites : feminist soldiers and feminist
antimilitarists / Ilene Rose Feinman.
p.   cm.
Includes bibliographical references (p.   ) and index.
ISBN 0-8147-2688-7 (cloth : acid-free paper)
ISBN 0-8147-2689-5 (paper : acid-free paper)
1. United States—Armed Forces—Women. 2. Women soldiers—
United States. 3. Women and the military—United States.
4. Feminism—United States. 5. Militarism—United States.   I. Title
UB418.W65 F45 1999
355'.0082'0973—dc21   99-6784
                                  CIP

New York University Press books are printed on acid-free paper,
and their binding materials are chosen for strength and durability.

Manufactured in the United States of America

10 9 8 7 6 5 4 3 2 1

For Bessie, Rose, Jean, and Judith

women of power who taught me well

For Ben and Maia to a future of justice and peace

CONTENTS

ACKNOWLEDGMENTS

This book is a product of deep and abiding commitments, long engaged conversation, substantial field work and thus community input, and the often seemingly invisible support of my life companions. My first debt and gratitude, then, is really a collective one. Without my community, political and social, this book would not exist. With them, it will hopefully have meaning and contribute to our collective endeavors for justice and peace.

My community began with my parents, Judith and Lewis Feinman, who first taught me to think about justice and peace by living in just ways and yearning for peace, and who always supported me unfailingly through everything I have ever done. I thank them for all that they gave me and continue to give. I hope this book gives some small token in return.

Many people helped to shape my thinking and hone my intuitions for this project. My first debts in this regard are to the activist communities through which I learned my politics. This work grows directly out of my activism for justice and peace. Without a community of activists and a commitment to that yearning there would be no inspiration to engage these questions; therefore, I owe the most to that vision and to the people who keep the magic alive. In the early 1970s I was introduced to antimilitarism in Coconut Grove, Florida by Cindi Carmichael, a schoolmate, Scott Herrick of the American Friends Service Committee, and a wonderful group of activist teenagers. I have had many friends and associations in the Santa Cruz political community where I cut my teeth as an organizer and developed the commitment for this work. I thank them all, but especially Éva Brunner, Dan Hirsch, Deena Hurwitz, Scott Kennedy, Julie Litwin, Peter Lumsdaine, Bill Pratt, T.V. Reed, Adrienne Rich, Ted Rico, Shelly Sella, Noël Sturgeon, Katherine Weddingdress, and all the people who participated with me in nonviolence preparations and actions to bring about a just peace. Especially important to me were the members of the Santa Cruz Nonviolence Preparer's Collective; Stop First Strike Collective; my first affinity group for the Mothers and Others Day Action in 1987 at the Nevada Test Site: "Incite, In Site, Insight"; my Gulf War affinity group, the "Post Mod Squad"—a motley crew of graduate students; Kolaynu/New Jewish Agenda and especially Deena Hurwitz, Adrienne Rich, Shelly Sella, and Julie Litwin—for the work we did in support of the Intifada; and the long-standing community support and inspiration of the Santa Cruz Resource Center for Nonviolence.

Barbara Epstein, Donna Haraway, and Gwendolyn Mink were each crucial field guides for this project's first incarnation as a dissertation, and their theories and methods leave indelible (although mutated) marks on my own.

I have the honor and pleasure of Wendy Mink's continued friendship and have benefited enormously from her intellectual generosity and her voluntary duty as my personal librarian. I am indebted to her sense of humor and her precise, pragmatic, and unflinching dedication to justice; I am grateful for our many political intersections, discussions, jokes, and especially for her early and perhaps too frequent readings of this book in its dissertation pre-life.

I owe so much to Noël Sturgeon, my personal editor and long-time affinite, who read and commented on too many versions, coached me through the publication process, and aided and abetted my field work in feminist antimilitarism. Which is more fun: organizing an action, or writing a book? Well, writing a book gives you a sense of deep satisfaction, after years of anxiety and many unnecessary gray hairs. Participating in organizing an action brings a level of "public happiness" unsurpassed (and its own gray hairs); democratic process is my greatest love. I suppose, after all, that both are indispensable parts of my work. And both are more like dancing in the revolution when we are privileged to bring them together. Thankfully, Noël and I have been able to share some of that dance.

Carol Cohn has been my long-distance writing buddy extraordinaire, with whom I gradually came to trust collaboration when, as she put it, our projects are barely six degrees apart. Our careful negotiation of the boundaries of each other's work still leaves me thinking that her thoughts are fully entangled with mine. My work is all the better for her generous critical eye and ear. Her clear thinking is fully woven into chapter 1. And our discussions there, on the edges of what a feminist take on the military ought to be, have been pleasurable and constitutive of my thinking.

Francine D'Amico began as my anonymous reader and then willingly reread the manuscript with detailed and enthusiastic feedback. Many refinements of my account are indebted to her commentary. Her depth of engagement reaffirmed the possibilities of this project.

I am also indebted to Cynthia Enloe for her critical trailblazing work of thinking through the connections between feminism and militarism in the context of international relations. Testament to Enloe's importance in this field is the number of books on women and the military and militarism that cite her work. When I first read *Bananas, Beaches and Bases*, I was awestruck and thought I would like to write a book someday that was in conversation with her project. She has set the tone and paved the way for this work. I learned a great deal through her writing, and she generously volunteered to read the manuscript, offering encouragement and valuable suggestions. And so, I am honored to be in conversation with her after all!

Special thanks go to Jennifer Hammer for following me around until I agreed to send in a book proposal, for her belief that the project was important, for her professionalism, and sense of humor as we revised each other's revisions of the revisions. She has handled the book and my persistent novice questions with grace and wit. Despina Gimbel, as managing editor, guided me and the book through publication with speed and grace. Special thanks to Ann Hirst, Andrew Katz, and Andy Fotopoulos for copyediting the manuscript.

My work is more urgent because of the responsibility I assumed in having two children; it has also been the greater challenge. The pleasures of growing with Ben and Maia are immeasurable. My partner, Kenny Welcher, in his gleeful detachment from the academy has been a wonder of grounding support for me, the co-parent of my dreams, and has made this work better by always insisting that it be readable by the uninitiated. Indeed, he read and read and read, and kept coaxing the text back to a common language. Of course, I do not always understand the inner workings of community development lending practices, or of softball season, but we manage to bridge the jargon gaps with our shared political commitments, and the pleasures of our wacky domesticity.

Many other friends and family have supported and encouraged me and kept my humo(u)rs in balance when this project threatened to overwhelm. I especially want to thank Cathy Feinman, Arthur and Diane Welcher, Lisa Welcher, Jon Welcher, Gale Frances, Michele Indira Garns, Radha Mallery, Kathy Pouls, and T.V. Reed. T.V. willingly and enthusiastically answered all my questions about professional life in the academy . . . and apparently is very good at being a juggler and a believer, because his interpretations encouraged me to stay! Jyoti Patricia Florio Prather has been my second self and soul mate for so long that I am sure my work and my life perspective are at least half hers. My brother, Mike Feinman, has been my cheerleader from day one. He has always seen my work as important and will not let me forget it. Baba Hari Dass taught to me how to breathe and the seed of that teaching has balanced my work. Claire Delano helped me to make sense, or at least make lemonade, of a series of teachable moments so that I could reclaim my voice in this work. Jenny Kreugman, long worshiped high school English teacher, encouraged me to write and believed in my intelligence: I promised her a book someday.

I received material support in many forms and from many places. Billie Harris, Sheila Peuse, and Alexandra Armstrong of the History of Consciousness Board office staff each helped me through the administrative labyrinth during the graduate school phase of this project. Their generosity, good humor, excellent office snacks (chocolate), and willingness to laugh were above and beyond the call of duty. I have received financial support from numerous places—a key component of being able to accomplish writing work. Judith Feinman and Lewis Feinman provided for me at many crucial moments. The University of California at Santa Cruz' financial aid programs and staff were crucial to my survival as a single parent undergraduate. Barbara Epstein funded me through several university research grants. The Regents Fellowship funded me through the University of California and the History of Consciousness Board provided me fellowship money. The rest of my graduate career was financed by my labor as a teaching assistant/graduate student employee: a category that continues to defy jurisprudence.

My experience in graduate school linked me with colleagues who contributed to my understandings as a scholar. Among those colleagues were: Bettina Aptheker, Megan Boler, Wendy Brown, Margaret Daniel,

Acknowledgments

Marcy Darnovsky, Giovanna Di Chiro, Joe Dumit, Julia Earhart, Yvonne Keller, Lorraine Kenny, Katie King, Nanci Luna Jimenez, Tim Murphy, Maria Ochoa, Ekua Omosupe, Will Roscoe, Chela Sandoval, Vicki Smith, and Marita Sturken. In the UCSC government document library, Jan Becking and Joanne Nelson, reference specialists, helped me locate and relocate government documents, make sense of the government numbering system, and track hearings, through the shelves and on the net.

Linda Grant De Pauw deserves much thanks for her magical labor of assembling a community of scholars and soldiers to study women in the military together, through the Minerva Center, and for her deft handling of flames, fallouts, and feminist antimilitarists on the listserv. I have benefited greatly from her resources, including the fact that my editor found me through the conversations I was having on the Minerva listserv!

My colleagues at California State University Monterey Bay demonstrate daily the possibilities of multicultural interdisciplinary work and collegial support: Rina Benmayor, Diana Garcia, Alberto Ledesma, Debian Marty, Cecilia O'Leary, Josina Makau, Amalia Mesa-Baines, Frances Payne Adler, Raul Reis, Gerald Shenk, David Takacs, and Qun Wang. Thank you.

Finally, I dedicate this book to all the border-crossing activist scholars that ever were and will be. This book would not exist without your presence and the promise of finding our voices, validating our collaborations, and attaining justice and peace.

INTRODUCTION

Two very different approaches to women in the military have developed from common roots in the second-wave women's movements. While each is invested in women's empowerment, and each uses the tools of the new discourses and policies of equal rights, their respective analyses of what that empowerment should look like are fundamentally different. Feminist antimilitarists oppose the military for its use of violent diplomacy, and associate that violence precisely with the military's culture of virulent masculinism. Their analyses demonstrate that the social, political, and economic apparatuses shaping masculinist militarism depend on the oppression of women. Feminist antimilitarists use a variety of theoretical and activist tools to explain military culture as opposite to women's culture and feminist goals, and moreover, they judge the military and militarism as impediments to justice and peace. On the other hand, women interested in joining the military, scholars recovering histories of women in the military, and supporting policies to expand women's professional roles in the military, a cluster of approaches that I call feminist egalitarian militarists, insist that it is women's right and even responsibility to perform martial service, because the military is the *sine qua non* of full citizenship and thus, equality. Feminist egalitarian militarists use equal rights discourse and policies to insist that women play a full and unimpeded role in the military.

These two perspectives, for and against the military on seemingly feminist terms, seek to expand the quality of women's citizenship; however, they define that citizenship in markedly different ways. These two perspectives on women and citizenship are generally not engaged with one another. Events in the last ten years, and especially since the Persian Gulf War, have pushed them together, or at least side by side.

Feminist egalitarian militarists fought for women combatants and continue to push for women's complete access to all Military Occupational Specialties (MOSs). They argue that women and men should be

assigned jobs for which they are qualified based on the job's requirements and not on generalizations about gender. Access to these MOSs
on par with men, they argue, present women citizens with the full range
of access to first class citizenship and career opportunities. Feminist
analyses in liberal feminist terms are needed to understand the stakes of
women in combat, of sexual harassment of women in the military, of lesbian and gay culture and policy in the military, and of military culture itself. Analyses of women's histories in the military and current policy
struggles over how women are to be integrated into all ranks are needed
to remind us that women are interested in joining for a complex of reasons. Women are participating directly in the transformation of military
culture from its masculinism. Feminist egalitarian militarists critically remind us that women have been working inside military ranks, incognito
or not, past and present, without being recipients of the benefits and
honors of a formal recognition of their soldiering as heroines and citizens.

Feminist antimilitarist analyses teach us that the military is a deeply
masculinist institution. Feminist antimilitarist analyses suggest that motivations for war are lodged in the traditional modalities of economic and
political domination and sexual conquest, and the masculinist dynamic
of militarist discourse. Feminist antimilitarist analyses and activisms uncover the violence of military diplomacy as it affects civilians, as it shapes
the sex-workplace around military bases, and as it destroys communities
and ecosystems. Feminist antimilitarism connects peace activism more
precisely to justice struggles and, last but in no way least, feminist antimilitarist direct action has also influenced policy via participation in
broad public opposition to the nuclear industries and to war. This connection is evident in public demonstrations from the Women's Pentagon
Actions (1980, 1981), the Mothers and Others Day Action (1987), and
the feminist antimilitarist involvements in the subsequent actions of the
1980s and early 1990s connecting environmental justice, antimilitarism,
and ecofeminist concerns.

These two broad analytical frames need to be brought together to create a dialog about women in the military that simultaneously acknowl-
edges the horrors of militarism and the achievements, interests, and
longings of women soldiers. Without figuring a way to discuss the various feminist and peace-oriented interests in masculinist militarism be-

tween feminist antimilitarists and feminist egalitarian militarists, we leave the field open to the antifeminist militarists, like Elaine Donnelly of the Center for Military Readiness, who would keep the military as a place where men alone can exercise the privilege and terrible responsibility to wage wars. These antifeminist militarists suggest that feminists (they call all feminists "radical feminists") are destroying the armed forces. Their work, since Phyllis Schlafly's infamously successful pitch about the spectre of co-ed bathrooms and women in combat as the core of the Equal Rights Amendment, has been to promote the masculinist version of the military and the presumption that women do not have what it takes and men don't want them to. We need a strong feminist analysis of militarism, wedded to an understanding of the legacy of women's soldiering and the history of opposition to women as soldiers. Without this analysis it will be, as I argue elsewhere,[1] difficult to respond to and account for women soldiers from a feminist antimilitarist perspective.

This book works to investigate women's entry to the military through an analysis of the discourse of citizenship that runs through both feminist antimilitarist and feminist egalitarian militarist work. I approach the questions from a feminist antimilitarist standpoint, with the aim of bringing a deeper understanding of women's presence in the military to feminist antimilitarists. In other words, although my investments undergirding this project are antimilitarist, I take women's entry to the military seriously. I listen to the ways that military women talk about themselves, and I listen to the ways that the elite and public political cultures are talking about them. I suggest ways that a feminist antimilitarist standpoint might engage the fundamental commonality of expanding women's citizenship and contribute to our understanding of what it means for women to have access to the military at this particular historic moment. Both perspectives stand to gain sophistication from one another's attention to the components of debate around women's citizenship and thus to work toward refinement of the notion of citizenship toward peace and justice combined.

The central discourse of military recruitment is embodied in the Army slogan, "be all that you can be," and laden with the promise of achieving a valorous martial citizenship. My study examines several episodes of late twentieth-century United States political history where the elaboration of women's citizenship and the articulation of a proper role for women as martial citizens took center stage. I ask what was at stake for various racial/ethnic women in the debates about women soldiers, women's citizenship, feminist antimilitarism, and the culture of patriarchal militarism.

This approach situates the debates over military women in the context of the sea change in United States social and economic politics since the middle 1970s and through the debates and representations of these issues up through the present. The book looks from the pivotal moment of the ERA debates about women and the draft to the most recent representation of a military woman in film: *G.I. Jane.* The analysis I present centers on two major transitions for women and women soldiers: the 1970s and 1980s Equal Rights Amendment struggles and the 1990–91 Persian Gulf War. These two periods saw the development of new policies on the parameters of women's martial service. They are also interesting to me because of the interactions of national and global political-economic processes, particularly the rise of second wave feminisms, the transformation of the U.S. political economy, and the related transformation of the United States military.

This book addresses the history and politics of women's inclusion to the military, then, from a feminist antimilitarist perspective. This kind of crossreading to understand the common ground of citizenship discourse has not been done before. A great deal of writing on women in, or and, the military has been generated over the last ten years, and especially since the Persian Gulf War. A variety of approaches to the topic of women in the military are developing, both in academe and in popular scholarship. These approaches include the scholarship that uncovers women's histories of, and types of, participation in military enterprises;[2] the antimilitarist analyses of the intransigent masculinism of the military;[3] and the approach that argues that the military has submerged its dependence on women's racially and ethnically stratified work in support of the military (thus not necessarily as soldiers)[4] while being nonetheless wedded to women's various labors that operate to make masculinist military life appear as an independent and valorous performance. Cynthia Enloe's work in this area informs mine quite thoroughly. I have learned from her methods of studying international militarized and racialized gender relations and applied them to my United States–based study.

Each of these literatures develops positions about the degree to which women's inclusion as fully vested soldiers will or will not transform the military. These literatures, and their popular interest, have been expanding since the Persian Gulf War brought broader attention to military women in the early 1990s. Policy changes that allow women access to combat MOSs; the military academy and boot camp sexual harassment cases emerging in the post–Gulf War period; and the successful court challenges to the old publicly funded male-only militia colleges in the South have each been part of this shift in discourse about women, the military, and equality. We need analyses that connect the general push for women's inclusion in the forces with a more broadly cast analysis of the *meaning* of women's inclusion when considered in terms of the discourses on citizenship and the transformations of social and political economy characteristic of late modernity. We must pay attention to the construction of new frameworks for women's citizenship, anticipate progress and regress in transforming masculinist militarism, and still insist that citizenship itself be freed from its entwining with martial service.

This project, thus, updates the history of women's inclusion in the military, including public representations of that history, but brings to bear several different perspectives on the meaning of that history. I argue that the positions for women's further inclusion in the military and the positions for feminist antimilitarism do not speak to one another. I work to generate a reading of one through the other. I take women soldiers' self-depictions seriously and understand them through their desire for full citizenship and for career advancement. I read for the ways that gender is defined and redefined in the configuring of a co-ed military that still refuses to allow open homosexuality.

I find the military a critical site for analysis because of the ways that it reflects and contributes to the construction of the social, legal, and political configurations of race/ethnicity, gender, sexuality, and class in the United States. More precisely, militarism is an infusion of both the institutionalized and cultural materials of that construction. At this moment, in the late 1990s, the United States military seems to be receding in importance with reorganizations, base closures, and more frequent military action through the auspices of the United Nations. This change is occurring simultaneously with the uncovering of women's military histories and women's inclusion in all but the most direct combat jobs. What this means for the future of women in the forces is yet unknown. Conversations about women in the military need to be wrested from their round robin about what women can do (with their bodies or their psyches), and grounded in conversations about the role of martial service in citizenship and the rights and responsibilities of women as citizens.

My methodological approach is interdisciplinary. I combine historiography, sociology, ethnography, and political theories of both the state and social movements to interpret these events. This book's chapter layout offers both a historical reading of women's entry to the armed forces since the advent of the All Volunteer Forces in 1973, and a reading of the social and political debates over how, why, and where women would be allowed to participate in the forces. I read for feminist antimilitarists' influence on those debates and interpret women in the military from an engaged feminist antimilitarist standpoint. The book utilizes a mix of sources looking for the elaborations and articulations that illuminate the debate about women's (militarized) citizenship: congressional transcripts and congressional commission reports; histories of women in the forces; Department of Defense-sponsored think tank studies; histories of martial citizenship and reliance on martial valor, including women's martial citizenship; literature (historical and political) on the rise and fall of the ERA; political-economic studies of the late twentieth century; feminist antimilitarist demonstrations and writings; gender and international relations literatures; popular film representations since the 1970s of women in military service; and my own experience and writing as a feminist antimilitarist activist/organizer. I use these texts to piece together a story about the ways that women's citizenship claims are being presented, taken up, and negotiated through the symbolic and practically lethal issue of combat. The political moments I discuss illuminate the question of women in combat as being about basic challenges to the "traditional" order of gender roles in United States political culture, always laden with power. These materials are investigated for their political importance in shaping public understandings of the military as gendered and racialized, for their importance in building a discourse of expanded citizenship claims, and for their contributions to the shifting definitions of equality.

*

In the first three chapters of the book I discuss the theoretical underpinnings and contextual background that I see as ways of interpreting the questions about women, the military, citizenship, and militarism. Chapter 1 lays out the positions of feminist antimilitarism and feminist egalitarian militarism to think through the ways that these two clusters of positions and ideas might come together for a more just and peaceful world. I frame this debate through my own experiences in the antiwar movement that led me to this study from my work as a feminist nonviolence workshop preparer and university teacher in gender and politics studies. In chapter 2, I elaborate on the rationale for reading the subject of women in the military from a race, class, sexuality, and gender sensitive angle in order to produce an informed and forward reaching approach to feminist antimilitarism and the study of women soldiers. I elaborate on this approach by placing the advance of women soldiers in the U.S. military into a global economic context to sketch the kinds of questions I think we should be asking about "Why women soldiers?" and "Why now?" I am especially curious about women soldiers' inclusion at a time of general downsizing of the military and watch for the race inflected effects of that downsizing, given the predominance of soldiers of color in the less secure ranks of the forces. Chapter 3 sketches the advance of women into the forces from World War II to the early 1970s by setting it in the framework of the historic importance of martial service to first-class citizenship. I begin with an analysis of martial service as a masculinist enterprise and use the history of women's incorporation to display the progressive challenges to that masculinism. This discussion develops the connections between martial service and citizenship, and suggests that women may not attain as much in terms of formal citizenship claims in the military as their predecessors (men of color). I attend to military women's history, disrupting the notion that women's incorporation into the forces is a happy progression of the logic of women's rights and moreover testament to the "equal opportunity model of military employment," by demonstrating the continued unequal treatment of women in the forces, based on their gendered and racialized status. My review of women's histories in the military will necessarily be a brief overview, and readers familiar with the history of women in the forces will not find any surprises here; my focus is on the ways that the masculinism of the military has been politically entrenched or challenged.

Because I read the history through a feminist antimilitarist standpoint, I am able to suggest that a combination of factors: military demographic necessity due to a very effective anti–Vietnam War movement, specific pressures and changes due to equal rights feminist activism, and international political economic shifts all contributed to the creation of opportunities for women to pursue careers in the forces.

The next several chapters develop the stories of debates over women's inclusions that have been particularly strong since the ending of the draft and the transformations of the post-1973 period. In chapter 4, I begin my discussion of events that have shaped and reshaped the debates over what roles straight women, lesbian women, and gay men might play as martial citizens. Highlighting the Equal Rights Amendment debates, I also use chapter 4 to discuss the feminist accomplishment of shifts in legal status for women's equal rights through the courts, demonstrating along the way how the discourses of equality changed the shape of women's expectations in the forces and the strategies used to fight for those changes. Opening of the All Volunteer Forces also created demographic shifts in what kinds of women would have access to what levels of the forces. Not surprisingly, demographic studies reveal significant residual racism and ethnic antagonism in the forces, resulting in disproportionate numbers of women of color in less skilled work. This chapter demonstrates the growth of public interest in the topic of military women and the unsettled relationship between military service and citizenship in women's discourse about equality. Feminist antimilitarist activism and inactivism also played significant roles in the military's absorption of women recruits and inattention to the increased numbers of women soldiers. This latter point, feminist antimilitarists' inattention to the increased numbers of women soldiers, led to a facile association of masculinism and militarism which left feminist antimilitarists unable to respond to the new conditions of militarism.

In chapter 5, I demonstrate how the haphazard and often contradictory impulses of the 1980s Reagan administration's massive Defense Department build-up created more space for women in the forces. This space was ultimately irrevocable without compromising military efficacy. I present this as an ironic counterpoint to the intensive feminist antimilitarist activism of the period as it (we) fiercely articulated masculinist militarism as the problem. Equal rights feminist activisms certainly helped create the pressures that kept women in the forces and continued to push the boundaries of exclusive masculine access to military culture. My discussion of this period illuminates the ways that women's gradual inclusion through the 1980s continued to be somewhat of a deliberate mistake, but more importantly, women's access in this time period allowed for a more entrenched presence of women soldiers, although the presence and practiced expertise of women soldiers was not common knowledge. Women's deep integration in to the military was not "known" in the public until the several military interventions of the late 1980s and early 1990s. I look at government documents and formal political discourse in this period, as well as the films *Private Benjamin* and *Top Gun* to think about the ways that women soldiers and military experts (teachers) were being acknowledged and represented publicly. *Top Gun* is of especial interest here because of its conscious function as a recruitment tool for Navy flyers. (The Navy consulted on the production, notwithstanding subsequent complaints about misplaced pins and lapels.)

Chapter 6 looks at the first major public displays of women's deep integration into the forces through the Grenada invasion, the police action in Panama, and the Persian Gulf War. In this period, women's integration challenged the forces' culture of masculinity and raised public awareness of the extent of women's participation in the forces. I investigate these public displays of force, with women included, to view the function of women's integration on its own terms and to view the public response to women's integration. I investigate the case of the Gulf War here as an opportunity to examine the direct feminist antimilitarist response to sustained military action with women soldiers present. This period is also an important study of feminist antimilitarism in action; it was the first antiwar movement with a defined and mobilized feminist antimilitarist presence. The debates over how women were to fulfill their responsibilities as soldiers, the intense foregrounding of real or potential motherhood, and the permeable—and oft crossed—boundaries of combat, set the previously quiet relationship of women to the military squarely onto the public stage. This was a moment when feminist antimilitarist analyses could be fruitfully applied and have been emerging since, as I suggested earlier in this introduction.

Chapter 7 reviews the hearings and report of the Presidential Commission on the Assignment of Women in the Armed Forces, convened after the Persian Gulf War, which set out to resolve the question of women and combat but instead demonstrated the depth of anxieties about women and their proper place as citizens. The commission was finally ineffective due to growing support for women's advancement as soldiers, and a changing of the White House guard to the Democrats; however, the discourses of opposition to women in the forces evidenced in the commission's work remain an important site for understanding the breadth and depth of opposition to women's changing work. The chapter finishes with a discussion of the ultimate decisions to open combat roles for women, except ground combat, and the meanings of those decisions.

I conclude, in chapter 8, by reviewing the tensions raised by women's entry to the forces, and discussing the questions this work should raise for feminist antimilitarists in imagining future responses to armed interventions by the United States. I stake these questions on the valuation we want to give to martial citizenship in the first place and suggest that we must begin by rethinking our national attachment to martial valor as first-class citizenship. This chapter takes up several film representations of women in the military since the Gulf War and suggests a possible feminist antimilitarist reading of the films, particularly: *Independence Day, Courage Under Fire,* and *G.I. Jane.* This last film is of particular interest not only because of its placement of an avowedly nonfeminist woman in the most elite combat unit, but also because, unlike its predecessor *Top Gun,* it was rejected by the Navy. They refused to consult on it. The film stands as a much more gender challenging view of military culture, albeit almost hysterically attached to its heterosexism. These films together each contribute different readings of the legacy of women's presence in the Gulf War and provide interesting departure points for imagining what the terrain of women's martial citizenship will look like in the coming years.

In sum, as we move into the twenty-first century I suggest some ways to think about women soldiers, martial citizenship, and feminist antimilitarism that might hopefully contribute toward stronger imperatives and strategies for justice and peace.

| ONE |

Feminist Antimilitarism/
Feminist Egalitarian
Militarism

[I]f we permit the current debates to start from the
premise that the military is the place in this society
where ultimately a person must earn first-class citizenship, then we leave unchallenged the militarization of
citizenship itself. . . . First we must argue persuasively
that the military is too important a social institution to
be allowed to perpetuate sexism for the sake of protecting fragile masculine identities. And second we must
argue persuasively that the military is too important.

—Cynthia Enloe (1993a)

United States feminist antimilitarism's core symbol and analysis has been
reliant on a fundamental connection between patriarchy and war.[1] Antiwar signs during the Persian Gulf War were frequent iterations of the
connection.[2] Feminist antimilitarist arguments to dismantle militarism,
in which militarism is defined as the use of military force for diplomacy
and the deep conditioning of the society to valorize military cultures, are
securely wedded with arguments to dismantle patriarchy. Such arguments rest on the assumption that militarism and patriarchy are in effect
and construction consanguine, and moreover, the antithesis to justice
and peace.[3] Feminist antimilitarists argue, alongside Enloe, that "the
military is too important," but diverge from Enloe to argue that the military *is* a fragile masculine identity and needs to be abolished.[4]

Yet simultaneously, and from common roots in the women's movements of the 1960s and 1970s, various equal rights feminists have been fighting for women's full membership in the United States armed forces, a position I call "feminist egalitarian militarism." This position follows from the core of the Equal Rights Amendment that women, as a category, should be allowed full access to the social, political, and economic spheres alongside men. Feminist egalitarian militarists would agree with Enloe that "the military is too important a social institution to be allowed to perpetuate sexism for the sake of protecting fragile masculine identities," but they carry the analysis elsewhere by fastening it to a logic of martial citizenship as the ticket to first-class economic and political citizenship.

In this chapter I sketch the broad characteristics of feminist antimilitarisms and feminist egalitarian militarisms to sketch some of their central theoretical practices, and some of the differences between them. In the chapters that follow, I will take up feminist antimilitarisms and feminist egalitarian militarisms again via some chronological case studies to think about the ways they have each affected the debate over women as soldiers and military culture more broadly. I then elaborate this framework in the political moments I highlight to model the ways that they might fruitfully converse.

I use the categories of feminist antimilitarism and feminist egalitarian militarism, not to foreclose on them, or to fasten people to positions within them, as much as to suggest that the folks who appear in my discussion are those who appear publicly as spokespersons and meaning-shapers for each side. Thus, I am most interested here in describing what I see as the general terrain of each position and a way to align them for a more effective feminist response to masculinist militarism as first class citizenship. I hope, after all, to present a method for articulating the two and to demonstrate that by bringing them together we can avoid abandoning the field to antifeminist rhetoric and perhaps even move toward more precise feminist antiracist understandings of the military, of patriarchy, and of militarism.

But first, I want to tell a story about how I came to this project. The story outlines a logic of feminist antimilitarism as I understand it and demonstrates how the gendered United States experience of the Persian Gulf War served to mark out my questions and method.

Theorizing My Activism: Signs of My Stakes in the Work

I came of age at the end of the Vietnam War, in the growing antinuclear movement and the ongoing civil rights activism for lesbian and straight women, for gay men, and for nonwhite racial and ethnic groups. At age 14, in 1973, I became an activist at the American Friends Service Committee's Peace Center in Coconut Grove, Florida. I participated in United Farm Worker pickets against commercial grapes and lettuce, and in meetings of teenage peace activists learning about the military and the developing arsenal of nuclear weapons. My antimilitarist and class conscious politics were developing well; my feminism was rudimentary and quite pragmatic. After a seven-year hiatus to study yoga, I returned to my activism in 1985 while I was a reentry student at the university. There my feminism and my peace and justice activism grew deeper and more thoroughly articulated to one another, in part because of my experiences in the meantime, and in part because of my exposure to the activist student environment.

I organized against the United States interventions in Central America, I organized for women's rights, against Star Wars-SDI, and generally against things nuclear. I organized on campus against the SDI (Strategic Defense Initiative) via Student Pugwash (the student offshoot of the Federation of Atomic Scientists, who stand against nuclear war), and organized a debate for the eve of the Reagan-Gorbachev Summit between Dr. Peter Vajk, of the Heritage Foundation and formerly with Lawrence Livermore Labs, and Dr. Robert Bowman, President of the Institute for Space and Security Studies, regarding the development of SDI.

I was organizing with a student group against the U.S. interventions in Central America, in the early spring of 1987, when I decided to attend a meeting discussing the upcoming "Mothers and Others Day Action" for the Nevada Test Site. I was impressed by the action plan and the feminist analyses that shaped it; I was already convinced that the connections between militarism and patriarchy were powerful and that both needed to be challenged. I was an antinuclear activist, although I had not been part of a civil disobedience action to that time. I attended my first nonviolence preparation after that meeting. On May 7, 1987, I went to the Mothers and Others Day Action at the Nevada Test Site, and woke up the next morning in the desert across from the Test Site with thousands of other activists. Being there in the exquisitely stark and expansive desert to reclaim the land for our many peace-loving imaginations of a nonnuclear future served to strengthen my focus and resolve. Feminist antimilitarism would be my strategy.

I became a nonviolence preparer and an active feminist antimilitarist organizer (in mixed groups of men and women activists) inspired by what I had experienced through the Mothers and Others Day Action. This was several years before I started thinking about women in the armed forces; indeed I was barely aware of their presence. I knew the *Private Benjamin* image and the recruiters had been targeting young women since I left high school, but the presence of women as soldiers was a bare whisper in the back of my mind. My explanation was that they were the subjects of false consciousness and that they—like the men— were motivated by the "poor draft," as in the argument that no one would join the military unless they had no other option for obtaining job skills. I did not entertain the notion that any woman did it for love of the military, and especially not the military as a career!

I learned more about feminist antimilitarism through teaching nonviolence preparations for civil disobedience activism. The preparations always entailed a discussion of the nature and practice of nonviolence, what counted as nonviolence along a continuum of behaviors, storytelling about histories of nonviolent practice and its uses, and finally role playing and other practical discussion about the potential encounters in a civil disobedience action. My storytelling about the origins of nonviolence and the logic for nonviolence connected to legacies of women's nonviolent activism and civil disobedience to secure the right to vote and against slavery, the bravery of women civil rights activists, and so forth. Often the participants in the nonviolence preparations (antinuclear activists, members of NOW, antiwar activists, among others) would associate the quest for nonviolence with "women's" (which women's?) traditional (whose?) practices, and either directly or ironically embrace these practices as the sign of and validity of nonviolence. Earth-based spiritualities (re-created and adopted by these activists) and feminisms that described antihierarchical relations were central informants to the culture of nonviolent civil disobedience.[5] Women and men activists, for the most part, embraced the critique of the dominant patriarchal militarist culture: the women were peace-loving and the warriors were men, with the interesting assumption and practice that men could be—and peace activist men were—practitioners of peace and nonhierarchical politics (although many internal struggles occurred over men's actual practices, and some women's as well).

I began organizing in a collective for demonstrations at Lockheed Corporation's ordnance research facility, at the top of Empire Grade, in Santa Cruz County. Part of our activism was to inform the local residents about the explosives that traveled their mountain road, to and from the site. Once again, the activists' discussions and action strategizing, their direct theorizing of the meaning in their practice, precisely articulated (for both women and men) the connections between patriarchy, militarism, racism, and capitalism.

Over the next several years, I helped organize a local chapter of Women in Black (at the time, during the height of the Intifada, many Women in Black groups were forming in solidarity with the Israeli organization) to stand against the Israeli occupation of Palestine and in support of the Intifada. Our weekly vigil marked, again, women's prominent role in "fighting" for peace. (I am a third-generation, born-in-the-U.S. Jew and I do not believe in the fortress of the Israeli state; short of no states anywhere, there should be two states at peace there.)[6] I taught nonviolence preparations for the Santa Cruz County chapter of NOW to help stand against Operation Rescue, and I was being called upon by miscellaneous groups to teach nonviolence strategies. I developed my stories and teaching routines for questions of women, feminism, and nonviolence, with ironic and practical uses of the notions of motherhood, to a largely (90 percent) white audience in a community that is roughly 30–40 percent of color. Civil disobedience and other forms of direct action against the military-industrial complex were not the terrain on which the communities of color in my area were focusing their struggles for justice at the time. Instead, the largely Chicana(o) part of my community was organizing against injustice in the agricultural industries where they labored. Racism, labor exploitation, discriminatory immigration practices, substandard migrant housing, and packing house flight to free trade zones were the critical issues to be addressed.

Suddenly there was Desert Shield and Desert Storm: the Persian Gulf War. It inflamed the complex layering of racial/ethnic conflict in the colonized and subdivided Middle East. The Persian Gulf War also presented a series of gendered predicaments for students of international relations,[7] and specifically for those of us who study gender, politics, and peace. The strange and exciting vision of Saudi women driving cars to protest the restrictions on their mobility by their masculinist culture. Driving cars! I immediately went to work with my activist tools participating in organizing meetings, teaching nonviolence preparations, and attending marches and rallies. I collected clippings about women being deployed to the Gulf. I wondered about them: the clipped representations of the women and the women soldiers themselves. During a brief organizing hiatus I joined my family in San Diego for Thanksgiving (odd moment though it was) and on the drive down from Santa Cruz we saw Army truckloads of young men, the majority Latino,[8] being transported to the bases. Even though women were centered on the news reports, the soldiers I kept seeing were men, and men of color at that. I kept teaching nonviolence preparations and organizing teach-ins about the war. Students in my classes and participants in the preparations were confused about the images of women. Some gleefully attested to the "be all that you can be" rhetoric of the Army and proudly stated that the armed forces *were* the equal opportunity employer they said they were. Others, who wanted to keep the distinction of women as nonviolent, saw the women soldiers as living a false consciousness, being the victims of a poor draft, and so forth. I felt confused in my work about the topic of feminist antimilitarism. Here was the center and vital heart of my interests: end militarism. Now it was stacked up against a strange collision of terms—end gendered militarism? Allow women in combat? Celebrate Phyllis Schlafly's fear that we had "lost our manhood"?[9] How would I reconcile the positions of women as peacekeepers with women as warriors, and fighting for status as combatants to reap the career and citizenship benefits (albeit less tangible) of martial service?

During the Gulf War I was teaching as assistant in a course entitled "Gender and Politics," with Sonia Alvarez and Gwendolyn Mink, and I was also teaching nonviolence preparations with the Santa Cruz Nonviolence Preparer's Collective. The former was planned and convened before the Gulf War began. The latter was a scheduled series in early response to the war's build-up, beginning in August 1990. In both of these contexts, I was struck by the ways that the practices and presumptions of feminist nonviolence and the histories of martial citizenship could not account for women's explosive presence in the Gulf War. I found myself in numerous conversations attempting to develop new ways of thinking about gender and nonviolence, and the ways that notions of women as peacekeepers, although most often rhetorical and symbolically deployed, were losing their meaning in the face of the visible presence of women in the war as soldiers.

A long history of feminist antimilitarist analyses inside the antinuclear, environmental, queer, and anti-intervention movements enabled an immediate reading of the Persian Gulf War through gendered and environmentally astute assessments of militarism: George Bush's performance anxieties; the relationship of oil subsidies to the regional conflict ("no war for oil" was a major rallying cry); and numerous analyses of the war's global and local, social and economic effects on women, men of color, working-class citizens, and the planet.[10] These feminist informed analyses were not monothematic, nor did they always invoke the same causal framework. There was, and is, a great deal of tension around the terms of feminist antimilitarism as a question of biologically or socially constructed peacemaking skills. Nevertheless, easy associations between masculinity and violence were abundant in the antiwar demonstrations, and generally in feminist antimilitarist discourse.

The Persian Gulf War challenged me to rethink the relationships between feminisms, the military, and antimilitarism. Although women never exceeded 12 percent of the deployed forces, they were constantly headlined, photographed, feature storied, and placed squarely on the congressional agenda. The woman soldier, even though she was formally restricted from combat deployment, represented a potential sea change in military culture. The remarkable presence of women in the war received only slightly less coverage than the "video game" combat footage that the Pentagon allowed in news accounts.[11] Pictures of women soldiers were constantly displayed in the press: as heterosexual married moms saying tearful good-byes to their children, as soldiers deployed in Saudi Arabia cleaning their gunbarrels (an ironic image given women's restriction from offensively shooting the guns), loading weapons onto fighter jets, loading and unloading supplies. These images of women as soldiers, the contradictions embedded in the images, and the experiences of women soldiers (including the post-war revelations about women soldiers being raped by male compatriots and being prisoners of war) sent

traditional notions of martial citizenry and female pacifism and inno-
cence reeling. At the same time, U.S. congressional battles raged over
women's fitness for combat duty and antiwar demonstrations were
thickly peopled with feminist antimilitarists and their analyses.

Women soldiers' presence was so controversial, in terms of accepted
masculinist military culture, that the incidents of male soldiers' violent
behavior toward them were not analyzed publicly as the fault of the
males, but rather underlined the question of whether women should be
in the forces in the first place. To highlight this point, witness the cultural and legal sanctions (however unevenly applied) against raping and
sexually harassing (although less so) women in other institutions. These
sanctions in other public institutions are such that while the enforcement
is still uneven, women are not immediately discussed in terms of how
they should not be there in the first place. Enloe suggests to us that "the
military is too important a social institution to be allowed to perpetuate
sexism for the sake of protecting fragile masculine identities."[12] As
women enter the ranks of the military, which they have been doing in
small but persistent numbers since the lifting of the 2 percent quota in
the early 1970s, we have to address this other side of the relationship between men, women, and the military.

I rely on my experience in the antimilitarist movements to ground my
theoretical and case study work to understand the predicaments of militarism, women's work in the military, debates about equal rights, and visions of justice and peace. The antimilitarist movement, heavily influenced by feminist antimilitarism, theorizes in practice. Noël Sturgeon has
called this the "direct theory"[13] of the movements. She argues that the
movement actions develop theoretical understandings tangentially, collectively, and by their very enactment. Thus, my ways of describing and
thinking about the material are embedded in my activist history, are a
product of that history, and are intended, ultimately, to speak a future to
that history bringing sharper understanding back to peace movement activism, and grounded in the imperative that we "must argue persuasively
that the military is too important."

This project emerged from my abrupt confrontation with the enormous contestation over the meaning of women's presence in the forces.
In my practice of antiwar work the notion of an automatic, easily recognizable and embraced linkage between feminism and antimilitarism was

eroded by women's increased presence, pride, and visibility in the U.S. armed forces. To this day, the rage over women in the forces is not about the numbers of women, but the challenge women pose to traditional military culture, presumptions of abilities, and fixed roles for men and women therein.

Women's entry to the armed forces challenges two major social forces to rethink their modus operandi. First, the masculinist military is challenged to incorporate women fully. Second, feminist antimilitarism is challenged to rethink movement strategies and rhetorical frameworks that have previously relied upon models of femaleness, however ironically deployed, as symbols for peace. Both of these challenges hold promise for a deepened understanding of how U.S. citizens envision themselves as a political community, and the opportunity therein to create a paradigm of belonging and valuing of self-sacrifice based not on bravado, but rather on the imperatives of social justice and peace. Feminist antimilitarism and feminist egalitarian militarism each have much to contribute to this process.

Feminist Antimilitarism

The myth of women as antithesis to militarism and to soldiering takes its particular United States shape by design, if not always by practice, through women's historic (and often imaginary) exclusion from the battlefield and relegation to the so-called private reproduction of citizens. Different women, of course, have had and continue to have, a variety of relationships to productive and reproductive labor, due to their differing class, ethnic, and racial locations in society and the market. Women have been expected to be the camp followers or homefire tenders. The predominance of men and male-oriented cultural practices in the armed forces has done little to dilute this myth. Therefore, I felt that, to point out the connections between the military and male dominance, the use of the myth was clearly justified. In short, until the Persian Gulf War in 1991, I primarily argued that the military was too important, and that women were in the distinct position to understand this and to lay morally persuasive claim to arguments for peace and disarmament.

I used this rhetoric while problematizing the reification of women's claim to caregiving, nurturing, and life protective behaviors/roles. I recognized that the argument of women as peaceful was dangerous, precisely because it contributed to the fastening of women to caregiving reproductive roles. The dangers for peace activists, in particular, rest in assuming, or hoping, that women by something in their nature (or nurture) can pacify the armed forces.[14] I think it is always a dangerous move to claim that women are deeply and broadly nonviolent caregivers, uniquely suited to keeping the peace and raising babies into citizens. There are some very sobering moments in history regarding the symbolic use of mothering to serve the needs of a state, and the particular ways that such calls for mothering consciousness have worked for fascist states.[15] I do not wish to be a junior architect of such a framework. I agree with Micaela di Leonardo's worry that morals and motherhood were becoming too well mixed in feminist activism against the military and militarism in the 1980s.[16] I also witnessed and participated in the ironic and contested use of those icons of mothering.[17] I was aware, as a student of women's histories, that the position of women as peacekeepers and peacelovers had political and moral purchase, despite its great political dangers. So, I used the image and worked its dubious magic in action.

My understandings of feminist antimilitarism emerged in the context of feminist, antinuclear, queer, antiracist, and environmental movements. I understand these movements to be shaped by the legacy of the early civil rights movement and the "second wave" of feminism.[18] They incorporate notions first developed in the civil rights movement, and adapted to feminism, that elaborate the connections between the personal and the political. These new social movements act within a paradigm that takes as its first rule that the political infuses and makes common the state, civil society, and private spheres.[19]

Civil rights activists first developed the sense of the personal as political by bringing the work of politics directly into the community through articulating the effect of social structures on people's daily lives. The New Left took up this model and the women's movements particularly furthered it to challenge the privatization of gender politics.[20] Women of color activists theorized the interlocking oppressions and positionalities that shaped their relationships to the movements for social change and their experiences in the broader culture. Gloria Anzaldúa's theorizing of the mestiza,[21] or border consciousness that develops is a critical contribution to this understanding, as were the numerous early challenges to a feminism that was markedly white in its practical understandings.[22] Feminists brought these practices of interrogating the personal as political into the antinuclear direct action movement, helping to shape the process and internal texts of the movement.[23] While feminist antimilitarists were largely from the white activist communities, they were influenced either directly, by their participation in the civil rights movements (Barbara Deming and Ynestra King immediately come to mind), or by the women of color's written and verbal critiques that were ongoing and available from the earliest stages of the women's movement. It is, however, now classically recounted that it took African American women's activism and the formation of their own presses, for example, Kitchen Table Press, to actually get women of color's writings into print.[24]

I have spent much of my activist life arguing that the military is too important—that we give too much money, too much in human life, and too much credence and power to the military as a political institution. In this I have concurred with other feminist antimilitarists who argue that military spending is out of concert with other kinds of spending for national security and indeed harms the social fabric, that human lives are too precious and human rights too important to resort to gunboat diplomacy, and that we are far too reliant on the military for political power and place too much emphasis on martial citizenship. This analysis is linked in feminist antimilitarism with an analysis that the military is saturated with destructive versions of racialized masculinity. This means that the most violent aspects of human relations have been sanctioned in military culture and lodged in, encouraged as part of, masculine behavior.

Feminist influences in nonviolence preparations and nonviolent direct action readily, albeit ironically, present the powerful symbols and stories of women as nonviolent. This reifies an equation of women and nonviolence, not necessarily true but certainly embedded in our gendered myths of social history. These associations have worked by relying on texts such as the Mother's Day Proclamation of the 1800s[25] and the Women's Pentagon Actions' Unity Statements of the early 1980s. The "Unity Statement," of the Women's Pentagon Action (WPA), first drafted by Grace Paley, but later revised (both prior to the first action and again prior to the second), says in its first version:

We are gathering at the Pentagon because we fear for our lives. We fear for the life of this planet, our Earth, and the life of the children who are our human future. . . . We have come to mourn and rage and defy the Pentagon because it is the workplace of the imperial power which threatens us all. . . . We women are gathering because life on the precipice is intolerable. We want to know what anger in these men, what fear, which can only be satisfied by destruction, what coldness of heart and ambition drive their days. We want to know because we do not want that dominance which is exploitative and murderous in international relations, and so dangerous to women and children at home—we do not want that sickness transferred by this violent society through the fathers to the sons. (Excerpt from "Unity Statement" 1980 WPA, rptd. in Harris and King 1989)

Interestingly, although each version presented a critique of racism, the 1982 version of the Statement most strongly articulated the racist classism of the Pentagon's apparatus:

We are in the hands of men whose power and wealth have separated them from the reality of daily life and from the imagination. We are right to be afraid. At the same time our cities are in ruins, bankrupt; they suffer the devastation of war. Hospitals are closed, our schools deprived of books and teachers. Our Black and Latino youth are without decent work. They will be forced, drafted to become the cannon fodder for the very power that oppresses them. Whatever help the poor receive is cut or withdrawn to feed the Pentagon. . . . (Unity Statement, 1982, rptd. in McAllister 1982)

Feminist antimilitarism in the WPA was developed as a broad-reaching analysis of the interconnections between race, class, gender, and militarized capitalism.[26] This analysis itself is critically important for understanding how militarism works and it has developed in complexity over time as evidenced by the two progressive versions of the Unity Statement. The trouble is in its reliance on women as the antithesis to militarism, thus positing men as militarism. Feminist antimilitarists base this opposition most often on the socialized roles of femininity and masculinity; Sara Ruddick (1983) turns the argument on its head to say that men can also develop these caregiving qualities through the practices of "maternal thinking."[27] Jean Bethke Elshtain (1987) suggested that war is perpetuated through the binary of the "beautiful soul" and the "just warrior." She suggests that the way out of this binary is for men to take on the qualities of Ruddick's notion of "maternal thinking." However, there is a certain purchase to using this binary in feminist antimilitarism in that it serves to highlight the existence of the political inequities and argues ultimately for a complete transformation of gender roles, while naming them as they operate. Reed (1992) and Sturgeon (1997) have both demonstrated that these public presentations of "unity" or "uniformity" in political activism are prone to accusations of "essentialism." Through participant observation in these movement politics it becomes clear that in their enactment the internal differentiations and even disputes are placed in the background to effect strategic political unity.

The ambivalence and ongoing struggles over defining the conditions of feminist antimilitarism within the movement are apparent in various articulations. Witness these remarks by the Cambridge Women's Peace Collective. Their position neither takes women's peace-keeping proclivities as a given, nor lets patriarchy off the hook: "If the qualities of caring and nurturing are ascribed to those in society who have no political power, and the influence of those qualities banned from international relations, the opposite attributes of forcefulness and competitiveness rule unhindered."[28] Thus, the work for those who have minimal political power (in this equation "women") is to not only transform their position to one of power, but to bring along the influence of caring and nurturing to the halls of power. This equation presumes women to be caregivers and capable of transforming "forcefulness and competitiveness" by their nature (or nurture).

As I suggested earlier, in my participation as a feminist antimilitarist, I have contributed to the myth that women are the antithesis to the culture of militarism as gunboat masculinity. I used that analysis of power in the feminist antimilitarist participation and organizing work that I did in the antinuclear actions at the Nevada Test Site, the Lockheed Space and Missiles Corp. sites, and against the Persian Gulf War in 1990–91. In doing so, I drew on the feminist antimilitarist work of Barbara Deming and other writings in the feminist antimilitarist genre including the often reprinted materials of the direct action civil disobedience handbooks of the antinuclear movement.[29]

Contemporary United States feminist antimilitarism is represented broadly by feminist individuals and organizations (some organizations were solely convened around sets of actions and thus ephemeral) and has included such figures as Bella Abzug[30] and Women Strike for Peace,[31] Lourdes Benería, Susan Brownmiller, Barbara Deming, Adrienne Harris, Ynestra King, Barbara Omolade, Grace Paley, Sara Ruddick, Starhawk, Donna Warnock, the Unity Statement for the Women's Pentagon Actions (and the participants), WomanEarth Peace Institute members, Cambridge Women's Peace Collective, Women in Black, Mothers and Others Day Action Collective, and the various antinuclear action collectives, to name a few.

Ruth Roach Pierson suggests that the cluster of feminist antimilitarism ranges through the most elementary "moral mothers" position to "women against patriarchy in all its forms."[32] She presents a helpful study of the way that feminist positions about war and peace have changed in historical contexts. She suggests that "feminists have posited conflicting theories on women's relation to war and peace and women have, according to changing historical circumstances, responded to warmongering and peace movements in a great variety of ways" (225). In my discussions in subsequent chapters of the developments in feminist antimilitarism during the late twentieth century I will highlight some of these changes, and of course, suggest others.

Feminist antimilitarists have argued, even at their most intentionally ironic, that women are closer to nurturance and thus more protective of life than men. Even when they accept that women are not necessarily simply nurturers, they continue to argue that it is women's socialized qualities of caregiving that will save the day. In a sense this is the same argument that right-wing women use to place women "back in the home"—that women are caregivers and nurturers, while arguing simultaneously that men are better suited for the brutal responsibilities of warfare.[33] Of course, feminist antimilitarists disagree with the second part of the right-wing equation which says that women are to be protected and defended by those brutal warriors. Feminist antimilitarists instead argue that there is a direct association between patriarchy and violence, as I have elaborated earlier, and that the military is constructed irrevocably on that connection.

By making such a connection, feminist antimilitarists become unable to account for women who love to be in the military for all the reasons that men may be attracted to it: for the various kinds of power, the desire to feel capable and in charge,[34] and for the kudos of political and economic citizenship. The problem for feminist antimilitarists becomes an inability to develop effective analyses of and opposition to a military that may be becoming less reliant on its masculinism to feed its militarism. This immediate linking of masculinism and militarism betrays the complexity of our situation as feminist antimilitarists. By assuming that the military is dependent on its masculinism, by presuming that only men can and will use gunboat diplomacy, feminist antimilitarism is left unable to account for women who love power-over. We should think straightaway of Margaret Thatcher in our not-too-distant past. Moreover, this position does not account for those like former representative Patricia Schroeder who argue for women's access, not from a notion of "pacifying the forces," or for a love simply of power, but for sheer equality. Furthermore, there are those who argue simply for the rights, or pleasures, of pursuing a career laced with bravado and danger.

While most feminist antimilitarism is enacted by white women, the analyses of the movement were attentive at least in their position papers, handbooks, and nonviolence preparations (activist group trainings) to the intersected problems of race, class, and gender.[35] Often treated as separate sections in the direct action handbooks, nonetheless action participants received short primers on: "Overcoming Racism," "Unlearning Racism," and "Connections between Race, Class, and Gender" as minitreatises designed to get activist participants discussing the connections between racism and militarism and class politics.[36] Nevertheless, much of the public presentations and manifestations of feminist antimilitarism were constructed around the oppositions of feminism as peace and patriarchy as militarism. By the mid-to-late 1980s women of color and white women's critiques of the white middle classness of the movement had come forward enough to be published in movement anthologies such as Harris and King (1989). For instance, Barbara Omolade, an African American scholar and antimilitarist long active in the civil rights and women's movements, criticized the narrow focus of feminist antimilitarism on "nukes" saying that

> The antiwar and antinuke organizers and their supporters have gathered
> millions to march and demonstrate against nuclear war and for a nuclear
> freeze as if only nuclear war threatens humankind. . . . The peace move-
> ment suffers greatly from its lack of historical and holistic perspective,

practice and vision that include the voices and experience of people of color. . . . The peace movement's racist blinders have divorced peace from freedom, from feminism, from education reform, from legal rights, from human rights, from international alliances and friendships, from national liberation, from the particular (for example, black female, Native American male) and the general (human being).[37]

Omolade's critique presents an important analysis of the workings of militarism seen from a broader political and more precisely economic perspective, and she cites other scholars, such as Damu Imara Smith, who specifically connect military spending to social and economic degradation. In the Harris and King volume, Lourdes Benería and Rebecca Blank do this work in an article called "Women and the Economics of Military Spending." This kind of critique, and according to Sturgeon's retelling of the history the influence of Barbara Deming, led Ynestra King, Barbara Smith, and others to produce a remarkable organization attempting to address the problem: the WomanEarth Feminist Peace Institute.[38] As Sturgeon tells us, this organization, founded on Smith's notion of racial parity, foundered in part through its inability to move past the binary of white and of color. A more hopeful location for work now is the shift of feminist antimilitarism and ecofeminisms toward international, multiracial, and multiclass coalitions. Certainly some work is being done in this direction though admittedly not nearly enough. An interesting development in this direction is represented by Gwyn Kirk and Margo Okazawa-Rey's work on the "East Asia-U.S. Women's Network against U.S. Militarism." They have been calling for renewed feminist antimilitarism through genuine international linkages that "press for a public debate on many key questions not addressed in the U.S. media coverage of Okinawa or in mainstream political discussion generally surrounding U.S. militarism."[39] Women have been organizing in international coalitions against militarism and especially U.S. militarism. Organizations such as Okinawa Women Act Against Military Violence, BUKLOD, and Kirk and Okazawa-Rey's group, all work toward international antiracist feminist antimilitarist visions.

Feminist antimilitarism has provided us with a critique of the late twentieth century that articulates patriarchal hierarchies as seen in racist/imperialist/colonialist pursuits, oppression of women and all others who are not white male, capitalist exploitation (though not always capitalism), and in the treatment of the environment (seen as "nature"). Feminist antimilitarists began to articulate the connections, and indeed the imperatives, between feminism and nonviolence in ways such as Donna Warnock, one of the organizers of the Women's Pentagon Action, suggests:

> Despite major theoretical commonalities, feminists are not necessarily nonviolent, and nonviolent activists are not necessarily feminist. This merger is our challenge. We are saying that feminism is crucial to pacifism, for we must dismantle the mental weaponry as well as the military. For us, nonviolence is a logical extension of feminism. To call ourselves feminist pacifists is to use neither as an adjective, but to integrate both. We are talking about a philosophy of its own. We are experiencing a leap in consciousness and we are recognizing that as revolutionary.[40]

The issues which became the focus for feminist antimilitarists included a far-reaching analysis of the dynamics of patriarchal oppression, in contrast to earlier (and ongoing) pacifist movements, in that feminist antimilitarists both identified and opposed what they articulated as the masculinist construction of militarism. The connections iterated were about the predominant masculinism in social, economic, and political power relations, the overwhelming degree of violence encouraged in and by that predominant masculinist culture, and the sheer destructive force of its enactment. They presented this critique by enacting rituals which reclaimed the possibilities for birth, life, love, and nurturance over those identified in militarism, namely death, destruction, and violence against women and children, and especially through the specter of nuclear annihilation as the purview of powerful military and businessmen.

Webs have recurred as a central theme and metaphor for feminist antimilitarist and ecofeminist practice. They originated in an early Seabrook occupation slogan: "Weave a web of resistance against nuclear power," by the affinity group "The Weavers" in Vermont, and were taken up by the feminist antimilitarist activists at the Women's Pentagon Action and in San Francisco during Women's Pentagon West. Epstein describes the scene as follows:

[I]n San Francisco, 300 women calling themselves "Women's Pentagon Action West" gathered outside the San Francisco Bohemian Club, whose members are men in positions of corporate and governmental power. The women set up cardboard tombstones inscribed with names of women who were victims of violence. In response to the Shakespearean motto of the Bohemian Club, "Weaving spiders come not here" (and reflecting the influence of Paganism, witchcraft, and women's spirituality) they chanted: "We are the flow, we are the ebb/ We are the weavers, we are the web."[41]

The web of interconnected yet distinct life is simultaneously the web of resistance to a militarized and undemocratic culture. The web of resistance is invoked against militarism and the degradation/destruction of the planet. It also signifies a mirroring and mocking of the conditions of globalization of late capitalism, patriarchy, and postmodern culture by insisting on a widely differentiated yet necessarily interconnected environment of social-economic-political organization. More recently, and not part of the realm of possibility in the 1970s and 1980s when the symbol of the web of resistance gained popularity, the web has come to represent both the possibility of networked communication and sites of resistance in the form of computer web site home pages and organizational networks.[42]

Feminist antimilitarism of the late 1980s worked harder to develop critiques of the racism in the culture and to incorporate models for transformation of racist practices in the direct actions. For example, at the Nevada Test Site, on several occasions beginning with the 1987 action there, I could see the ways that the interconnected oppressions were addressed by the participants. For instance, at the Test Site, for each of the demonstrations held there, leaders of the Shoshone Nation invite protesters on to Shoshone land that had been renamed the Nevada Test Site and claimed by the United States government for national security work: the underground testing of atomic weaponry. In this way, the Shoshone refuse to acknowledge U.S. federal control over their land and other antinuclear activists, as their guests, both affirm the Shoshone right to the land and refuse the federal government's claims, thus challenging the concept of "national security" at multiple levels. Much was said by the rally speakers about the ways that the U.S. government has reneged on treaties and claimed "national security needs" over Native sovereignty that have resulted in federal confiscation of vast tracts of land.[43]

The antinuclear movement more broadly has used strategies of civil disobedience that ranged from site occupations and symbolic transformations, such as that described above, as well as setting up villages inside Seabrook,[44] and literally weaving the doors of the Pentagon shut as a "web of resistance" to militarism in the Women's Pentagon Actions of 1980 and 1981.[45] These symbolic actions represent various methods of marking the limits of state power and challenging the state to assert itself publicly, through arrests and other violent responses. By doing women's work of nurturing and protecting, and calling for life to be preserved in the face of such destruction, one of the feminist antimilitarist activists' hallmark strategies was to demonstrate "the passion to make and make again where such unmaking reigns," as Adrienne Rich wrote.

Sturgeon has argued that the direct action movement as a whole incorporated the feminist antimilitarist analysis in ways crucial to its self-conceptions and thus its practices:

> The direct action movement, through its insistence on feminism as an important part of its repertoire, and its conflation of feminism with key parts of its political action and organizational structures (non-hierarchy, nonviolence, consensus process, ecofeminism) theorizes the integral nature of feminist critiques for its construction of an oppositional politics. . . . Thus feminism can act as a connective discourse for the movement because of the way in which shifts in gender relations are central to the process of restructuring. Analyzing these shifts is central to any effort at social and political change.[46]

Sturgeon elaborates on the promise of such an analysis for the movement precisely because of its utility in fashioning intersections between various struggles for justice. This is one of the great strengths of feminist antimilitarism as a model.

Feminist antimilitarism is often linked with ecofeminism. It is an interesting phenomenon born precisely of the connections between feminist antimilitarist concerns and feminist environmental concerns. Sturgeon (1997) tells the story of U.S. ecofeminism that tracks its emergence from the conference of women activists, "Women and Life on Earth," to the 1980 and 1981 Women's Pentagon Actions. Sturgeon argues persuasively that ecofeminist analyses helped shape the antinuclear direct action movement's practices and were not simply emergent from or the next step from antinuclear protest.[47] Beset with similar problems to those faced by the more generic antimilitarist movements, in terms of the predominance of white activists, ecofeminism actually has much less of a presence in activist communities and is most visible in the academy. Ecofeminism provides a model for simultaneously understanding the world from a feminist, nonviolent, socially and economically just, and ecologically sustainable set of criteria.[48] My work on women and the armed forces attempts to employ and develop this model. I am also stretching ecofeminism to re-embrace its roots in the antinuclear/antimilitarist activist movement.

Demonstrations of feminist antimilitarist ecofeminism have ranged widely. These demonstrations have included performance art, such as webs woven across rivers to filter garbage,[49] and anthologies and articles of ecofeminist perspectives.[50] They also include direct actions at military sites, such as the Women's Pentagon Actions, weaving webs across the doorways as I mentioned above; the Mothers and Others Day Actions at the Nevada Test Site, which included animal images such as batik butterflies held on both sides of the fence to connect people committing civil disobedience and those not, animal tunnel/birth canals under the fence, rituals of levitation, purification, and the reclamation of the land by the Shoshone Nation as they invited people through the fence, the performance of rituals, and the planting of food and flower seeds. All these actions were strong counteractions to deadly masculinist militarism, and all had rejuvenating references to women, mothers, nature, and native peoples. In other words, the theme of a patriarchal militarism albeit sometimes ironically was projected over and over, placards read: "war is a dick thing." Thus, interconnection and peace are a feminist thing—"a vulva thing (?)"

Feminist antimilitarists have presented important maps of the late twentieth-century political scene that articulate full citizenship and women's rights, and demonstrate some of the context for women's claims of access to military jobs. However, feminist antimilitarists have been unable to reconcile their critiques of patriarchal militarism with the display of women soldiers in the forces. Feminist antimilitarism needs to develop its analysis of militarism to mark the resilience of masculinist militarism in the face of pressure to incorporate women, without dismissing the possibility that militarism could function without masculinism. Feminist antimilitarism also needs to create more complex analyses of the relationships between feminism and nonviolence, and women as soldiers in the forces.

Ironically, many of the strategies and actions taken against the military by feminist antimilitarists are the product of the same rupturing of the liberalist illusion of separate private and civil spheres by and for women that become the impulse for women to seek equal opportunity employment and fully invested citizenship in the armed forces. However, the powerful critique of the patriarchal military which has emerged since the Women's Pentagon Actions at the beginning of the 1980s and literally fed the antinuclear movement since, has depended on an antimilitarist stance which obscures the role of women in the military who share the belief in women's equality.

Feminist Egalitarian Militarists

The second cluster of feminists I am concerned with here are those that I am calling feminist egalitarian militarists. These are women (and some men) who argue for women's full inclusion to the military. They have done so, as Jane Mansbridge argued, on the "egalitarian" terms of the premise of the Equal Rights Amendment.[51] These feminists have followed the argument that women's equal rights require concomitant equal responsibilities. In the *Rostker v. Goldberg* (453 U.S. 57, 1981) case, the court decided that women were already exempt from combat, the draft was intended to produce combat-ready troops, and therefore women should not be drafted. The NOW *amicus curiae*, however, argued that universal conscription was a critical next step for women to attain first-class citizenship. The 1990 NOW National Board's policy on women and the military restates the case in terms of career opportunities, since it is not currently a debate over conscription: "Therefore be it resolved that NOW demands equality for women in joining the military and in training, job assignments and benefits in the military; and be it further resolved, that NOW actively supports elimination of statutory restrictions on women in the military."[52] Feminist egalitarian militarists have also presented a more utilitarian argument, that women want access to the careers afforded by and within military service. For instance, former representative Patricia Schroeder (D-CO), arguably the leading political elite member of the equal rights feminist cluster, said in response to criticism that she was working against the feminist agenda by fighting for military women: "I keep saying feminism isn't about opening up the jobs you want, its about opening up the jobs some women may want. If I just opened up the jobs I wanted, I wouldn't have to work so hard."[53] Her arguments both rest on the presumed connection between equal rights and responsibilities in the exercise of equal political and economic citizenship and on the argument that martial citizenship is the ticket to first-class citizenship. Nancy Hartsock cautions us that for women "to be equal participants in the political community . . . either the nature of the political community must change or some women too must become warriors."[54] NOW has moved to the latter strategy.

While feminist egalitarian militarists agree to the linkage of equal rights and equal responsibilities, they differ in how much access they think women should have. For instance, although Reps. Beverly Byron (D-MD) and Patricia Schroeder (D-CO) worked together to get women flyers assigned to combat duty, Byron would stop short of allowing them to perform ground combat. During the Persian Gulf War, Schroeder was also on the opposite side of the fence from her colleague Sen. Barbara Boxer (D-CA), who pushed for parental leave policies for soldiers with children. Schroeder argued against it saying: "You can imagine who they'd love to throw out first! It doesn't make any difference how well they perform. Having people on the outside raising all these questions is really helpful to them because it gives them the license to say, 'Well, gee, it's been really nice having you here. Now go home.'"[55]

Jeanne Holm in her book *Women in the Military: The Unfinished Revolution*,[56] details the history of women getting into the military and then argues that women still have a way to go to achieve full equality. Carol Barkalow, an Army captain whose book *In the Men's House*[57] details her experiences in the military, argues that women should have full and equal access, that women "have what it takes." This having what it takes is again modified between different feminist egalitarian militarists. In an article that appeared in the *Atlantic Monthly*, Brigadier General Evelyn "Pat" Foote suggested that pregnant women and single parents should not be deployed.[58] She favors men and women being held to the same standard and excluding women from things they cannot accomplish at those standards. According to Charles Moskos, Foote "hope[s] for a future that harks back to an era when women soldiers, in the main, were unmarried, had no children, and few outside distractions and were more committed to military service than their male counterparts."[59] Now women sign up for the military as a career move, a jump start on higher education, and so on, while also juggling other commitments. Furthermore, as the military has become a more generically acceptable profession for women, albeit with dastardly pitfalls such as sexual harassment, women have been willing to see it as part of a more complex set of commitments, in the light of most job choices. Foote would argue that it most certainly is not.

Some egalitarians are not necessarily enthusiastic supporters of the military, but nevertheless argue for women's access,[60] witness Mary Fainsod Katzenstein:

> Feminist consciousness in the military does not embrace a radical agenda that seeks an end to U. S. interventions abroad, drastic reductions in military spending, or a world constructed on nonviolence. It is only just beginning to make connections among the practices of sexism, racism and homophobia. Nevertheless, *it would be wrong, because of differences in feminist visions, to read military women's activism as a case of co-optation.* Feminism in the armed forces has set its sights largely on making the military sex-blind. In another institution, at another time, such an objective might be thought conservative. In the U.S. military at this time, the vision is deeply challenging [italics mine].[61]

This brings me to an ongoing dilemma in sorting out the views of the women who support opening up the military for women. In much the same way as I have done for feminist antimilitarism, I am exploring the nuanced views of equal rights supporters of women in the military. Some supporters believe in precisely equal rights terms, some even suggest we have to do it to fulfill the logic of citizenship as it stands although they may be fully against militarism. People like Judith Stiehm make this sort of argument. Although her first book explored the concepts and practices of nonviolence in such organizations as the Committee for Nonviolent Action (CNVA) and the civil rights movement organizations, she comes to argue, by the end of it, for strategic nonviolence, yes, but not for the elimination of force in political life. Stiehm's later work has been a perhaps reluctant acceptance of the military and women's role in it as evidenced by the following statement: "What I do not respect and what I even fear, is a position which accepts violence as effective, as necessary, and as appropriately exercised by men only. . . . [A] society of defenders, a society composed of citizens equally liable to experience violence and equally responsible for exercising society's violence is, I think, stronger and more desirable."[62] Stiehm is cautionary though. She does not think that the forces are changed by women's presence alone. Witness this comment from *Arms and the Enlisted Woman*: "If the military does depend on women's absence, it can be subverted or radically altered by joining it, especially by joining it in large numbers and as full partners. One must be clear though: the women in today's military have not altered it. In fact, their limited numbers may have made them more conventionally loyal and uncritical than military men."[63] This point must give pause to feminist antimilitarists and equal rights feminists alike. Will it finally be the case that the small numbers of military women, less than 15 percent, will hold and ultimately not have a great impact on military culture? How will this determine the impact of Fainsod Katzenstein's view of feminist influence inside the armed forces? Will they not be the bare hope of, or threat of depending on where you sit, a Trojan horse to the Pentagon? This is a question as yet unresolvable. More to the point is the level of heated debate that persists even with these small numbers of women in the first place. That, of course, is our signal that the numbers are far less interesting than the symbolic effects, the tremors created in military culture's meaning systems.

I think it is fair to say that even national NOW originally made the argument for women in the military in order to fulfill an equal rights logic, but not in support of militarism since their statements were always, until 1990, qualified with statements, such as in National Conference 1971, about the effects of militarism:

WHEREAS, women are victims of the military in war, through rape and forced prostitution, and WHEREAS, military training relies upon sexual slurs against women to inflame soldiers into aggression, and WHEREAS, military decisions are exclusively made by male supremacists, and WHEREAS, men themselves are subject to loss of life and personhood by being subject to compulsory military service from which women are exempt, and WHEREAS, women in the military are restricted on the basis of sex in job training, education, area of service and are confined to low level, non-policy positions, THEREFORE BE IT RESOLVED, that NOW condemns the degradation of women by sexist practices within the military and the sexist basis for compulsory military service [emphasis in original].[64]

NOW's *amicus curiae* of 1980 in the *Rostker v. Goldberg* case of unequal protection regarding selective service of men only more precisely argued that compulsory conscription was the key to first-class citizenship. As their published policy adopted by the National Board in 1980 they wrote: "NOW opposes the reinstatement of registration and draft for both men and women. NOW's primary focus on this issue is on opposition to registration and draft. However, if we cannot stop the return to registration and draft, we also cannot choose between sisters and brothers. We oppose any registration or draft that excludes women as an unconstitutional denial of rights to both young men and women."[65]

Finally there is another group, the Brigadier General Evelyn Footes of the forces, who have always felt a place for themselves in the military and think women should have the career access and citizenship status bequeathed by martial service. This position stands for a truly equal rights military. Feminist egalitarian militarists are predominantly career military women, and women soldiers, who aim to have women accepted as the capable career soldiers that they have, of course, already proven themselves to be! Witness Carolyn Becraft of the Women in the Military Project for WEAL (Women's Equity Action League): "In order to assure continued assimilation of women in the military, it will continue to be necessary for civilian political officials in the Department of Defense and Congress to provide guidance and oversight of the military in the interest of equitable treatment of military women and preservation of the effectiveness of the All Volunteer Forces."[66] Becraft has for years collected and reported on the changing conditions for women in the military and was just promoted from being Deputy Assistant Secretary of Defense for Personnel Support, Families, and Education to Assistant Secretary of the Navy for Manpower and Reserve Affairs. Becraft founded the Women in the Military Project currently located at the Women's Research and Education Institute (WREI), and formerly at Women's Equity Action

League. WEAL, WREI, and NOW, especially since bringing in Karen Johnson, USAF (ret.) as National Secretary and then as Vice President of Membership, have each contributed to developing the formal equal rights feminist position on women in the military. It is a position that rests wholly on fighting the inequities within the military as an institution on the basis, as I suggested earlier, of the simple logic of equal rights. At times this position takes on a combative tone, as in this statement from Johnson, written in response to the 1997 panel report from the Federal Advisory Committee on Gender Integrated Training:

> Over the last 25 years women have increased from 2 percent to 13.5 percent of military personnel. As women have increased our presence and roles in the military, some of the old guard among military and civilian leaders have greatly resisted the further integration of women in the armed forces. To these old guards I say, "So, your mothers, sisters, daughters, granddaughters, and nieces wear combat boots. Get over it! Resistance is futile!"[67]

Women's Military Histories

While many are fighting for policy changes directly to insure women's access to the full range of Military Occupational Specialties (MOSs), or military job classifications, there are also a number of scholars of military women's histories who are recovering those stories and using them to "normalize" women's participation as a heretofore unacknowledged part of the composition and history of military life. All of these historians and scholars of women's military history deal with the masculinism of militarism; it is likely impossible to avoid! What the majority of these scholars do not do, and thus part of why I classify them still as militarists, is to challenge the militarism of the military itself. This means that the arguments for women in the military are posited as a question of inclusion in an important public/government institution, but not as a question of the nature of that institution itself.

It is also instructive, I think, to note that in the late 1990s, as MOSs are increasingly opened to women, the unilateral activities of the United States military are seemingly receding in importance. This change is simultaneous with the moment when women's histories of their place in the forces and women's inclusion in all but the most "direct" combat jobs are occurring. What this means for the future role of women in the forces cannot yet be told. What is clear is that conversations about women and the military need to be wrested from their round robin about what women can do (with their bodies or their psyches), and grounded in conversations about the role of martial service in citizenship, the masculinism of martial service in citizenship, and the implications therein for the rights and responsibilities of women as citizens. This, from a feminist antimilitarist point of view, requires a reexamination of the premises for martial citizenship as first class. At that point we can also begin to discuss and foreground broader questions about the use of the military itself. The women who write about their experiences in the forces and push for women's greater access therein, consistently point to citizenship as one of their primary impulses.

The majority of the books about women in the forces are being written by women who have been there. In this burgeoning literature on women and the armed forces, the "fact" is also being rediscovered that women have participated in United States martial service (informally) since the colonial struggle to found the nation. Many of the authors write about their branch's history and detail the struggles and achievements of integrating women into the forces. Major General Jeanne Holm, USAF (ret.) has written a definitive work on women's incorporation into the forces in the twentieth century, with special emphasis on the Air Force, and she is quoted widely.[68] Jean Ebbert and Marie Beth Hall have written on the Navy and, as they describe themselves in the preface of their book: "Both authors have ties with the Navy and bear it deep affection. We are both married to retired Naval officers. Marie Beth Hall is the daughter of a Naval officer and the mother of two more. Jean Ebbert is a former Naval officer and the author of books and articles about the Navy and for thirteen years was a Naval Academy Information Officer."[69] Two authors, commissioned by the Center for Military History, have each written part of the history of women in the United States Army, Colonel Betty J. Morden, USA (ret.) and Lieutenant Colonel Mattie Treadwell. Their work is published through the Center for Military History's Army Historical Series.[70] These representative and widely accepted texts begin to uncover the extent of women's participation and certainly set the stage for women in the forces to chronicle that history.

More recent books have focused on particular historical moments or demographic groups.[71] A number of other publications have worked to biograph the career of a particular military woman:[72] a tendency to use oral history and autobiography is quite strong in the literature on women in the forces.[73] In addition, as I finish this book numerous others are recently or almost in print reviewing various women's military histories, and analyzing current gender dynamics in the forces. The field is expanding with new insights about the ways that women are and have been situated in the military.

The Internet list for information about women and the military, H-MINERVA, has many subscribers who are present or former military women, many with, or pursuing, advanced academic degrees. This list is the H-MINERVA@H-NET.MSU.EDU and a spin off from Professor Linda Grant De Pauw's Minerva Center and her two periodical publications on women and the military: *Minerva Quarterly Report on Women and the Military* and *Minerva Bulletin Board*. All three publications are excellent sources of information and contacts with people interested in studying the topic. De Pauw herself has written on women and the military,[74] and is responsible for much of the wide-ranging scholarly network in the field of women and the military.

Several important trends are emerging in this literature. The first is the tendency of the historical literature[75] to create narratives of the struggles for women to be incorporated in the various levels of the forces and then end with high hopes for women's complete inclusion on the logic of equal rights and equal responsibility, their merits as fine soldiers who have already proved themselves worthy of martial citizenship, and the fact that they are already practicing martial valor and sacrifice without the benefits of martial citizenship.

The second trend is a nascent dispute regarding the historical numbers (read actuality) of lesbians in the armed forces.[76] The illegality of homosexuality in the forces, despite "don't ask, don't tell," makes this dispute difficult to resolve, because of the necessarily closeted stature of lesbians in, or veterans of, the military. This debate is being engaged by various groups of women in the forces trying to recover the history to validate their relationship to the forces, and it is steeped in the structural homophobia, heterosexism, and masculinism of the forces. This is a struggle laden with the policing mechanisms for women's nontraditional accomplishment in the military and for reinforcing the bounds of ultimate masculinity in traditionally masculinist military culture.[77]

The trouble in trying to mark out authentic sexual orientation demographics in the forces is linked precisely to the confounding of sexual norms that occur as soon as a woman is located in the forces; in other words, *nice* girls don't shoot guns. This trouble is then compounded by the changing political meanings of claiming the identity (even the notion of the identity "lesbian" is a historically located label) over a period that ranges at least from World War II. A recovery of long-standing women's culture and lesbian camaraderie in the ranks is also readable as the non-lesbian bonding between heterosexual women in a sex-segregated, career-oriented, that is, nontraditional context. Homophobia, both cultural and legal, in the forces feeds the difficulty by leaving no room for women to identify themselves safely in the most public sense. Thus, disputes over the numbers of women in the forces who were, or are, lesbians are unresolvable because of their restraint by martial law, and because of the uneasy and unclear gender crossings in cultural signs such as dress, marital status, career choice, and association.[78] Finally, the vigorous claiming of a lesbian identity in the forces, and the vigorous marking of a history of lesbian identity over time, are both charged with political meaning and great civic importance in the contemporary struggles for inclusive citizenship rights. In other words, we cannot argue for inclusive citizenship rights without also tackling the question of who gets to claim that citizenship.

This historical recovery works in similarly noninnocent ways as the historical recovery of the "woman" in battle. Both kinds of recovery remain controversial acts because of the amnesia about the recurrent debate that Fenner points out and the literal erasure of the record of women's war work; that is, they are at the front lines but not technically combatants. Therefore they received no combat duty pay. It is common discussion among women soldiers, although seemingly impossible to document, that women pilots' flight records were altered in Grenada, in Panama, and in the Gulf, to erase any proximity to combat. This impossibility is due both to the hearsay nature of the information over the Internet, and that the evidence was, precisely, erased.

Overall, feminist egalitarian militarists argue from several overlapping positions. They argue for complete gender equality: women should have both rights and responsibilities the same as men. This, feminist egalitarian militarists suggest, is the track for first-class citizenship. They also argue, and this shows up ironically in our most outspoken politically elite feminist egalitarian militarists' discourse, that women need to have equal access to the careers afforded by the military. These are strategically necessary points for *justifying women's inclusion* in the military as an institution. What they do not do is to *justify the military* as an institution.

Feminist Antimilitarisms and Feminist Soldiers: Upping the Anti *[sic]*

As Enloe (1992) argues, the position of feminist egalitarian militarism has assumed preeminence in national, and possibly international, figurations of the construction of women soldiers. I am interested in finding a way to shape a feminist antimilitarism that engages this construction of the woman soldier, but draws together Enloe's two-part concern with which I began the chapter: that the military is too important an institution to let its sexism go unchallenged *and* that the military is too important. Equal rights feminists need feminist antimilitarists' analyses of the military as a patriarchal institution to better assess the structural integration of masculinism in the military. Feminist antimilitarists need to grapple with the class and the citizenship rights and responsibilities issues to better assess the draw of the military, in particular for women soldiers, but also to cast the analysis of militarism more broadly and with more precision at the same time.

In this light, while feminist antimilitarist arguments contribute critical insights regarding sexism, heterosexism, racism, and patriarchy as an interlocking system that clearly continues to operate in and shape practices of the military culture, they do not serve to explain women's interest in the military and the acts of performing war —except as an inadequate claim that military women are subjects of false consciousness or a poor draft. We have to heed Katzenstein's warning here that feminists in the military are indeed challenging its sexism; they are not merely being pulled along by job prospects. We also have to recognize and account for the intense pride and entitlement felt by some military women regarding their abilities and successes in their military careers.

Feminist egalitarian militarists, on the other hand, argue for egalitarian practices on the basis of citizenship rights and responsibilities, and for career goals. While these are important approaches to defining equality and citizenship, resting them on access to the military's strata is no sure guarantee of success. Women have gained access to many levels of the military since the opening of the All Volunteer Forces, however they still remain less than 15 percent of the forces overall, and their position in the broader culture has not noticeably improved in relation to their military access. In the past, men of color gained access to formal citizenship rights, freedom from incarceration or bondage via martial service, as I document in chapter 3 on martial citizenship, but women already have those formal rights. In fact, military access for women is in part symptomatic of the achievement of those formal rights, not a precursor to them. I agree with Barbara Omolade of Hunter College, quoted in an article by Annette Fuentes in the *Nation,* "African-Americans seek heroes. Even people who think we shouldn't have been in the Persian Gulf look at Colin Powell with awe. People have always said black people can't fight. So we joined the Army to prove it. That same thrust has picked up around women. But blacks have not found true equality through military service. And having Powell at the top won't change foreign policy."[79] Feminist egalitarian militarists need to be clear that they argue for women's access to the military as an end in itself. They produce no critique of the patriarchal underpinnings of militarism, no question of how the impulses of militarism thrive on sexual domination (including the "friendly fire" rape of female U.S. troops by male U.S. troops, such as in the Gulf War), racism, prostitution in the oppressive brothel industries, pornographic literature—such as the pin-up calendars sold in the Pentagon bookstore pre-Gulf War, pornographic films played before bombing raids, or publicized demeaning of other cultures' women, such as the "nicknames" for Saudi women during the Gulf War: BMO or Black Moving Object.

Both movements, feminist antimilitarism and feminist egalitarian militarism, have effected the terms by which and terrain on which the military operates. Feminist antimilitarism has done so by restraining military actions, and feminist egalitarian militarism by challenging the patriarchal culture of military action through women's inclusion. They have achieved this through their own criticisms of the military, and in conjunction with the transformation in military technologies and strategies since the Vietnam War, with the economic transformations globally and in the United States, and with the broader social changes resultant from feminism's challenges to masculinist culture beyond the military and reflected back on it. These changes include a myriad of litigation for women's rights to their bodily safety and integrity, to equal treatment in the workplace and schools, and to the general improvement of women's status as citizens. This labor is ongoing and feminists bridging the gaps between equal access and antimilitarism are critical to furthering a project for justice and peace.

Enloe's statement guides me in thinking through how important it is to push these two agenda into conversation. It is critical for feminist antimilitarists to pay attention to the points made by liberal feminist militarists and visa versa. If we do not, we allow the debate to be shaped in great measure by antifeminist masculinist militarists like Phyllis Schlafly (as I will suggest happened with the ERA), who oppose women in the military altogether, and then we lose the point of equal rights, access, responsibility, and peace. If we allow the terrain of struggle over these issues to be defined only by equal rights feminists, we allow it to be discussed as a simple matter of letting women in and thus perhaps partially transforming the institution, without challenging the military's ongoing problems: for example, racism and (hetero)sexism are litigated out, but still persist structurally and culturally in the forces. Homophobia remains legally entrenched. Racism that emerges as class/rank stratification still functions: witness the placement of white women as combat jet flyers. In other words, we lose the feminist antimilitarist critique of the military as part of the system of patriarchal domination that encloses it.

Finally, if we allow the debate over the military to be defined only by feminist antimilitarism, we lose the ability to see several things: (1) an important terrain on which to argue about the defining terms of first-class citizenship; (2) the ability to converse with women soldiers about militarism; (3) the opportunities to view changes in the patriarchy and understand how it moves, diffuses, or falls apart, and then what? (4) The makings of an important class analysis with both domestic and international implications—not just a poor draft; and finally, (5) the dilemma that we cannot simply say "war's a dick thing" when women also want to fight: moved by bravado, skill, patriotism, and so forth.

The following two chapters work to set up a broader theoretical framework in which to pursue answers to the questions I raise here. I turn to theories of gendered and racialized state power in order to understand how prerogative state power, in the form of the military, is continuing to shape women's relationships to it. I then look more closely at the question of attaining first-class citizenship in the United States and wonder what is to be gained for women by this approach. These two foci serve to build on my analysis of the separate approaches feminist egalitarian militarists and feminist antimilitarists already take and to model what we might gain by bringing those approaches together for justice and peace.

TWO

The Soldier in the State

The master's tools will never dismantle the master's house. —Audre Lorde (1984)

As the sites and registers of women's relationships to the state expand in late modernity, both the characteristics and the meanings of the state's maleness transmogrify. Ceasing to be primarily a domain of masculinist powers and an instrument of male privilege and hegemony, albeit maintaining these functions, the state increasingly takes over and transforms the project of male dominance. However, as it moves in this direction, the state's masculinism becomes more diffuse and subtle even as it becomes more potent and pervasive in women's lives. Indeed, while the state replaces the man for many women, its jurisprudential and legislative powers, its welfare apparatus, and even its police powers often appear as leading agents of sex equality or female protection. —Wendy Brown (1995)

In this chapter I consider women's entry to the military as a process embedded in the development of postmodern late capitalism and effected by the transformative influences of social movement politics. In other words, I want to suggest that to understand women's entry to the military and respond to it—from either anti- or pro-positions—we are much better able to do so by understanding the conditions of that entry. By contextualizing women's entry to the military in these broad political and economic terms, I foreground and engage the intersections of class, racial, and sexual hierarchies in the United States as they operate through the military. This approach presents a clear view of the ways that the military as a social institution both reflects and creates cultural assumptions that undergird United States society. By bringing the political and economic fields together, arguments about the military in the culture and the culture in the military are more effectively presented.

Feminist antimilitarist analyses that suggest militarism as a cultural hegemony[1] can be bolstered and sophisticated by this approach. Jacklyn Cock's analysis of the definition of militarism is instructive here in that she lays out three interconnected aspects of militarism and suggests an approach to analyzing it: "the military as a social institution," "militarism as an ideology . . . an acceptance of organized state violence as a legitimate solution to conflict," and "militarization as a social process . . . involv[ing] a mobilisation of resources for war at political, economic and ideological levels."[2] Cock tells us it is precisely in the analysis of the interconnections between these three, with close attention paid to their political-economic context, that we see how militarist culture is constructed, how it is regenerated, and what are our points of collusion and resistance. I learned from Cynthia Enloe's work that to understand international politics and militarism precisely, we need not only to look at the apparent, masculine contributions, but that we also need to look at women's participation to see the fullness of gendered militarism. I suggest here that to understand women in relationship to the United States military and militarism we must look at such a broader context. I suggest, alongside Cock, that we limit the analysis of militarism if we simply identify it as the aspect of the state which houses prerogative governmental power. I see militarism as operating in Cock's three-part process in the United States, particularly bolstered by the economic linkages via the military-industrial complex and fully integrated into the social structuration of the culture via everything from children's war toys to corporate dependence on Defense Department contracts.

My focus is on the masculinist apparatus of the military and militarism as they are impacted by debates over women's inclusion. My understandings of the masculinity of the state, and more precisely its patriarchal modes of operation, are keyed by Audre Lorde's insight in the epigraph, echoed by Wendy Brown.[3] In framing the state thus, my view of the possibilities for women as soldiers is definitively narrowed. In this chapter, I describe what I think are some of the larger-scale reasons for women's entry to the military and what that might indicate for us about women's place therein, about the shape of the military, and about the possibilities for feminist antimilitarism.

I rely on the, perhaps now classic, triumvirate of race, class, and gender as my analytical framework for studying the dynamics of the United States military. I describe my understanding of this framework through its component parts, but primarily as a whole to read the state of the state, and through that to read the constellation of women soldiers, feminist antimilitarists, and the military. Truth be told, I am unable to think about the workings of the world, of feminism, of militarism, of even my backyard garden without noticing the interconnections of these aspects of our culture. For instance, I—a white middle-class woman with heterosexual privilege, regardless of how I think I muck up the boundaries in practice—garden in a backyard because I want to, not because it is my wage like so many of my neighbors in the Pajaro Valley who work very unromantic rows of strawberries under the constant toxic cloud of methyl bromide, my neighbors of whom the wage workers are almost all Latinos and Latinas, currently struggling to unionize, many of whose children sit in my college classrooms working with me to figure out the possibilities for our collective futures. I have come to see this triumvirate as an indispensable tool for understanding how we are who we are, and what to make of it after all.

I am indebted, as are most theorists of models of interlocking identities and social positions, to the feminist theorists who have blazed the trails by modeling for us the ways that these linked identities shape our living conditions. Both first-wave United States feminists, emergent from the abolitionist movement in the middle 1800s, and second wave feminists, in the civil rights movement in the middle 1900s, have presented us with understandings of the connections between slavery and patriarchy, civil rights and women's rights—even if white women, by and large, have proceeded on both occasions to distance themselves from those connections in order to win concessions from the liberal patriarchal state. Nevertheless, mid–twentieth-century antiracist feminist theorists including Gloria Anzaldúa, Angela Davis, Barbara Deming, Audre Lorde, Adrienne Rich, Chela Sandoval, Barbara Smith,[4] and many other activist scholars of the 1970s and 1980s—as I argued in chapter 1 about the feminist antimilitarists—developed the models of interlocking oppressions in their work to try and understand the precise ways that government policy, and economic, social, and political practices differentially effect and were effected by communities of citizens in the United States.

To understand the social construction of race,[5] the masculinism in the state,[6] and the layered and multiplied effects of social and political exclusions of women as a way of understanding the reasons for women's entry to the forces, I am interested in taking up the analytical tool presented by Kum Kum Bhavnani and Margaret Coulson: "racially structured patriarchal capitalism." They suggest this term, in a longer conversation about feminist theorizing and racism,[7] as a way of thinking through the complex intersection of modalities of oppression. Bhavnani and Coulson insist that the elision of the term "racism" for the term "ethnocentrism" dilutes the very point of connection between these modalities of oppression. They ask socialist feminists, "to examine how 'race,' class, and gender are structured in relation to one another. How do they combine with and/or cut across one another?... To take these questions on does require a fundamental redrawing of the conceptual categories of socialist-feminism, and it may help us to develop a more adequate politics."[8] I think their formulation predates and answers Judith Butler's more recent worry that when we list terms such as race, class, gender, sexuality, and so on, we are demonstrating that we are not sure exactly how they fit together. Rather, Bhavnani and Coulson present us with a phrase that indicates precisely what the relationships between oppressive modalities in the United States look like.

I am setting this complex (and interestingly cumbersome) term as a guide for my analyses and as one important key for understanding the dynamic of late twentieth-century militarism. I find the analytical and political tools of an antiracist socialist-feminist perspective help me to answer a set of questions about how these cross-cutting categories shape women's experience in the military. I hope to contribute to our understandings of the social/economic structures of the armed forces, and suggest some strategic shifts for antimilitarists in our work to dismantle militarism.

My first sense of this tool is that it helps to simultaneously foreground and magnify the varying forces that encumber the issues of women and the military, and feminist antimilitarism. As I have stated in the previous chapter, feminist antimilitarism has unevenly applied, but frequently accounted for, the interlocution of these terms. It will not be surprising to note that women of color most frequently used the combined tools as their method for analyzing militarism's differential effects on women and their communities, since women of color bear the double (or multiple) jeopardy of these arrangements.[9] Of course, having presented a tool leads to the mythic assumption that it will provide the appropriate rubric for all subsequent analysis. In practice, the mutations to masculinist militarism and racially structured patriarchal capitalism, the ways that each groans against its own boundaries of description, are part of what we get to use in discovering ways out!

One of my quarrels with feminist antimilitarism, as it should now be apparent, is that it does not adequately address the conditional absorption of women into the military. Women (of all colors and socioeconomic backgrounds) do not all behave in predictable ways (for the sake of the gender), race emerges and submerges as a salient category in determining access and discrimination in the military, and even big bad bogeys such as the Reagan administration have complex contradictory relationships to this story. Given those conditions, I will use the tool to reflect on the various moments I address and look for ways that it helps me, and hopefully you the reader, to understand how we got here.

In other words, while I take up this tool as a framework for analysis and a method of inquiry, I also recognize that the systems I am studying are embedded in the process of change via their own institutional requirements and activist pressures on various fronts; therefore, they are not fixed to any one set of strategies. That, of course, is part of the object of my study, in that the question of women in relation to the military is open and in flux now, which I highlight in the section of the book on temporal changes in the military and antimilitarism through the late Twentieth century. The constant threat of war, in our war-centered culture, means that feminist antimilitarists must be prepared to respond. This means that feminist antimilitarists need an activist bag of tricks that can expand on the current repertoire to include critical, dynamic reflection on the changing structures and meanings of national, racial, class, and gender hierarchies in United States' citizenship rites.

As I will demonstrate in the next chapter, these citizenship rites, especially in relationship to martial first-class citizenship, are precisely and historically masculinist. I follow Brown's suggestion that "the state's masculinism becomes more diffuse and subtle even as it becomes more potent and pervasive in women's lives."[10] I concur with her analysis that the masculinism of the state is changing, but not eroding. I contend, following Stiehm[11] that women are entering in small enough numbers to have minimal impact on the forces' role in providing masculinity a proving ground for citizenship, and precisely, women are entering just enough to be superficial evidence that the military is an equal opportunity employer. My attention below to the racial demographics even within women's ranks demonstrates that racism continues to distort the formal equal opportunity policies of the armed forces. On the other hand, I want to be sure to claim the changes in the state, which have made significant differences in women's lives, to the credit of the women activists that have launched them. I just share Brown's suspicion that working within the state's apparati leaves us subject, in the simplest of terms, to co-optation by that very state.

While I am working with the implications of such reflections on domestic U.S. conceptions and practices of citizenship, my understandings of the domestic situation are shaped by the international ramifications of the functions of the state and particularly the militarist state. Cynthia Enloe's work has guided me here as she maps the intersections of gender, race, and international politics, with specific focus on the United States militarism and its international support structures. While she carefully shows us the ways that women are being absorbed as soldiers, she also suggests that the professionalization of women soldiers might lead to the reconciliation of the contradiction between women and the masculinist "violent sacrifice under state discipline in the name of the nation."[12] Enloe is right to suggest that this current turn toward women as professional soldiers and soldiering as a profession is interesting and interested in legitimizing women's place as citizens. We have to be careful to note this within its quite limited application. That is, as a symbolic legitimization particular to a small number of career soldier women within a small number of soldier women overall. Several turns of this agenda are not so benign. First, the professionalization is at the highest ranks, and not in the general and increasingly poor ranks of soldiers. Second, as computerization and automation of the military come to predominate, as Gray[13] tells us it shall via his readings of military planners' documents, the role of foot soldiers will diminish, thus devaluing women's work as they enter.

1973: Political Sea Changes

We arrived at this demographic of women soldiers and these debates over women's soldiering through a constellation of changes over the late twentieth century that are critical to this discussion. My approach to this material serves to remind us that it is a public activist legacy which has helped to shape the current conditions and provides us with a way to map out future appraisal and action. My attention to the influences over the changes in women's access to the military is informed by the sea change in international relations since the early 1970s. The period is usually marked as beginning roughly in 1973[14] during the confluent events of the end of the Vietnam War, the end of mandatory conscription and the beginning of the Vietnam Syndrome—the discrediting of U.S. foreign policy of force and the refusal of many male citizens[15] to participate in martial sacrifice. It was shaped economically by the first major oil crisis and post–World War II recession. This sea change was also wrought by international transformations through new racial and national identities as a result of migrations and decolonizations, corporate capital's flight to the free trade zones (which had been occurring since the mid-1960s but stepped up pace in this period), heavy recruitment of women into the armed forces (the 2 percent quota was dropped in 1969) and their inclusion in United States military academies. This last pair of events were occasioned by the rise of second-wave feminism, represented in part by the struggle for the Equal Rights Amendment and in large measure by a myriad of activist pressures and broad-based cultural, sociopolitical transformations. The proliferation of liberation/anticolonial struggles, and new forms of social protest around issues of identity politics, nuclear arms and power, environmental activism, and social justice issues helped to shape this transformation. The combination of these social and political changes, acting on one another in a multiplicity of ways, has opened a space for women to assert themselves in areas heretofore prohibited, and to be "used inside of the current social and economic system in particularly exploitive ways."[16] The loss of factory jobs in the United States, the increased demand for technically skilled workers, and the discourse of equal rights have all contributed to women's push for access to the military.[17]

This connection implies that women entering the United States military do so primarily for economic reasons, and not necessarily for access to notions of noble citizenry or martial valor. The predominance of working-class volunteers, coupled with the armed forces' marketing strategy that promises access to increasingly inaccessible educational opportunities in marketable technical fields, supports this argument. Of course, for women recruits the actual conditions inside the military remain freighted with difficult barriers of racism, sexism, and harassment. Nevertheless, women of all colors are being targeted for recruitment, and the economic draw is sufficient in the first instance to at least create the circumstance of women's increased enlistment.

Racially Structured Patriarchal Capitalism and Women Soldiers

We need some way . . . to represent all the shifting and churning that has gone on since the first major post-war recession of 1973, which does not lose sight of the fact that the basic rules of a capitalist mode of production continue to operate as invariant shaping forces in historical-geographic development.[18]

By analyzing the discourse (equality) and the material imperatives (class, gender, and racially/ethnically based economic insecurities) of women's recent claims to be included in the "opportunities" afforded by participation in the military, feminist antimilitarists can locate one of the more severe repercussions of global arrangements of late twentieth century capitalism. While, as Enloe suggests, we now have the image of the woman as "professional soldier citizen" representing women's aspirations to military service, rather than the older "poor draft" model, I argue that there is still a disproportionate number of women, and men, joining for the equal opportunity that the forces promise. In fact, the forces have been increasingly unable to deliver on that promise as more cuts in personnel, downsizing of bases, and general increase in poverty amongst base families occurs in the forces of the late 1990s. The Defense Authorization Act (FY2000) includes proposals for access to food stamps. This poverty continues to show along racial lines, reflecting the continued interpersonal and structural racism in the society, even in the face of the equal opportunity model of the armed forces recruitment policies.[19] The Reserves provide a flexible secondary labor pool to draw from in times of crisis. The ranks of the infantry and the Reserves contain disproportionate numbers of people of color to the civilian population, and disproportionate numbers of women of color to white women.[20] Infantry ranks are being squeezed by downsizing and the criteria, although as yet unofficial, are being shifted to prefer recruits with high school diplomas. This occurs at a time when the military's downsizing allows it to be more selective, with the result that poorer potential recruits, those who have dropped out of school to earn subsistence wages, will not be as readily brought on board.[21] Interestingly, this shift in informal criteria remains informal. This should be a reminder to military demographics scholars of how important it can sometimes be to recruit any and all bodies, thus the need for recruitment flexibility. This flexible secondary labor pool creates potential crises of its own, such as when Reservists, unaccustomed to the possibility of actual deployment, found themselves being called up for active duty during the Gulf War.

If we articulate patriarchy, racism, and capitalism as a larger, albeit permeable, system, then we must stretch Harvey's plea to note that the basic rules of a racially structured, patriarchal capitalism continue to operate by virtue of their flexibility. Enloe suggests that the professionalization of soldier women "relegitimizes the military during an era of changing relations between women and men."[22] Certainly Brown[23] instructs us in this regard, theorizing the "postmodern" character of late twentieth-century state masculinism. As it grows more diffuse, harder to track, it nonetheless leaves its mark on political power arrangements. The military is such an interesting case study because of the ways it has incorporated some women as soldiers, creating trauma waves in the system, but has managed to leave its masculinist lore, culture, and practices intact. Even, as I will discuss in detail later on using the film *G.I. Jane,* the showing of women in the forces is not presented as a "feminist" success: "I don't want to be a poster girl for women's rights," Lieutenant Jordan O'Neal says in *G.I. Jane.* O'Neal relies upon her own merits, seeing her success as the result of being a "professionalized woman soldier," as

Enloe (1992) would suggest we are seeing framed now. Moreover, the ease with which this transition is occurring has more to do with the changing nature of the military operation than the changing nature of the military as a masculinist culture. In the operational sense, the increased reliance on and planning through techno-warfare presents us with a situation where, as Gray and Addis[24] suggest, soldiers being women matters less as war technology automates and becomes the core of war's "technostrategy."[25] As the military system shifts its weight toward automation and a privileging of computer expertise over the arts of hand-to-hand combat there is a flurry of nostalgia over the art of combat. The recent Disney adaptation of the Fa Mu Lan myth from China, *Mulan,* and the film *Saving Private Ryan* both tell us of the bravery and martial sacrifice of hand-to-hand combat. As martial valor's defining acts are transformed[26] so the soldiers' identities will follow; though perhaps not without some resistance. This does not mean that the military is any less interested in war, or in the kudos of masculinist martial valor.

Cultures of the State

Mainstream theories of postindustrial society have failed to appreciate the profound impact that civil rights and women's liberation movements have had on postindustrial (especially but not exclusively the United States) society's organization and political economy. Although the recent theories of the postindustrial and postfordist world help us to sketch initial pictures of the "new world order," they fail to account for the vast influences of feminist practices and survival strategies on this new political economy, both through progressive effects and through the state's reactionary national and economic restructurings. The intrusion of women to these models generates a remarkably more nuanced and more hopeful reading of the potential ruptures in the new world order and thus some possibilities of creating more hope-filled stories and strategies for justice and peace. More precisely, they provide us with a way to revisit the debates over women in the armed forces as part of a broader context of social and political transformation, and as fraught with cooptive dangers and misleading promise for women's citizenship. As Ferguson argues in her study of bureaucracy:

Militarism is a threat to women, not an opportunity. The military establishment is one of the most powerful organizational constellations in bureaucratic capitalism; recruiting women into it will not keep it from un-
dermining Third World experiments in socialism, or fueling a wasteful,
war-based economy, or escalating the arms race. The liberal argument that
'equal rights entail equal responsibilities' for all citizens is grounded in the
abstract conceptual categories of juridico-legal discourse. But the actual
public domain within which these rights and responsibilities take their
meaning is a barren bureaucratic realm, where there are few genuine opportunities for the collective, public activity that is properly called citizenship. (Ferguson 1984:195)

Wendy Brown tells us that it is the "theoretical problem of the state
itself, specifically that paradox that what we call the state is at once an in-
coherent, multifaceted ensemble of power relations and a vehicle of massive domination."[27] She argues that to ask for redress and protection
from the state for patriarchal injury when the state embodies patriarchy
is the wrong strategy. We have to notice the ways in which the state and
its military system continue to be masculinist. It is no great victory to
find women soldiers serving the masculinist state! On the other hand, we
have to be able to wrest any improvements in the conditions of women's
lives from the state and strategize our challenges so that they and we are
the most effective in disrupting the masculinist business as usual of the
state. As feminists, it is critical to map the transformations of patriarchy
in itself and develop a clear sense of the articulations between patriarchy
and capitalism as they accommodate, or fail to accommodate, interest
group demands for inclusion.

Racially structured patriarchal capitalism is undergoing a series of
adaptations to accommodate certain claims of the women's movements
and of nonwhite racial/ethnic groups of women and of men, and yet it
has not been dismantled, nor adequately impacted. I suggest that the inclusion of women in military ranks and academies has minimally shifted
the power, although it is a necessary starting point.

If, as Brown (1995) tells us, "leftists have largely forsaken analyses of
the liberal state and capitalism as sites of *domination* and have focused
instead on their implication in political and economic *inequalities*,"[28]
then what kind of project is it to argue for women's increased access to
the upper echelons of the military? This is precisely the danger in moves

to open the military on the basis of redressing inequalities inside what Ferguson calls a barren bureaucratic realm. While fighting for women's unfettered access to the military as an institution, as an important first step—witness Enloe's exhortation—this strategy by itself (much of liberal feminist militarist thrust) forgets the question of the military as a far-too-important apparatus of force—the second half of Enloe's exhortation—and also forgets the inevitability of women soldiers being effective on and affected by the masculinism of the institution.

The Racially Structured Patriarchal Capitalist State

Frederic Jameson provided a model to read postmodernism as the logic of late capitalism. He suggested that we could better understand postmodernism by seeing it as a piece of late capitalism and thus be able to map the transformations in our late twentieth-century life through that understanding, rather than give in to the fragmentation as it were. I use several texts[29] which attempt to combine and explain postmodernism and postfordism. Their models are helpful to a feminist project of social and economic justice, and in some ways they can illuminate the entry of women to the military. These stories generate maps whose partiality leaves much to be desired in terms of understanding the conditions of women's lives, and yet they do provide a first stage of conceptualizing the predicaments we face.. I find that their omission of a consideration of racialized and gendered conditions obscures the ways in which women's expanding roles in the formally civil (and previously male-dominated) spheres of socio-economic life have been central to the transformations of which these authors speak. The disruption of social meanings they attribute largely to the changing industrial economic conditions of the postmodern/postfordist period, were in fact producing, and produced by, women's and men of color's new (and old) economic and social locations. The fissure in the military apparatus which has enabled women to pressure their way in is also a result of, and in relation to, these changing conditions and civic activisms.

I use the military as an example of the applied and integral relationship among racism, patriarchy, and capitalism. I anticipate the "feminization" and "color-coding" of certain sectors of military work and pay, simply by following the pattern of other sectors of wage labor that have opened to white women and women and men of color in the late twentieth century. As such, women can be incorporated into the male-centered military as long as they are placed within clearly marked female and racially tiered roles. Even with the 1993 entry of women to limited combat roles as fighter pilots, the women consistently profiled are white.

The Radical Economists

To place the radical economists in proper perspective, inside the debates about Marxism in the late twentieth century, it is important to recall that Marx predicted that the capitalist system would dig its own grave through the increased concentration of capital itself. This concentration would bring with it economic crisis and through the acute polarization of the working and capitalist classes, would sharpen the conflict to revolution. Over the course of the twentieth century many Marxian theorists have complexified this picture. Lenin's addition of the dimension of imperialism enabled him to point out that through expansion and foreign domination capitalist nations could manage their internal contradictions and sustain themselves more effectively than Marx had foreseen. Gramsci incorporated the notion that the culture arising through mass consumption would serve as a motor for continuing capitalist development once the early stages of monopoly capitalism were stabilized, and the creation of basic industry no longer served as the catalyst.[30] From the 1930s, the Frankfurt School developed critical theory to argue that ideology as such had become the central organizing factor of capital/labor relations and that this was a socially structured motor.[31] Others, mostly since the 1960s and largely working and/or inspired through the Frankfurt School, have pointed to the key role of social and economic reform in regenerating capitalism. This theoretical frame is most thoroughly expounded now by the theorists in the Regulation School.[32]

French Regulation School theorists, and Social Structures of Accumulation theorists in the United States, have a common agenda of continuing to assert a key role for the working class and arguing for a longer-term and more nuanced development of capitalism than was previously mapped. They see this development as stages that are catalyzed by crises in over-accumulation, which lead to further expansion and colonization of new natural and labor resource pools. It is here that they are most useful in explaining the logic of women's inclusion in the United States military.[33]

The Social Structures theorists present a logic of capital management that I think can be seen as the driving force behind the military establishment's willingness to recruit women. The inclusion of citizens' agency by the U.S. theorists establishes the argument that the simultaneous pressures from a changing labor pool and from the workers themselves combine to create this opening for women soldiers. In general, this gender shift in the workplace has important ramifications for wage relations, that is, the "family wage," and specifically for the armed forces it has the further stunning effect of calling into question the male-centered culture of martial service.

Because of their focus on the complex terrain of economy, culture, and the physical ability of capitalism to expand, these theories have all helped explain why the class system has not polarized with the severity Marx predicted and why economic concentration did not lead immediately to crisis and revolution. In essence, the concentration of capital has occurred over a broader field and a longer time, enabling an analysis of internal stages. Furthermore, capitalist networks can manage these crises. On the other hand, grounded in Gramsci's insights and brought forward by theorists of postmodernity, the notion of power intimately tied to resistance[34] has complexified the "class struggle" by recognizing the agency and consciousness of the oppressed as opposed to their assumed false consciousness. This agency also presents a different strategic challenge for feminist antimilitarist activists in engaging with women in the armed forces. In other words, feminist antimilitarism cannot afford to dismiss women's attraction to the armed forces as simply a "poor draft." Nevertheless, much of the appeal for women seeking to rise in professional status in the forces is certainly tied to economic benefits, at least in part. However, this raises the question of the "professionalized women soldier-citizen."

Several writers are working to combine analyses of late twentieth century economy and postmodernism. Lash and Urry[35] argue that, as the postmodernist "culture" is characterized by disorder and fragmentation, so goes the global economy. They posit the concept of "disorganized capitalism" to argue that monopoly capitalism is in fact in a structural crisis, that class polarization in general, and the working class in particular, are no longer the models of the revolutionary moment. They are less concerned with pointing to a revolutionary moment as such and rather see that the disarray itself is the source of changes in relations of capital. While this is an accurate reading of the conditions, it obscures any notion of conscious agency in the process. The service class, in their account, is the center of this disarray in the United States. However, it is not apparent what kind of agency the service class might have, nor do Lash and Urry make clear who is in this class by description of racial and gender tiers, who have long been exploited.

Ernest Mandel and then Frederic Jameson have used the term "late capitalism" to imply a transition from capitalism to yet something new. Jameson uses late capitalism as a framework for discussing social and economic fragmentation as a basis for postmodern culture. Jameson points out that the late capitalist economy and postmodern culture are in effect merged and that struggle on the cultural level is just as critical as economic struggle. Furthermore, he writes that this period is one of crisis in liberal capitalism, which is reflected as a crisis in social meaning.[36] As such he presents the possible location of seams in the new world order fabric. This model, of a crisis in liberal capitalism, reflects back on the question of women's roles in the military and in particular on the question of citizenship, because the pace of change for women in gendered liberal capitalism is also contested in this period via questions of what kinds of practices are anointed with tickets to first class status. Precisely, the political terms of late liberal capitalism are at stake here, precipitated by activist struggles to expand citizenship's terrain and by the state's (in its myriad forms) response. Thus, we see the logic for a "professional woman soldier-citizen."

Both Lash and Urry and Jameson mark this merging of capitalism and culture as if for the first time. Lash and Urry more subtly, Jameson more overtly, argue that postmodern culture and late capitalism need one another to sustain the production/consumption cycle. This map assumes that in a different market schema, there could be a separation of culture and politics, production and consumption. A more precise reading of the situation is that the insights and practices of the political movements of the late twentieth century, in particular the civil rights, women's movements, and direct action movements have enabled and insisted upon a reading of culture, politics, and economy as necessarily entwined.[37] As such, the revelations of both the postmodern and radical economic[38] theorists all told owe much to the refiguring of the political arising from these movements.

Lash and Urry, in an arguably reductive reading of Marxism, write that where Marxism sees capitalist development as driven by economic forces, they see a more complex picture that includes the workings of the state and culture. In this they develop accounts of the arbitrariness of meaning, the replacement of the word with the image and the consumption of the image over the product. This move goes beyond Aglietta's[39] assertion of fordism as generating the integral relation between production and consumption; that is, the commodification of social life. Lash and Urry emphasize spectacle over meaning, and the boundary breakdowns between culture and "private" lives in the ways that identity gets decentered and commodified. T. V. Reed reminds us that spectacle is also a critical form of creating meaning and thus the two are not only not vying for position, as in Lash and Urry's formulation, but rather the spectacle and the meaning are read within one another after all.[40]

While their account is in some ways persuasive, its critique of Marxism is far too curt. Not all Marxist analysis centers around the economy—in fact much of the Marxist analysis that is being generated contemporaneously with their work is greatly infused with the Gramscian-based insights regarding culture and consumption. For instance, Laclau and Mouffe point out the ways in which this commodification of social life has led to "numerous new struggles [expressing] resistance against the new forms of subordination . . . from within the very heart of the new society."[41] Indeed, a racially structured and patriarchally organized capitalism is at once more centralized and more thoroughly intrusively dispersed as the state takes on economic regulation. For example, this structure is enacted through AID policies which subsidize international industrial development, and increased social regulation through racially coded "family values" struggles, including surveillance of welfare clients, domestic drug wars, and a dismantling of the privacy rights upheld in *Roe v. Wade* (1973).[42]

A strong component of Lash and Urry's argument is their analysis of the service class, its role in organized and disorganized capitalist societies, and the role of the university in capitalist society. Their argument is that the service class inserts itself between the working class and the capitalist class and in the process restructures capitalist society, or in their terms, helps along with other factors, to "disorganize" it. The university and the research foundations are the major bases of power in the service class; they are thus the leading agents in the re-structuring of capitalism. If this sounds like a revisitation of the late 1960s assertion of the university student as the new working—read revolutionary—class, I think that may be close. However, they seem to assert that the service class is not a revolutionary subject, and at times they cast it as reactionary. Postmodern culture, according to Lash and Urry, is the culture of the service class and of disorganized capitalism, and like the service class itself, leans in both reactionary and progressive directions.

Overall, they argue that the "political," or perhaps better the site of resistance, is now in the process of consumption rather than at the site of production. This is a dangerous move given the way that the actual sites of production are being moved to the free trade zones leaving many of these potential consumers without income with which to consume. This account erases the potential power of workers to control, and even keep, their work sites, and leaves the "political" in general without much of a map for agency, except as a kind of "Consumer Reports" activism[43]— which, of course, assumes some modicum of buying power/choice. It is further countered by the argument I presented earlier, that the "site" of the political is not confined to a particular location, but rather infuses social, economic, and "private" life.

I think Lash and Urry's concept of the service class and its role, and the role of the university within it, contributes to a descriptive understanding of the late twentieth-century shifts in the United States economy. It does not, however, account for the place of the working class, or the nonworking poor—nor even note the predominance of racially stratified women in these categories, nor does it end up effectively tying these shifts in the United States economy to the global economic picture. In essence, we are left with flatly descriptive and differing accounts of the center of disorganization in several of the focus countries. Their account also rests more on description than theory—in Germany it is basic industry that counts, in France it is the state, in the United States of America it is the service class. They do not tie these descriptions together to support their argument about international and disorganized capital. They propose no relationality between these systems, yet by virtue of their existence as a detailed "list" subsume them under the notion of "disorganized capital."

This organized cacophony of disorganized capital locations does not adequately describe the context of labor relations in the armed forces. Especially in light of the enormous military Reserve Forces and their significant proportion of working-class enlistees, it is important not to lose sight of this concentration of what can rightly be characterized as service workers. In a society that continues to rest so heavily on its military prowess, we need to be careful to mark the crucial function of, and experiential existence of, working class soldiers. In Lash and Urry's account of the New Deal and the creation of the welfare state in the 1930s, the working class plays virtually no role. One need only look to Mink and Piven and Cloward[44] for more accurate, nuanced, class- and race-centered accounts of this period. Lash and Urry argue that the service class created the New Deal. I would say, along with many historians of the period, that the motor behind the New Deal was the organization of the working class and that the service class developed in response. Instead, Lash and Urry use their interpretation as the first evidence of their theory that the service class is the center of the disorganization of capital. Two factors are simply missing from their account that, like the working class and the New Deal, are not the effects of disorganized capital but have a more complex agency: (1) the transformation of gender roles alongside incorporation of women into the wage labor force with the transformation of society and culture that this entails, and (2) the transformation of the notion of race and nation.[45] Again I would argue that these two positions—gender and race—have, in their shifting relationship to political and economic power strongholds, simultaneously impacted international capitalism. In order to develop a clear picture of the forces that shape late twentieth-century life, we need to represent the agency involved accurately.

There is another cluster of radical political economists who see the late twentieth-century social economy as one of many stages inside the logic of capitalist development. David Harvey[46] reviews the assertions of the postfordists, postmodern cultural theorists, and the Regulation School Marxists in order to bridge these perspectives. He tells us that while we are witnessing surface changes in the organization of capital, in fact, the logic of the regime of accumulation still operates. In this way he breaks with the position of Lash and Urry, as he generates a host of examples of capitalism's dispersed organization. He examines "peripheral Fordism,"[47] which is the move of industry to less-developed, cheap labor sites, typically in Third World countries. He develops the concept of "flexible accumulation," to describe capitalism's adaptation of, and to, the global economy. Harvey describes "flexible accumulation" as a "flexibility with respect to labour processes, labour markets . . . characterized by the emergence of entirely new sectors of production . . . and, above all greatly intensified rates of commercial, technological, and organizational innovation."[48] He suggests that capitalism has become more, not less, organized and that "the tension that has always prevailed within capitalism between monopoly and competition, between centralization and decentralization of economic power, is being worked out in fundamentally new ways."[49]

I would go further than Harvey here, following Laclau and Mouffe,[50] to say that the economy is not an autonomous and self-contained universe, but rather, influenced more generally by the struggles in social relations themselves. Harvey marks this transition as containing "a revolution (by no means progressive) in the role of women in labour markets and labour processes" as well.[51] This revolution is in part caused by women's demand—both social and economic—for inclusion in wage labor. Industry's use of women is at least partially informed and structured by patriarchal assumptions about women's stability as workers, thus categorizing women as ephemeral, low-investment labor. This connection is carefully developed in a series of studies that focus specifically on the sites of production: free trade zones, maquilladora shops, the revival of sweatshops in the cities, and domestic piecework that I will review in this chapter. These working conditions and their reliance on female labor are a central piece of this new stage of capital. They represent an accommodation of certain links of "feminism" in that they seem to encourage female opportunities for independent wage labor. However, the manifestations of this new set of "opportunities" are carefully orchestrated by the corporations and the local governments to contain the workers in a strict hierarchy of racial and gender-based limitations. This pattern is also visible in the project of including women in the United States armed forces with the debates over women's access to combat (career-oriented) roles and women's acceptance in the elite military academies. Another aspect of this project to include women in the forces is the foundational exclusion of particular groups of women from particular job classifications, as I illustrate in each of the book's historical foci. The difference for U.S. military women is the stratification of women in the professional class—privileged elite combatants and career soldiers—and the soldier workers of the lower-echelon and lesser-skill occupations.

Racially Structured Patriarchal Capitalism Diffused

While there is not necessarily an essential connection between capital and patriarchy, I make a case that patriarchy is mutating in a co-constitutive fashion with capitalism. For instance, superficial changes in social relations such as slight increases in wage ratios, entry of larger numbers of women to the military, and an increase in the number of female politicians, have not yet disrupted the basic fabric of racialized patriarchal modes of accumulation. In other words, paralleling the notion of capital accumulation, power still accrues at a greater rate for men, especially white men, in the United States.[52]

Postmodern culture and flexible accumulation-based economies of the late twentieth century can be seen as coupled with and complemented by flexible meaning in patriarchy. To map women's relationships to power in the late twentieth century, we need to comprehend racially structured patriarchal modes of accumulation in the same sense as capitalism. To accept the notion that both capitalism and racialized patriarchy are disorganized or in some form of postmodern disarray is to lose the moment of understanding that, while both systems are riddled with seams and vulnerable to a myriad of interventions, both are capable of adapting to social and economic pressures, and historically have done just that. Racialized patriarchy itself has incorporated certain markers of feminism, on its own and in cahoots with capitalism. As Brown has suggested in the epigraph to this chapter, the masculinism of the state has become more diffuse, not disappeared via its attentions to demands for redress and rights expansion.

This absorption of some of the markers of feminism has been possible and necessary due to changes in the organization of and relations between culture and capitalism. With mass consumption as the driving force of late twentieth-century capitalism, multiple sites of contestation over social and economic practice have emerged. Pressures brought to bear by expanding consumer awareness, and the flux of expanding and retracting economic opportunities for women have reshaped women's expectations for themselves and necessitated a response from the culture and the economy. Harvey comments on this development and its connection to flexible accumulation:

[T]he emphasis upon ephemerality, collage, fragmentation and dispersal in philosophical and social thought mimics the conditions of flexible accumulation. And it should not be surprising either to see how all of this fits in with the emergence since 1970 of a fragmented politics of divergent special and regional interest groups.[53]

I would differ with Harvey here and argue that the political actions and the modes of accumulation are acted upon and reflected through one another. The activists do not simply reflect back as mimes; they act upon and in their action contribute to the revaluation and repositioning of political claims. These groups both reflect and mimic the conditions of flexible accumulation and postmodernity by accruing symbolic gestures/practices, such as web weaving in the case of anti-nuclear activists, and existing simultaneously inside and outside of the capitalist culture system. While they re-emphasize the temporality and the local/global tensions of the late twentieth century, they do not always mimic the actual diffusion of capitalist modes of production through a parallel understanding of the shifting, strengthening, and dissolving national boundaries. It is my experience that the movement actors are both embedded in the context of racially structured patriarchal capitalism, and struggling to come to terms with their location and to respond in politically savvy and effective ways: sometimes these are to critically reflect and sometimes they are to remain as fully outside as possible.

Epstein tells us that these movements often eschew a sense of global or long-range strategy;[54] however, I would suggest that it is less due to a sense of futility than a sense of trying to formulate specifically located strategies and an understanding of the precise formations of late modernity in which the state's apparati are flexible and responses as well as visions need to be flexible and collaborative to be effective. By this I mean that the movement actors looked often to the context of the particular action, such as the Lockheed Corporation, and formulated a response directly. For instance, stopping workers at Lockheed's gates and accepting the Shoshone invitation onto the Nevada Test Site. Likewise, police response varied. For instance, at the Nevada Test Site where actions became a regular fixture in the late 1980s, the authorities responded by building an outdoor stockade of cyclone fencing directly inside the gate where protesters could be corralled easily and then bussed to Beatty (the next "town"). Connections to larger economic, environmental, political, and social injustices were indeed made; however, the planning and activity itself was localized. We need partial, specific explanations to see the patterns of our age if we hope to imagine and manifest more equitable social, economic, and ecological relations. As Haraway comments: "Partiality, for me, is about the possibility of connecting conditions and analyses from within people's movements and interpretations."[55] My use of a notion of partial perspective is not a position of depoliticization; it is a position of immediacy and responsibility in terms of the direct ramifications of the current conditions. It is a perspective and political claim to the moment which presents political actors of the late twentieth century with a means and vision for action. This partiality enables a response grounded in the particular conditions of the lived relations of power in the particular nexus of relations at stake. Furthermore, a claim to partial knowledge allows for the inevitable mutations of theory/planning through their encounter with practice. In fact, one might say that positions of situated partial knowledge[56] are the only honest positions one can expect to take.

Signs of Women in the New World Order

Capitalist patriarchy, by dividing and simultaneously linking these different parts of the world, has already created a worldwide context of accumulation within which the manipulation of women's labour and the sexual division of labour plays a crucial role.[57]

A number of feminist political historians and sociologists[58] interpret the stakes of global capitalism by studying the free trade zones which are packed with women workers in some of the most exploitative working conditions of postmodernity. Their methods of centering analyses on the direct experience of the workers present a critique of global capitalism through the ways it is written into the bodies of female industrial workers themselves. Feminist studies of the free trade zones make generalizations about different peoples' experiences of the postmodern, postindustrial world fall away, presenting a more nuanced and hopefully more sophisticated grasp of the conditions we face. A reading of the free trade zones themselves becomes an unavoidable picture of the particular ways that racism and sexism permit the radical exploitation of "host" countries' cultures. Furthermore, study of the patterns of social and economic "opportunity" development in these zones presents a critical parallel to the existing and potential conditions facing women in the United States military. This critical parallel is seen in the ways that both environments devalue the particular labor pools where women are engaged and present hollow renditions of the pretensions toward economic or political freedom they purport to grant women via their participation.

In the accounts of economic restructurings in response to organized labor and community interests there emerge some strange confluences. Examples are, the move of international corporations' factories in search of cheap labor, typically female, in the free trade zones, and the shift of dirty technologies to neighborhoods where the more influential and wealthy citizens do not have to see them—such as the Not in My Backyard (NIMBY) movements of urban activism. These kinds of economic restructurings also highlight the critical intersection of race and class with gender in that the dirty technologies are often relocated to the poorer communities, for example, the dumping of toxic waste and the proposals to dump (store) radioactive waste adjacent to poor communities along with toxic waste incinerators. Another example is the struggle between loggers and eco-activists over the questions of labor activism and sustainable agriculture and tree harvesting.

I explore several feminist analyses[59] of racialized late patriarchy and late capitalism, noting the vastly different vantage point of these feminist authors from my prior examples and asking what difference their accounts make in understanding the conditions of the late twentieth century. These feminist authors look at the particular manifestations of global racially structured patriarchal capitalist relations through foci on the literal sites of production. Their accounts demonstrate that this system continues to organize the workplace far and wide by exploiting the racial and gendered positions of women's lives, in both their productive and reproductive terms. The stories I choose are exemplary of a structure that was in place during the same period in which the initial transformations of the relationship of women to the forces takes place. By highlighting these stories I hope to question the liberal feminist assumption that getting women "equal access" to jobs in the military automatically means parity in status and pay.

There is a burgeoning literature of site specific studies of the conditions of the sexual and racial division of labor in the late twentieth century. These studies read the global political economy through localized pictures of the conditions of women's work lives and the kinds of resistances played out within them. As such they present substantial pieces of the puzzle of the broader conditions of the late twentieth century. This is a different approach from that taken by the radical political economists I reviewed earlier. The situated accounts provided here in combination with the maps reviewed above can generate a more nuanced picture of the effects of postmodern postfordism on women's lives in the late twentieth century. This combination then enables a multilayered reading of United States women's unprecedented entry to the military in this period. In order to flesh out this analysis I turn now to the accounts of women in the global workplace.

The racially structured patriarchal capitalist economy has dealt with some of its crises of overaccumulation by continuing to expand its horizons. This colonization is part of the mechanism that arose in response to organized (mostly white male) worker demands in the industrialized nations (i.e., strong unionization in some cases, and at least higher wages) as well as the influx of women to industrial economies with parallel demands. In other words, workers in the developed industrial economies, especially in established industries, were effectively resisting the capitalists' "need" for large margins of surplus value and have become unprofitable labor power.[60] In turn, beginning in the 1960s[61] manufacturing corporations have been moving production subsidiaries into "export processing" (or free trade zones), which are predominantly located in the so-called underdeveloped nations.

Some feminist scholarly and activist practices help us to understand both the impact of the new world order on women—who remain literally and figuratively on the periphery[62] of racially structured patriarchal capitalist accumulation—and the ways that women work to explain the conditions of the late twentieth century through these situated knowledges. The majority of free trade zones, maquilladora, domestic piecework, and urban sweatshop workplaces are populated by women of color. This advancement in the employment of women in the factories of the free trade zones "reveals the function that women fulfill in the industrial wage labor force at the present stage of capitalist development, and . . . it enables the understanding of the particular impact of multinational investments upon local labor markets."[63] Fernández-Kelly is referring here to the fact that while women are being recruited and employed in record numbers in these factories, the unemployment rate among men has remained high. Aihwa Ong[64] points out the calculated hierarchy of race layered into the hierarchy of male to female in the Malaysian labor market. The combination of assumptions that the corporations are making about women's ephemerality as workers—potentially married/pregnant (not around long enough to unionize)—in terms of racial hierarchies that demand assimilation and attempt to discipline the women into universal workers, and factory locations in poor communities, either on national borders or in the inner cities, consistently target women as the most easily exploitable workers. While, as the case studies demonstrate, there is a history of resistance to these forms of worker control, the issue here is the way that the corporations actually attempt to manipulate race and gender as disciplinary tools.

Material Conditions for Women's Work

Women in general in the late 1990s make up an increasingly disproportionate percentage of persons below the poverty level in the United States.[65] Inside of this figure, black and Latino women, are below the poverty line at twice the rate of white women. This is typically true for women, even with full-time work, because of the racial and sexual ghettoization of women's occupations, and the inequity in the male to female pay scale.[66] As a result of these conditions, for many women the push for equal pay is a serious and central concern. And yet, the impact of the transition to a service economy, which Lash and Urry discuss as the arrangement for disorganized capital in the United States, is primarily a plethora of part-time burger flipping jobs with few benefits and little job security.[67] As Kuhn and Bluestone insist, "the basic issue in any economy is not only the level of employment or unemployment per se, but the quality of the jobs that exist, the living standards that those jobs permit and the distribution of income that the economy generates."[68]

In the late twentieth century the majority of jobs available to females in the United States continue to be lower-wage, nonmanagerial, often part-time, and with few, if any, benefits.[69] For example, in the United States semiconductor industry up until 1982, production line jobs were 69 percent female occupied with a racial division of: 49 percent Euroamerican, 23 percent Latina, 19 percent Asian American, and 9 percent African American. In the same industry's managerial and professional jobs, only 19 percent were occupied by females and 88 percent of these women were white.[70] After 1982, roughly three-quarters of the available production jobs had moved offshore to the free trade zones. Job loss in this United States-based industry was high and critically impacted U.S. female workers, especially the 51 percent group of women of color. These women were forced to choose from the part-time work in the service industry. It is well known that many other production industries have followed the same pattern as the semiconductor industry and moved their factories offshore. In the late 1980s the agriculture business in California began to do the same, with production plants and fields moving to cheaper sites in other countries, mostly in Latin America. In the free trade zones where the jobs were relocated women were specifically recruited at a weekly pay roughly equivalent to a day's wage in the States. These statistics for women in the workforce must be augmented by acknowledgment that women production workers, in all these cases, are still bearing the double burden of carrying unpaid reproductive work as well. Ong cites the additional three to five daily hours of household work engaged in by factory workers at home.[71]

The typical industries in which there are a predominance of women workers operating in the free trade zones are what are considered "light" industries: textiles, garments, food processing, cigarettes, toys, shoes, electronics, data entry, and sex work. These industries are the "runaway shops," so-called because of their ability to pack up production and move it to best take advantage of new labor markets of unorganized workers. The subtext of this pattern is, of course, the fact that at some point worker consciousness and resistance to exploitation becomes strong enough to decrease the surplus value of the host country's labor. These industries rely on the sexual division in the pay scale, a country's political instability, and an absence of union activity.[72]

Hiring practices in the factories, exacerbated by infrequent minimum wage laws, have encouraged a focus on unmarried, 16- to 25-year-old females.[73] In Malaysia, the government's protective legislation laws "had the unintended effect of reinforcing corporate policy to discourage married women from applying."[74] This, coupled with the high turnover and layoff rates, mitigated against unionization. In Mexico, the maquilladoras operate in much the same way. Because they "rely on the use of cheap unskilled and semi-skilled labor to maximize productivity and profits, they are led to employ the most vulnerable sectors of the working class. These sectors are increasingly being formed by women."[75] As Fernández-Kelly goes on to document, the maquilla women are hardly supplementary wage earners. In fact, in the severe economic conditions in Mexico, the unemployment figures are not affected by women's employment in the factories, because the count is based on male employment. Frequently, women are the only ones in the family able to get jobs. As Enloe (1990a) points out, this is not just a situation on the borders, but rather also exists as far inland as Mexico City where there are numerous international garment sweatshops, again recruiting young women workers. Enloe recounts a radicalizing moment for some of these women in Mexico City when, after the 1985 earthquake, labor bosses came in to rescue sewing machines and not the women's trapped co-workers (1990a, 169).

The employment cycle for these free trade zone women is a maximum of three years, after which they are laid off, or quit due to exhaustion, failing eyesight, repetitive motion injuries (Ong 1987), reproductive pressures and desires (Fernández-Kelly 1983), or plant relocations. Most often these women are caught in an extended cycle of temporary hirings so that they are constantly shifting between the cluster of factories in the zone. This rapid turnover mitigates against the development of unions. Further problematizing unionization struggles for these women is the fact that in areas where there are even male-centered unions, these unions have difficulty incorporating women's issues or catering to women workers' needs. This is explained in part by differences in gendered needs, such as childcare, but predominantly by the nature of the job segregations themselves.

Host countries rely on traditional gender relations of inequity, which enable the state to ensure a cheap and docile labor force for the international corporations. Enloe ties the conditions of women's work in the free trade zones to the relations of debtor governments and the World Bank. "The most popular formula pressed on debtor governments combines cuts in government expenditures on 'non-productive' public services with an expansion of exports."[76] The governments, in turn, promise to keep intense worker discipline to insure smooth plant operations. Disciplinary strategies rely on local traditions of relations between men and women, and on religious particularities (such as the use by the Malay state of hierarchical Islamic and family values) drawing in various social forces to develop a sense of social responsibility among the workers toward the corporate "family." As Ong states, this is achieved by the "daily production and reproduction of relationships according to 'given' male supremacist principles" (180). Thus patriarchy is constitutive of labor relations in the free trade zones, not as ideological baggage, but in Ong's description, as part of the Foucaultian sense of the construction of knowledge/power systems.

Racially structured patriarchal capitalism remains a central organizing tool for the transnational corporations because of their reliance on the surplus value generated by unequal relations of power and wage between men and women and between racially marked groups. As Fernández-Kelly points out, "capitalism benefits from the exceptional. As long as women's role as wage earners may be viewed as the exception rather than the rule (even in situations where large numbers of women work outside the home) women will continue to be liable to sexist and discriminatory policies in wages."[77] In the Malay factories there is a racial hierarchy of Japanese male owners to Chinese male bosses to indigenous Malay female production workers.[78] In the United States semiconductor industry, as I have shown earlier, managerial positions are dominated by white males, of females in nonproduction work 88 percent are white and in production work 51 percent are women of color. Internationally, especially in the examples here taken from the 1980s, the owners are typically Euroamerican, Japanese, and Chinese males, while indigenous women of color make up the workforce.

Given the ways that international corporations have reconstructed production work to take advantage of pre-existing inequities among the sexes, what is to prevent the United States military from constructing women's expanding role in the forces to fit with this disadvantaged pay and benefits model? This is a more complex analysis in the United States military where pay grades are clearly institutionalized and do not in themselves differ between military workers by race and gender; however, and here is the liberal feminist approach, keeping women out of certain kinds of work generally and noticing the under-representation of women of color in the more prestigious career ranks means that women are also experiencing a financial disadvantage as the military organizes its Military Occupational Specialties to accommodate and control women's participation. Even with the recurrent struggles over combat duty we can still see that fighter pilots, who come from the elite military academies, are predominantly white males with the highest combat pay. Will these segregations of duties and pay still stand and perhaps become more deeply entrenched?

Economic Equality or Not

For women of all colors in the United States, the prospects for independent financial prosperity continue to fall behind men's: women still comprise the majority of adults below the poverty line, women can still expect to earn, at best, between 67 and 72 cents for every dollar earned by a white man.[79] Women continue to be kept below the glass ceiling in corporate life through old boys networks and sexual harassment. The loss of unionized industrial-sector employment to overseas manufacturing's highly exploitive labor practices, and the proliferation of part-time service-sector jobs leaves little in the way of quality occupation and prospects for women's work.

Turning to the armed forces for training and career opportunity in the United States is not much of an improvement, although it is certainly marketed as one. The institutions of the armed forces are one of the few semi-equal opportunity employers, and yet they are also downsizing. The armed forces' equal opportunity employment is however tainted because, even though sexual harassment or discrimination is against the law, women in the forces still experience a great deal of harassment. Especially noteworthy here is harassment condoned by the policies against homosexuals that is frequently used to target and discipline women of any sexuality whose accomplishments are not properly contained in feminine boundaries.

The military has been suggesting to women that they can trade time in the forces for a wage-earning skill and a sense of belonging and importance in the nation's political economy. Women's aspirations for equality are being utilized by the forces to fill the ranks which young white men have been abandoning. Women are specifically targeted as recruits, with the lure of high-technology training, if the recruitment ad messages are at all universalizable. In other words, women are also joining the military in response to particularly acute economic needs. In order to address women's presence in the armed forces, attention must be paid to the economic imperatives that encourage them to seek military employment.

The New Political Actors

Piecing together fragments of a map of the new world order, we have the reorganization of the signs of capitalism, race, patriarchy, and the very forms of the political. In this section, I focus on the new political actor in light of the larger transformations of the political economy and the development of openings for women in the armed forces in the context of the women's liberation movement. This new political actor is both the cause and product of the transformation and as such is a critical component of the map for two reasons. First, s/he is a way of reading the specificity of the changes thus far—in other words the development of bodily centered politics, prefigurative politics, and the key role of direct activism. Second, s/he is a key player in the hopeful schema I wish to construct in terms of future antimilitarism.

Since the mid-1970s there has been a distinct shift in political activists' perceptions of themselves and their roles in the larger direct action movements. This change in self-perception led to a shift in the nature, characteristics, and purpose of the actions themselves. Arturo Escobar has argued that social movement theory arises from the particular political agenda of the theorist.[80] This is not a "new" perception and has been part of the postmodern theoretical enterprise, generally speaking.[81] There are important implications for social movement theory in the sense that "our theories might be validated only in terms of the practices they enable, of the effective actions they might make possible or to which they might contribute, not in terms of some absolute criteria of truth 'out there.'"[82] It is thus a particular task of social movement theory to be responsive to movement practice and develop avenues of communication between the two. It is a question of the traffic between theory and practice that interests me here; it is the very articulation of the practice of theory from within the movements themselves. This is an aspect of the movements that has received little attention from within the academy,[83] and yet there is a great deal of movement theory in movement publications and in movement practice. Laclau and Mouffe[84] explain a key characteristic of these movements as their temporality and suggest that they create useable hegemonic constructions fashioned out of particular nodal points of political salience. These articulations of political position, therefore, are transient, but only in the sense that they are subject to continual internal review in the articulation of the visions, analyses, and contextual priorities of the particular action(s) being planned.

The civil rights movements of the late 1950s and 1960s demonstrated the nonrepresentative quality of the United States political process and used strategies of protest politics to articulate demands for increased participation in the democratic process. These movements called for various degrees of inclusion, continuing to operate under the assumption that their demands would be taken up by the representative democratic state. Simultaneously, forms of prescriptive theory were being developed. Some of these theorists looked to older histories of social movements and did revisionist work, such as Lawrence Goodwyn's *The Populist Moment*.[85] Goodwyn showed us that the populists were modeling a form of radical participatory democracy, whose source and sustenance was derived extra-institutionally. In fact, it was the abrupt radicalization of the Farmer's Alliance at the nonresponsiveness of governmental institutions that shaped the movement's understandings of itself and its project. At the same time, a number of other theorists of social movements were beginning to develop a new framework for analyzing movement meanings.

The social movement theorists present a closer account of the lived politics of the actors whose terrain is described by the postmodern/postfordist theorists. In addition, most new social movement theorists have worked inside of, or around, the movements themselves, and as such they represent the possibility of a closer reading of the actual conditions of postmodern activism. Having said this, I would add that the new social movement theorists often lose sight of the movement practices' historical grounding in the civil rights movement and early second-wave feminism. Civil rights activists first developed the sense of the personal as political in bringing the work of politics directly into the community through articulating the effect of social structures on people's daily lives. This model was brought to the New Left and eventually helped form the context for the women's movement.[86] White feminists subsequently brought these practices into the direct action movement, helping to shape the process and internal texts of the movements.[87]

Resource Mobilization Theory, Political Process Model, and Other Explanations

A key theoretical school developed in the period of the mid-1970s around the concept of "resource mobilization."[88] These studies articulated movement strategies toward a series of steps designed to make the most of institutional resources by channeling them into movement agenda and then creating a kind of (unintentional) obligation to the maintenance of the organizations managing the resources, rather than the agenda of the movements themselves. In many ways, resource mobilization theories fit with the classical notions of participation in representative democratic forums as the proper channeling of conflict, albeit with the friendly modification that many groups need to organize extra-institutionally in order to influence the institutions. Thus theories of resource mobilization carry a logic of liberal conformity and the argument that inclusion in the system was the appropriate and most effective strategy for social change. Piven and Cloward[89] argued that movements must still be cautious of co-optation by the institutions from which they seek support; however, the key is to mobilize those elite resources to the movement's benefit. These theories, by their focus on organizations, neglect to examine the role of the political actor and thus obscure key components of the actual constitution of and theoretical ground upon which the new movements were beginning to articulate their separate and collective identities. Thus, resource mobilization theories remained unable to describe the cultural transformations, feminist and otherwise, which were occurring in the movements. The resource mobilization theorists were crucially limited in their ability to explain the newer forms of move-ment activity, which mocked, ignored, or simply tried to obstruct the op-erations of the state.[90] Furthermore, resource mobilization theorists op-erated under liberal notions of independent citizens in the "civil sphere" of society, as opposed to the "private sphere," which remained invisibly inhabited by "dependents." In this sense, the movement theories which emerged from the United States remained uninformed by civil rights and feminist perspectives regarding the inseparability of personal and politi-cal status which became increasingly central to the collective self-under-standings of the antinuclear, environmental, and social justice new social movements.

A second field of inquiry was being developed during the mid-to-late 1970s that took into account the increasingly foregrounded question of identity and the multiplicity of identities in social movements. In terms which took account of the actual subject collectivities, Michael Useem,[91] in his book *Protest Movements in America*, sought to describe the move-ments, especially the civil rights movement, as organized by expressions of solidarity via interest groupings such as race and class. In this way his work looked at expanded notions of collective consciousness based on common interest. His focus was primarily on the structure of group in-terest and did not thoroughly account for the interactions between the environment, or resources, and the actor. In 1982, Doug McAdam in *Political Process and the Development of the Black Insurgency*[92] began to problematize the connection between the actor and the field of action by attempting to synthesize Useem's solidarity theories and the resource mobilization theories. His argument more closely respected the actual location and effect of political actors while still attempting to account for the material conditions within which they operated. In addition, both he and Useem, by their focus on the civil rights movement, foregrounded an understanding of the personal as political reflected in the movement's processes and structures. In this way they were able to represent the ways that movement culture was part of the political transformation occurring through the movement's work.

Through the late 1970s and the 1980s, both the composition and modes of description of social movements can be seen to have undergone a significant transformation. These movements both develop their de-mands as points of pressure on the system, and generate new hegemonic discourses and alternative community practices in a common struggle against structures that are an interweave of the institutions of racism, patriarchy, and capitalism. This change in the agendas of the movements themselves has been accomplished by a change in their modes of analysis, which I hinted at toward the beginning of this section. Now I will turn to the new social movement theories and the ways in which they speak with the movements, as well as the largely unrecognized modes of theoretical practice which can be observed being generated by the movements themselves.

New Social Movement Theory

The more recent trends in social movements have been loosely fitted to the rubric of "new social movement theory." These theories have emerged in conversation with the Marxist and postfordist theorists, describing and reflecting in their methodology the transformation of movement dynamics in the emergent feminist, antinuclear, lesbian and gay, antiracist, and environmental movement(s) since the 1970s. What can be said as a general observation of these movements is that they are informed by the emergence and theoretical developments of the early civil rights movement and the "second wave" of feminism. They incorporate notions developed in feminism that elaborate the connections between the personal and the political first developed in the civil rights movement. They act on a ground which assumes that the political infuses and makes common the arenas of state, civil society, and the private.[93]

In effect these movements attempt to stake out a middle ground; a place that is at once independent of state, civil society, and the private, while claiming a deep interdependence and interconnection of all three. The general focus of the critique has been articulated to include patriarchal hierarchies as seen in racist/imperialist/colonialist pursuits, oppression of women and all others who are not white male, and all manner of capitalist exploitation. While this is a severe generalization, the thread it makes apparent is that the issues which became the focus for these movements included a more far-reaching analysis of the dynamics of oppression than prior organized movements. These issue clusters included particular identity struggles which intersected each other in ways which may be termed as deep coalitions outside of traditional formal political organizations, although they are more often temporary and strained coalitions.[94]

My education in these movements causes me to feel a strong resonance and value in the term "racialized patriarchal capitalism" as I have been attempting to pursue it in this book. In my experience, the terrain of struggle for justice has always necessarily encompassed all forms of oppression. This description is not a matter of the rote listing of, or ranking of, oppressions, but the actual interdependence of oppressions which becomes obvious upon close scrutiny. For example, at the Nevada Test Site I could see the ways that the interconnected oppressions operate and can also be used against themselves in antinuclear actions. At the test site Shoshone Nationals invite protesters onto their land which has been claimed by the United States government for national security work: the underground testing of atomic weaponry.

New social movement theories have developed which attempt to describe and prescribe for this new profile of movement activity. It is important to note the historical location and political stakes of the more contemporary theorists. Many of those now in the academy studying movements or theorizing about possible movements were involved in earlier movements and/or current ones and still look for a way to communicate with the movements themselves; in most cases, unlike classical social movement theory, more akin to resource mobilization theorists, and more reflective of the movement actors' self-perceptions, these are friendly studies. For this reason, new social movement theories have been primarily friendly to the movements on the left; however, some theory is more closely connected to the movements themselves. My interest here is to focus on those theorists whose work demonstrates an actual historical engagement with the movements in order to emphasize the activists' voices. A profile of these activists and their theoretical practice enables a more vivid portrayal of the rhetorical and actual political space available for late twentieth-century political actors and thus a more vivid picture of the openings provided for women in their pursuit of roles in the military, as well as for those activists who attempt to shut the military down.

Alain Touraine in his book, *The Voice and the Eye*,[95] described his work in action research in the new social movements. His method was to have his research assistants participate in movements directly, then go back to the academy to formulate strategy, and then bring this strategy back out to the movements to study its efficacy. His work was initially done in France with the working-class movement, and with the movements for democracy in Chile. His work was a departure from the earlier classical and system-bound theories in that he sought to study the political actors and to look for methods to do research that both described and directly informed the movement he was studying. He argued that the movements themselves were the transformative political actors and that they were, in effect, constructing what they were fighting for by their very existence. After ten years of research, he found that his method was not useful to movements; it was too much like rejected notions of vanguard politics for a movement that prided itself on its decentralized and leaderless forms. Even more to the point is that the movements' own self-conscious theorizing and strategizing encouraged the sense that outside "experts" were unnecessary.

Two other key theorists were developing analyses which furthered notions of the new social movements themselves as political actors, while also accounting for their interactions with the larger society and the formation of "new societies" within the movements. Claus Offe, in his study of the German movements, made the case that the new social movements were transformative of the political simply by their refocusing of the center for political change.[96] The autonomous communities and the practice of decentralized power bases were key to this agenda. Alberto Melucci began to study these political actors by analyzing the movement spheres and arenas for action and clarifying the defining characteristics of the movement strategy and milieu. He conceptualized the movement network as "not just instrumental for their goals. It is a goal in itself".[97] He elaborated a description of movement spheres as being "a form of collective action: a) based on solidarity, b) carrying on a conflict, c) breaking the limits of the system in which action occurs."[98] These conceptualizations help us to imagine ways that movements operate, and are sympathetic or "true" to the ways that the movements describe themselves. One key formal and informal agenda of the movements has been precisely to operate outside the power structures and to experiment with forms of power which are nonhierarchical and "prefigurative" of their notions of society.[99]

The methodology of the theorists discussed above was inclusive in all cases of some sort of relationship, that is, dialog with a movement sector. The studies were based on direct observation/participation and theoretical models. The theorists tested the efficacy of their models with the activists themselves. In some cases, Tourraine for example, the strategies did not work directly to enhance movements in their work. In all situations though, I would argue that the theorists were continually grounding their research in reference to the different movements. What each of these theorists omits in his or her work to explain this new conceptualization of the political is the groundwork done by civil rights and early feminist activists on the structure of democratic politics. Infused in New Left understandings and subsequently pervasive in political organizing, the concept of the personal as political was key to the development of the new social movements' self-conceptions. The multiple sites of identity and struggle were generated from this notion and deeply inform the structures of postmodern politics. It is precisely this sense of self-articulation experienced by political actors which allowed for the assertion of a variety of "rights," including women's articulation of their rights to be martial citizens and be availed of the privileges therein.

Laclau and Mouffe suggest a strategy going beyond Marxian notions of a clearly situated primary political actor toward a vision of "radical" democratic politics in which the relationality of political moments depends purely on those moments' articulation of points of resistance. In their frame, social movement actors are themselves a shifting terrain of hegemonic constructions serving particular purposes and coming together in the first place via nodal points of intersecting interests. They see no continuous or logical identity for political actors, but rather a series of articulations along a chain of equivalence.[100] These chains of equivalence are ephemeral, in keeping with the fluidity of postmodern politics. In this sense they are never construed as an essential revolutionary class, nor is there an essential revolutionary moment; rather the picture is one of politics constructed on a stage of ever-shifting meanings. A critical point to their work is the deconstruction of the notion of an essential revolutionary. Their model provides a useful sketch of the new political actor in the sense that they elaborate on the specific role of subject position and identity in the movements' work. Perhaps one of the most useful conclusions and developments in their work is to highlight the use of articulations and hegemonic moments; in other words, the concept of democracy, as such, can be deployed as easily on the right as on the left.[101] I find this particularly intriguing as I look at the use of the concept of "equal rights" encouraging women to join the armed forces. This is a problem which most of the other theorists, precisely because of their study inside particular movement milieus, omit. Its articulation enables them, in part, to develop their argument, using Althusser, that the social is overdetermined and there is no absolute revolutionary class, or identity. Instead, a radical democratic politics needs to create hegemonic discourse that can, at least temporarily, stabilize the various political contingencies through temporary coalitions. However, the concepts themselves, as Laclau and Mouffe suggest, remain mobile and subject to redefinition.

Epstein argues that although Laclau and Mouffe do describe the new social movements' political strategy, they do not look closely at the movements' own tendencies to assert a politics which in many ways yearns toward universal values.[102] As such there is a contradiction in the movements' own sense of their role, both insisting on the ephemerality of political positions and on the prefiguration of the just society. Arguably the prefiguration is most often articulated as a process which is never wholly complete, yet it is true that the yearning for a picture of wholeness is part of the story. Thus their positions are less ephemeral, rather than more.

In the antiwar movement, civil disobedience had as its goal the obstruction of business as usual and the mockery of state systems of control. The women's movement placed a great deal of its emphasis on the same kind of strategy, as well as a more reflective internal strategy of withdrawing support from the mixed movements and generating separate cultural institutions.[103] The antinuclear movement used strategies of civil disobedience which ranged from site occupations and symbolic transformations, such as setting up villages inside of Seabrook[104] to literally weaving the doors of the Pentagon shut as a "web of resistance" to militarism in the Women's Pentagon Actions of 1980 and 1981.[105] These symbolic actions represent various methods of marking the limits of state power and challenging the state to assert itself publicly, through arrests and other violent responses, thus marking its own position and making what typically rests under cover exposed to public view.

Epstein's 1991 account of the United States direct action movement traces the history of women's involvement with the movement through the women's movement alongside the credit she gives to the civil rights and earlier pacifist movements in shaping its political strategy. While Epstein argues that the presiding influence over the movement's philosophy and style is a combination of feminism and ecology, she calls into question the movement's viability without what she would identify as a coherent strategy. As she states, "anarchism, spirituality, feminism, and nonviolence all provide standpoints for the development of a critique and an alternative vision, but none in itself addresses the question of strategy. Strategic thinking is lacking in the movement no doubt partly because there has been no coherent intellectual framework within which it could take place."[106] Her argument redirects our attention to Laclau and Mouffe's assertion of the ephemerality of meaning in movement practices, yet they would posit that this is an important component of the new social movements due to their reflection of and engagement within postmodern politics. Sturgeon would likewise argue that the movements' actions and politics directly reflect the "project of teaching people how to struggle for themselves, how to work collectively, how to exercise their democratic rights, and how to interpret those rights to expand the areas subject to their control . . . it is in the effort of enlarging the meaning and expanding and renewing the practice of democracy that United States social movements have been most successful."[107] Thus the measure of what counts as political transformation is a key to each of these authors' readings of the movements. Unlike many of their predecessors, Sturgeon and Epstein clearly write with the strategic aim of influencing the direct action movement; and both would agree that their interests lie with helping to reflect the movements' politics back to itself as a strengthening act. Where they part ways is in the credit they give to the movement's strategic aims as I outlined above. Sturgeon's study of the movements' conception of themselves as both politically articulate and engaged in theory acting reveals a strong foundation of and conscious use of feminism in practice.

Both authors see the confluence of postmodernism, postfordism, radical pacifist, anarchist, and feminist thought and conditions as critical to the formation of the new social movement actor, and agree that the theories pertaining to these categories offer partial explanations of the conditions of the late twentieth century. Citing the use of strategies from feminist organizing, such as consciousness-raising groups, and the learned need to create some kinds of democratic structures to avoid what Joreen (Jo Freeman) called the "tyranny of structurelessness,"[108] Sturgeon argues for a critical and formative connection between feminism and the new social movements:

> The direct action movement, through its insistence on feminism as an important part of its repertoire, and its conflation of feminism with key parts of its political action and organizational structures (non-hierarchy, nonviolence, consensus process, ecofeminism) theorizes the integral nature of feminist critiques for its construction of an oppositional politics. . . . Thus feminism can act as a connective discourse for the movement because of the way in which shifts in gender relations are central to the process of restructuring. Analyzing these shifts is central to any effort at social and political change.[109]

Sturgeon's work presents an important analysis of the uses and limitations of resource mobilization theory and new social movement theories, citing the former as concerned mainly with the "micro-level" of organizational ties and the latter as concerned with the "macro-level," concentrating on the structural contradictions which produce the movements. Sturgeon sees the direct theory[110] of the movements as operating simultaneously on both these levels. As such, the new political actors, especially in light of her account, present a more nuanced reading of the conditions of late twentieth-century politics and possibilities. These political actors reflect an understanding of culture, politics, and economy as intertwined and mock and resist the systems of racially structured patriarchal capitalism which shape the "new world order." They have laid an active discursive groundwork in the political field of the late twentieth century which enables an articulation of rights, and both parallels and informs women's claims of access to military jobs. Simultaneously, these claims are reflected in the possibilities and conditions of women's work in the free trade zones, and other ephemeral economies.

Direct action participation and analyses of social movements enable me to understand some of the ways that political actors' discourse in the late twentieth century causes and is caused by postmodern postfordist relationships of power. Sturgeon's model of direct theory informs my understanding of these actions as part of the refiguring process and as a lived and locally based construction of alternative possibilities. Certainly the influences cross-cultivated between women activists in different movements: against nuclear proliferation, for environmental justice, for peace, and for decent living wages, are all traceable to this continual growth of understandings within and between the movements.

These conditions, this discursive shift developed over time by activists and in terms of women's rights exampled in this project, also work to create a space for women to assert claims of equality on the state and the military. Ironically, many of the strategies and actions taken against the military by other women are the product of the same rupturing of the liberalist illusion of separate private and civil spheres by and for women that become the impulse for women to seek equal opportunity employment in the armed forces.

The ironic and powerful critique of the patriarchal military which has emerged since the Women's Pentagon Actions at the beginning of the 1980s and literally fed the antinuclear movement since, has depended on an antimilitarist stance which obscures the role of women in the military who share the belief in women's equality. This invisibility of women soldiers both in the public eye and in the antimilitarist movement was to come to a shocking end in the course of the late 1980s and the early 1990s through several quite visible United States military interventions.

Conclusion

In this chapter I have examined a number of analyses which purport to explain the conditions of late twentieth-century life and the potentialities for projects of social transformation. In the process I have attempted to suggest ways in which the various analyses contribute to, but in themselves do not comprise, maps of the current situation. In using these analyses as various signs of the new world order, my attempt was to mark the problematic omission of women in many of these accounts, both for the sake of a more complete picture, and for my purposes in applying these models to help explain the situation of women entering the United States military. I have raised the issue of the high stakes of leaving women's positions and contributions out of these maps and in my own work sought to illuminate the gaps and begun to examine women's various locations in the new world order.

A key omission in the radical economists' study of the late twentieth century is the simultaneous and interpolated accommodations that racial hierarchies, patriarchy, and capitalism have made to one another. This linkage becomes quite clear when we examine the vitality of the transnational corporations which thrive on the position of inequality faced by women living in the free trade zones. The collusion between the state, the transnational corporation, and the World Bank in constructing these zones further entrenches women's inequality. The questions which need to be raised in this regard are: in what ways can feminist activists formulate strategy to achieve justice, given the entrenchment of racially structured patriarchal capitalism? In what ways does the global economic pattern foretell the circumstance of United States women entering the military?

With the military clearly an apparatus of the state that "does gender,"[111] I am thinking about the ways that the state can manage women soldiers' racialized gender while allowing them to participate in the sanctified role of citizen-soldier. Brown (1995) demonstrates that the state's disciplinary apparatus continues to regulate us in "unfreedom." I posit that the state continues to regulate distinct gender roles, even as it allows women to perform some parts (still not all) of masculinist soldiering as an "unfreedom" masked as an ultimate freedom, that of first-class citizenship. The strongholds remaining on certain aspects of soldier practices and the clenching "don't ask, don't tell" regulations outlawing homosexuality and inlawing regimes of heterosexism and control of mainly women's (manly) performance in the military work to reproduce these gendered effects.[112]

Agreeing to work within and for the state as a women soldier presents the predicament of being located in the belly of the beast. One cannot expect to either fully succumb to the policing of gender in such an environment, nor to be fully insulated from it. The woman citizen-soldier is about certain kinds of rights attained within the regulatory state, not about aspirations to "freedom"; rather about aspirations to "liberty" within a circumscribed terrain for some women. Perhaps this is the core predicament of the concept of citizenship thus cast. Women have articulated what is to be cast as women's citizenship in different ways over the course of U.S. history. Set aside from first-class citizenship as it has been defined by the man and the man in the state, women have struggled to define themselves into first-class citizenship through the masculinist means of martial valor, through a refusal, as Ynestra King once said, to demand a piece of a carcinogenic pie, and through various liberation struggles to redefine the terms of citizenship itself. To this question of citizenship rites—gendered, racialized, and classed—I turn in the next chapter.

THREE

Martial Service and Military (Masculine) Citizenship

The Challenge

Has our country sunk so low? Where is our manhood?
—Phyllis Schlafly (Huckshorn 1991)

A citizen has the courage to make the safety of the human race their personal responsibility.
—*Starship Troopers*

In the film *Starship Troopers* (1997) women and men experienced co-ed training, habitation, and showers. This thorough co-ed status was new in the movie compared with the book. Robert Heinlein made waves in the book by having women as naval officers and pilots. In the movie they were also ground combatants. Membership in the society, of the book and the movie, was two-tiered: civilians on the bottom and citizens on the top. You became a citizen if you served in the military. Citizens' privileges included various kudos of social status, education, and the license to raise a child. As the recruiters in the film said, "service guarantees citizenship." In the narrative, the grunts, or infantry, are the ones who become the true heroes, saving the day by their courageous capture of the brain bug.

At this particular moment in United States military history it is quite interesting to think that the infantry are being mythologically reinvigorated and revalorized in terms of combat lore, at the same time that women are able to fight from combat planes and arguments are made persuasively that women soldiers can do practically anything the men can do. This complicated public narrative hearkens toward futures *(Starship Troopers)* and pasts *(Mulan)* in which women were also heroic infantry. Of course, there is the recuperative *Saving Private Ryan*, the blockbuster hit in the United States with Tom Hanks as star, in which the narrative tells of men soldiers risking everything to rescue a fellow soldier. In rhetoric denouncing women in the military and especially in combat, a frequent refrain is that men will want to protect and rescue fellow women soldiers and thus will be distracted from the real work of warfare. The rescue presented in *Private Ryan* is only heroic because the private rescued is a guy. He represents the salvaging of the masculine martial citizen, though he himself raises the humbling question (or perhaps underlines the point) of whether or not he has been worthy. His wife and children surround him with a yes. It would prove the mistake of allowing women to become soldiers if the "fellow" soldier was a gal.

How is it that citizenship is entwined with martial service and martial service is entwined with masculinity? What are the possibilities, problems, potentialities of wresting the terms of citizenship away from martial service? Is it wise to do so? Can we afford not to? Nancy Hartsock tells us that the martial, the masculine, and the citizen entwined are as old as western (Greek) formulations of democracy. Moreover, she argues that "the masculine political actor . . . is indeed most at home in agonistic and competitive settings" and that "rather than war being politics by other means, political action as it appears in these texts is simply war by other means. And through this war, citizens attain and celebrate manhood."[1]

In this chapter I focus on the development of martial masculine citizenship since the American Revolution. I look at what has been gained through martial citizenship in the past and wonder what can be gained for women by being incorporated to martial citizenship. I discuss the legacy of United States martial citizenship as masculinist culture and demonstrate the challenges that women's presence in the forces have posed to that culture. I rely on Linda Kerber's work[2] regarding the gendered development of citizenship in the early United States, and Gwendolyn Mink's work[3] on the history of women's role as citizen-mothers in relationship to United States social welfare policies of the twentieth century. I draw on both authors' work to base my claims about the contemporary structures of gendered citizenship, and to link current women soldiers' and women military historians' insistence that soldiering, or martial service, is the ticket to fully invested citizenship. The claims for fully invested citizenship have been twined with military women's claims for full economic citizenship via the technological training that is part of the soldiering benefits package. This is not so different from the impulse in the newly formed United States to use principles of political participation as leverage for economic protections.

Martial valor is one of the defining moments of citizenship. Both citizenship and martial valor retain a strong impulse of the masculinism that Hartsock suggests is part of its legacy in western democracies.[4] Because of this connection between martial valor, citizenship, and masculinism, an important task for feminists interested in the military and in citizenship is to develop our understanding of the linkages between these three, and participate in rethinking that linkage, that is, arguing for the ways that the military is too important an institution to allow masculinism to shape it and that the military is too important to citizenship.

The struggle to define women's roles as citizens via the drafting of women (or not) and the assignment of women to combat both signify an interruption in previously uniquely masculine terrain. However, the strategies for attaining these roles for women have been fastened to claims of equal rights to first-class citizenship. While this was a successful strategy used by men of color to gain basic formal citizenship rights, it may not afford the same leaps in status for women. Precisely, women already have the formal citizenship rights that men of color won through martial service. One question we need to ask about citizenship is why women want to reinforce the relationship between martial service and citizenship in the first place, and if not, then what is the particular draw to martial service after all? The second question to ask is what martial service gains or what the institutions of the military gain from having women as part of the labor pool. This is a more complex question regarding the particular forms of labor management in the military and the ways that women are being utilized as women and by race in that process.

In this chapter, then, I set up my thinking about the role martial citizenship has played in defining gendered and racialized social and economic citizenship. I do this work by first elaborating on the foundational project of defining citizenships in the United States as a new nation, and demonstrating the continuities of the early ideological framework with the present. Second, I take up the construction of women's military histories and what kinds of meanings are imbedded in those proactive accounts of women's progressive inclusion. Third, I briefly review those histories of women's gradual formal inclusion in the forces. Finally, I discuss the development of a women's rights approach and the ways in which this approach also reifies the armed forces as an institution of citizenship bestowal, both in the social and economic senses of citizenship. It is precisely this willingness to bank on military participation as key to citizenship claims that concerns me here. I look to turn the argument around and suggest that to be full citizen participants we will need to develop our comprehension of the ways that we must re-create the military into something we as a democratic polity can live with.

Production of the Martial (Masculine) Citizen

My analysis of women's relationship to the military is informed by the assumptions upon which citizenship in this country was founded. In the framing of the Constitution, citizenship was defined through white landowning masculinity. One of the linchpins of that citizenship was martial service.[5] Tied to notions of liberal republicanism developed in the French Revolution and expanded in the revolutionary English colonies that became the United States, martial service was one of a citizen's several primary duties that *he* exchanged for the rights of first-class citizenship.[6]

Martial duty in the United States has historically been a constitutive part of male citizenship. Linda Kerber documents the formative connection between the valor of martial service and the possibilities for citizenship in the revolutionary United States, shortly after the Paris Peace Accords. She quotes Sarah Jay, revolutionary patriot and wife of a prominent politician, in her toast to the Peace of Paris, to illustrate this connection: "May all our citizens be soldiers and all our soldiers citizens."[7] Kerber suggests that the quote, "testif[ies] to the acceptance of a new relationship between the military and the republican state."[8] This relationship would key the definition of, and rightful heirs to, the new republic and serve to justify the various conquests that enabled the nation to expand. In short, it intimately ties soldiering to national identity.

Kerber discusses the development of republican political ideology as it framed United States definitions of citizenship. She demonstrates that the first stage of defining the parameters of citizenship ambiguously accounted for women. A principle reason for this ambiguity was that women were not officially allowed to soldier for the nation, yet, in the Revolutionary War martial valor was the key to claims for citizenship. Literally fighting to attain the "freedom" of nationhood, was the province of males as soldiers and was therefore also the preeminent vehicle for membership in the new nation. Of course this was also precisely racialized in that the simultaneous valorization of men fighting for the freedom of the nation and the valorization of men committing genocide on the peoples already living in the new nation's borders went hand in hand. Martial service was the ultimate form of patriotism and its performance accrued males prestige and honor. With this first defining characteristic of citizenship in place, the 1790 Naturalization Law further dictated that citizenship would be afforded only to white immigrants, thus citizenship was conceived as both gender and race restricted from its beginnings.

Martial service/sacrifice's counterpoint evolved to be mother-service, or the protective and reproductive duties of women, through the elaboration of a republican motherhood. Martial duty was the traditional passage to citizenship and manhood in the United States and reproduction of good citizens was the passage to women's (second-class) citizenship and womanhood. White supremacy was the foundation of both the martial citizen and the republican maternal citizen.[9] Benjamin Franklin's early vision of peopling the New World with the "lovely white"[10] was a widespread sentiment certainly traceable in republican motherhood ideology through the formation of the welfare state[11] and the development of stories about culture and evolution in nineteenth-century science.[12]

Liberal republicanism was a paradigm of political morality for the new citizenry. It defined citizenship through the paramount principle of civic virtue and was popularized by Thomas Paine in his revolutionary pamphlets and echoed in Sarah Jay's toasts to the revolution. The virtuous citizen was expected to participate in public life in a disinterested way. Prerequisite for this disinterested participation was a personal character of independence, productivity, industriousness, and the capacity for self-sacrifice. The measurements of this ability to be disinterested were property ownership and martial valor and sacrifice, both cornerstones of first-class citizenship and precisely gendered masculine privileges. In practice, these measurements were only available to Anglo men in the revolutionary United States, except for African males who captured English soldiers and thus were granted citizenship[13] and freedom.

The United States military is a critically contested terrain around notions of citizenship. While in the context of the late twentieth century it has become a central arena for contesting the terrain of women's citizenship, it has historically been a critical arena for contesting racialized masculine second-class citizenship. Early conceptualizations of citizenship founded on masculine martial valor,[14] were reenforced by granting freedom to blacks who fought in the Revolutionary War.[15] An enormous transformation of the terms of citizenship was fought for and then granted to African American men because of the twin pressures of their demands after martial service in World War II and the international scrutiny leveled on Jim Crow practices in the United States. As John Sibley Butler[16] suggests, there was also a pattern of recruiting men of color during wars and then reinstating quotas and segregation in the postwar periods. What this new integration actually meant for men of color varied; however, to be sure, the integration of the forces and the benefits bestowed through the G.I. Bill enabled them to gain some foothold in economic terms, albeit minimal. For instance, many of the men of color and poor whites used the G.I. Bill just to get through their interrupted high school education. Women, excluded from formal martial service until their auxiliary status in the world wars, were not afforded this peerless proving ground of loyal citizenship by virtue of being women, and even in their secondary status as auxiliaries were not considered.

By World War II, examples of men of color attaining citizenship rights through martial valor had formed an impressive list: African slave and free Africans in the North attain rights through fighting in the Civil War; Martin Delany, black nationalist of the late 1800s, argued for a respected black citizenry, by stating that blacks had participated as soldiers in the Revolutionary War: "Among the highest claims that an individual has upon his country is that of serving in its cause, and assisting to fight its battles," and that participation in the forces to save the Union in the

Civil War was the way to earn citizenship.[17] Irish immigrants, technically citizens, but socially outcast, created their membership as white citizens by fighting both in the Civil War and then in the Spanish-American War; and Japanese American men were released from internment camps during the World War II if they signed up for military service (an explicit affirmation of worthy citizenship. Many of these Japanese Americans served in the most decorated unit of World War II: the all-Japanese American 442d.[18]

Republican ethics were defined gradually in gendered and racialized terms through a series of oppositions: independence to dependence, productivity to domesticity, industry to servitude, martial vigor (sacrifice) to motherhood. Republicanism thus developed as a prescription for first-class white male citizenship, second-class white female citizenship (females could not hold property, vote, perform martial service, or keep their children in divorce or abandon), and exclusionary cultural/racial citizenship.[19]

White female citizenship was private citizenship based on the citizen-mother's role in cultivating subsequent generations of citizen-men-soldiers, citizen-mothers, and properly socialized Americans. The last of these included management of nonwhites' and immigrant whites' social assimilation to Americanism. Generally, nonwhites, barred from property ownership, franchised citizenship, and martial service were, functionally, noncitizens. The founding definitions and development of citizenship and belonging were stabilized in the oppositions outlined above. These discrete roles were solidified as the citizen-soldier and the citizen-mother.[20] As Mink describes it, "Virtue demanded courage as well as willingness to sacrifice self-interest and risk life in defense of the republic. The capacity to soldier was the *sine qua non* of fearless and disinterested citizenship."[21] The martial citizen, then, was unmistakably male, and the citizen-mother, female.

Martial masculine citizenship[22] proved quite resilient over the several centuries since the founding, although it has shifted its racial boundaries to accommodate men of color. The struggle in the Civil War over drafting Irish men and African men,[23] the use of the African American Buffalo Soldiers to help win the west from the Native nations who were its inhabitants prior to the winning of the Civil War for westward ho!, and the draft in World War I of African American men, all served to push the envelope of martial citizenship to begin to include more than the "lovely white"; however, without the same entitlement to social benefits as their predecessors.[24] Tensions over the inclusion of African American men in the armed forces were not structurally addressed until the end of World War II, when the G.I. Bill and the desegregation of the forces through Truman's Executive Order 9981 in 1948 began to make the playing field more level.[25] Congress also passed the Women's Armed Services Integration Act (WASIA), formally bringing the (still segregated) women's auxiliaries from the two world wars into the forces.

Women's Martial Service

Women have long been informal martial participants in the United States, although unacknowledged outside of the strict boundaries of "nurses," or water carriers, such as "Molly Pitcher." Mistaken identity discovered has been the main source of stories about women's unconventional roles in wartime prior to the world wars.[26] A growing literature documents women soldiers who dressed as men and fought alongside them heroically since the beginning of United States history.[27]

As with men of color's integration in the forces' leading to increased citizenship rights, women's soldiering and auxiliary participation has been an advantage in arguing for first-class citizenship since, arguably, the signing of the Nineteenth Amendment was an award for women's World War I participation. Women gained formal political rights by over one hundred years of struggle to redefine their place in society and reinterpret the Constitution to include their interests and identities as citizens. This long process is ongoing as women continue to struggle for basic human rights and social and political equality.

Women, as citizen-mothers, and their children, have been the sign of the homeland protected by the warrior men. Citizen-mothers are seen as vulnerable, "beautiful souls," as Jean Bethke Elsthain has suggested, as the purposeful opposite to the soldier as "just warrior."[28] Citizen-mothers, by definition, are critical to the reproduction of the nation state. Women have reproduced and produced for the national security. Until the World Wars, and the development of women's auxiliaries, women were largely excluded from formal participation in the forces.

Women have been war's producers for everything from uniforms to bombers.[29] Women have also, in both World Wars, been flyers and suppliers in the support teams for combatants.[30] In World War I, twelve thousand women served as clerical help in the Navy at equal pay to their male counterparts.[31] Nursing corps have long been the women's auxiliary to the combat wings. Clearly, traditional paradigms for women's roles in war are not stable. Rather, when troops mobilized, the forces have allowed(encouraged) intended and unintended gender bending. These bends have ranged from looking the other way while lesbian and gay base culture thrived, to earlier attempts by women to go to war disguised as men, to massive recruitments of women within specific vocational confines or time periods. These interruptions in the masculine martial structure of the forces have worked together with broader social changes to affect women's understandings and expectations of sexual labor divisions in the armed forces and in the society.

Women, in their roles as wives, mothers, and daughters, have also provided the social infrastructure for military bases and the sustenance of warriors in the military theater.[32] Traditionally, United States women have played the all-but-invisible roles of support to the military through their positions as diplomatic wives and base wives; other nations' women have served in that structure as prostitutes to service the bases' male soldiers.[33] Women continue to bear responsibility for reproduction of soldiers and children. Women continue to be overrepresented in the reproductive work associated with warring: in food services, nursing, prostitution, maintenance work, and so forth—all the jobs that are the traditional realm of female labor.

Internationally, in wars where the casualty rate has been high, women (particularly white women) have been encouraged to do the most basic work of reproduction—child bearing—to replenish the ranks.[34] This was a powerful transition post—World War II in the United States, when the government and industry coaxed and forced women who had been running the factories out of the wage market and into the "kitchen" to make dinners and babies. This assault on women's wage work was supported on every front: with factory layoffs, television shows modeling perfected nuclear families such as "Ozzie and Harriet," and elaborate menus and dinner party recipes in women's magazines such as *Woman's Day* and *McCalls*.[35]

These gendered arrangements of martial citizenship are being challenged in the late twentieth century, and especially since the Persian Gulf War. The connection between martial citizenship and manhood is eroding somewhat, though perhaps not at its combat core. This erosion comes from several major transitions in the world of things military. Women's rights activism and scholarship have changed our understandings of women's roles in society, including the military. Antiwar activism and feminist antimilitarism have challenged both domestic and international manifestations of masculinism and sexism in the military. Base cultures have been exposed by feminist antimilitarists for their structural and economic support of exploitative sex labor in bar brothels and feminist antimilitarists have also exposed the existence of U.S. soldiers' abandoned children.[36] Liberal feminist organizations and feminist policy makers helped create and utilize the pressures via these recuperated histories and civil rights victories in relation to the more broadly constructed liberal state to expand women's rights and secure a professionalized place for women in the military services. Current debates, uncovered histories, a proliferation of biographies and autobiographies, the establishment of archives, and women in the military organizations are bringing to light the participation of women in the U.S. armed forces as far back as the Revolutionary War. On-line networks such as the MINERVA listserv and H-WAR are creating instant information and debate arenas with a mixture of active duty, reservist, veteran, and non-service-member scholarly participation.

Women Soldiers in the Door

The history of women's entry to the U.S. armed forces as soldiers is a long one, and their inclusion has been the product of extensive struggle and fortuitous circumstance. As official armed forces workers (not solely in the auxiliaries as they had been in prior years), white women were first eligible to be in the Nursing Corps in 1947 as a result of the Army Navy Nursing Act (Public Law 80-36C). On 2 June 1948, Congress passed the Women's Armed Services Integration Act, Public Law 80-625, which was fought for and brought forward in the Congress by Representatives Margaret Chase Smith of Maine and Frances Paine Bolton of Ohio. The WASIA had also been widely supported because of women's contributions to the war effort in World War II, an interesting precursor to the pressures for change after the Vietnam War and the Persian Gulf War, though each is quite specifically set in its historical context. Public Law 80-625 allowed women into the services, albeit with severe quotas and restrictions. A quota was set of 2 percent maximum in each branch. WASIA had, as one of its restrictions on women's integration, instructions that no women were to serve in combat situations.[37] This formal process toward military gender equity compensated for the loss of male soldiers in World War II, and took advantage of, and gave advantage to, some of the women who were already trained in the machinery of the forces. This did not include the WASPS who were decommissioned before the end of the war amidst a flurry of anxiety over their proximity to male-appropriate roles.[38] In this process, the auxiliaries, which had functioned as external support organizations, were dissolved. They were replaced by female corps corresponding to the service divisions. By 1949 the special women's sections were: Women's Army Corps (WACS), WAVES[39] (Women Accepted for Volunteer Emergency Service: the Navy Women's Corps), Women's Air Force (WAF), Women Marines, Army Nurse Corps, Navy Nurse Corps, Air Force Nurse Corps, Army Medical Specialist Corps, and the Air Force Medical Specialist Corps.

Training, active, and reserve units were segregated by sex and race, on the basis of long-standing practice and justified by arguments about better unit cohesion. These arguments regarding race among the men were simultaneously being debunked. The heroic martial service of the Tuskegee Airmen, the 332nd in the Air Force during World War II that became famous for its record of never losing a bomber during its missions in the European battlefield, helped to prove that racial segregation was unfounded in the forces. The women, however, found deep structures of segregation persisted:

> 4,000 Black women served in a racially segregated WAAC [Women's Army Auxiliary Corps] during World War II. The Navy did not accept Black women until close to the end of the war; the Marine Corps opened its ranks in 1949. . . . Black WAAC nurses were not allowed to treat white servicemembers until the end of 1944. This came about as a result of a fear by government officials that white women nurses would have to be drafted if Black nurses were not more fully utilized. . . . One of the most frequent

complaints of the Black WAACs was that they were not being trained in technical skills, but were being sent to cooking and baking schools and assigned largely to custodial and laundry jobs.[40]

Truman ended formal racial segregation in the armed forces with Executive Order 9981 in November of 1948.[41] This executive decision was possible through the social, political, and economic pressures of the 1930s and 1940s. The New Deal era, and then the war, had created an opening in the discourses of race and citizenship rights. The extension of some citizenship rights, namely an integrated armed services, to African American males was in part a product of the revelations of the Holocaust. The United States hypocrisy in standing publicly for human rights while ignoring horrid racial and economic abuses at home was challenged by the growing civil rights movement. A base of union activism in the 1930s, and the superficial race liberalism inherited from the Roosevelt administration's New Deal, provided rhetorical and structural openings for the movement toward policy change in the forces.[42] The treatment of African American soldiers abroad, their martial sacrifices in the war, rising international pressure to secure human rights at home with the organized civil rights activism—including Phillip Randolph's March on Washington, and activism in the armed forces' Conscientious Objectors Prison Camps where a number of demonstrations were staged against segregated bunks and mess halls[43]—all served to increase pressure on the government to address the racial inequalities amongst the men in the forces. Straight and lesbian women and gay men's struggles for inclusion to full service in the forces during the later part of the century would come to echo this political moment.[44]

In 1951, Congress created the Defense Advisory Committee on Women in the Services (DACOWITS). It served as the advisory arm for the Pentagon on issues pertaining to the recruitment and retention of women in the forces within the WASIA guidelines. DACOWITS was a key government-based advocacy organization for developing women's roles and opportunities in the forces.[45] The DACOWITS was not challenging women's exclusion from combat roles during this period. While the law restricted women to certain occupations and quotas, the law granted men access to the Army Nurse and Medical Specialist Corps.

Over roughly the next decade, a series of openings for women in the Forces occurred. On 8 November 1967, Public Law 90-130 lifted the 2 percent quota, allowing women to hold high grades of service and to receive the same rank-associated benefits accorded to male veterans. In 1969, the Air Force opened Reserve Officer Training Corps (ROTC) to women. On 11 June 1970, the first two women, both white, received promotions to Brigadier General.[46] In 1971, a total of 1.6 percent of the armed forces was female, a legacy of the quota on women from the WASIA. Until the late 1970s most other WASIA restrictions on women in the forces remained, including exclusion from all but the Air Force's ROTC, and from education through the academies, as well as segregated training in women's training centers and assignments to the women's Corps in each branch.

In November of 1971, tensions over base conditions resulted in Army women holding demonstrations against racism at Fort McClellan, Alabama. Half of the arrested soldiers were African American women. At the time of the demonstrations, African American women made up 14.4 percent of all active duty enlisted women and 3.3 percent of all active duty women officers.[47] Very little information is available about these demonstrations. I have only found Harold Jordan's brief mention of it in his essay with Cynthia Enloe, and a brief discussion in Betty J. Morden[48] of the incident where she describes what occurred from the records in the Center for Military History. This is a site for further study as the connections between race and the strong lesbian culture on the base and the shifts to a sex-integrated training center all inform one another. Morden makes no mention of lesbian culture in the forces, of lesbians, or of homosexuality in her officially sanctioned history of the Women's Army Corps. On the other hand, Rogan does discuss the strong lesbian culture at McClellan.

The lack of coverage of racism at Ft. McClellan is a product of the continued scant attention paid to race in relationship to armed forces' women. Recent work, especially by Brenda Moore,[49] has recuperated African American women's work in the military from the founding but especially focused on the WACs. Her research also points to important questions regarding the reasons for African American women's overrepresentation in the forces and the meanings and strategies for assessing their presence.

As women attain access to higher-prestige jobs in the armed forces, analyses which disappear one category (race) to highlight another (gender) will be forced to reckon with the increasingly vivid differences in women's treatment by race. I hope that my gestures in that direction will contribute to such progression. I also hope to point, with this account, toward needed work on the intersections between racial and sexual politics as they merge, or at least parallel, in these accounts.

Fort McClellan was the training center for the Women's Army Corps and a cultural enclave for women in the Army. Before the dissolution of the separate armed forces' branches such as WAC, McClellan served as a strong, women-centered base with a quiet, but safe and largely high-ranking, lesbian population.[50] Helen Rogan discusses the way that the lesbian culture at McClellan shifted with the gradual integration of the forces. The increased acceptability of a military career for straight women made it possible, if not widely embraced, to imagine that women of traditional femininity could be in the forces. This increased acceptance of the military as a career for straight women was simultaneous to the initial shift toward integrated training. Rogan illustrates her point about the disruption of the women-centered and lesbian safe culture of the base with a story from a base member:

> The first of the big-time annual witch hunts was in 1972, when a corporal deserted, and she named thirty-two people. I was one of the people told to take a lie detector test to prove I was not gay. I was very hurt: I said tell the *girl* to take one. . . . Later I needed to get a security clearance for flight school, and the CID said, "You refused to take a lie detector test and so we assume you're guilty."[51]

Randy Shilts also discusses some of the lesbian culture in the forces, and demonstrates the allegedly large numbers of lesbians in the forces, especially before the integration of the corps. While he suggests from his interviews that there was a strong lesbian presence in the Women's Army Corps (active to the mid-1970s), as well as the other corps, WAF and the WAVES, there is no official count. There is a legendary story among lesbian and gay veterans of the head of WAC staff, Johnnie Phelps's, discussion with Eisenhower[52] that 95 percent of her WAC staff at Army headquarters were lesbians, including herself, after which he canceled a pending witch hunt. This story has been disputed by other veteran women who insist that there were few, if any, lesbians in the forces at that time. This only reinforces my contention that, regardless of the actual numbers, the perceived threat to the forces by the mere presence or suggested presence of lesbians, or for that matter the numbers of women generally, which have not risen above 15 percent of the overall forces, is enormous. I stretch this argument over women undifferentiated by their sexualities, because the naming of a woman as "lesbian" in the forces operates as a sign of unconventional, and thus inappropriate, female behavior. Melissa Herbert demonstrates the way that women "manage their gender" in order to navigate the fine line between career success and challenges to gender norms reflected in military practice.[53] This is so regardless of whether the actors are women disputing the Phelps story to protect themselves, or the command structure of the forces pointing to and prosecuting women for their unconventional behavior.[54]

In 1971, NOW National Board issued a statement on women in the military, regarding the placement of women in the ranks. Entitled, "Women and War," it addressed the contradictions of women's relationships to warring and soldier status:

> Whereas, women are victims of the military in war, through rape and forced prostitution, and whereas, military training relies upon sexual slurs against women to inflame soldiers into aggression, and whereas, military decisions are exclusively made by male supremacists, and whereas, men themselves are subject to loss of life and personhood by being subject to compulsory military service from which women are exempt, and whereas, women in the military are restricted on the basis of sex in job training, education, area of service and are confined to low level, non-policy positions, therefore be it resolved, that NOW condemns the degradation of women by sexist practices within the military and the sexist basis for compulsory military service.

Thus, NOW presented its guarded support for women in the military while arguing against the reinstatement of compulsory service. This position served to demonstrate the need for equal treatment and access while continuing to condemn the military's masculinist culture, for example, "women are victims of the military in war, through rape and forced prostitution," "military training relies upon sexual slurs against women to inflame soldiers into aggression," and "military decisions are exclusively made by male supremacists."[55] The insistence that women be able to advance in the military was made on equal rights grounds of citizenship. The Department of Defense recognized permission to develop women's roles as "manpower" within the shifting boundaries of femininity.

In 1972, the Department of Defense was already looking to expand women's roles and participation in the forces, not to enhance their citizenship status, but rather because of anticipating the effects of the Vietnam syndrome on male volunteer recruits and conveniently taking up the openings provided by equal rights activism. The DoD convened the Central All-Volunteer Task Force "to prepare contingency plans for increasing the use of women to offset possible shortages of male recruits after the end of the draft."[56] On August 7, 1972, Admiral Zumwaldt of the U.S. Navy, in "Z-Gram 116," recommended that more Navy jobs be opened to women, including training as pilots. His memorandum was a watershed for changes in the Navy, and more generally in the forces, as he was the first to push seriously for women's inclusion in a broader spectrum of Navy billets. He was also the first admiral to push for integration of the Navy and, later, to recognize the need to implement race relations awareness training. Oddly enough, this was the same Navy that twenty years later would be at the center of an enormous sexual harassment scandal over its Tailhook convention. With "Z-Gram 116," women could train to land aircraft on Navy carriers and be present on ships, albeit only on temporary status. Following this lead the Army and the Navy/Marines opened ROTC for women.[57]

The draft, or involuntary conscription, ended in 1973 after President Nixon signed the Paris Peace Accords marking the formal end to the war in Vietnam. Arguably, this began a shift of the military toward increased professionalization of and career status of military service. No longer were all male citizens required to respond to national security in like measure (at least theoretically). Rather, soldiers were and are recruited on the basis of their own patriotic, economic, social, or political assessment of the benefits of soldiering. Congress established the All Volunteer Forces in 1973. In that same year, the first women Navy pilots graduated. The institution of the All Volunteer Forces[58] was a serious blow to martial masculinity, because mandates were set for women to be recruited in the hopes of mitigating the expected dearth of white male recruits.

After the Vietnam War, the United States experienced several new phenomena regarding waging war. Michael Klare' referred to these phenomena under the rubric of the "Vietnam Syndrome."[59] These phenomena were characterized by United States male citizens, and especially young white males, declining military enlistment after the Vietnam War, and U.S. policy makers' reluctance to engage troops in another long war due to effective antiwar mobilizations and the widespread unpopularity of the Vietnam War. This, of course, did not mean that policy makers were becoming less hawkish or more reluctant to make war, but rather that warmaking policy shifted to planning for LICs, or Low Intensity Conflicts, such as the wars against Chile, El Salvador, and Nicaragua. In the 1990s, of course, this strategy of low-intensity conflict had shifted to the Middle East.[60]

By the middle of the 1970s, the institutional restraints on women's participation in the armed forces were rapidly falling away. Major General Jeanne Holm, then Women's Air Force Director, recommended that the Air Force also allow women to train on jets; however, the Air Force delayed until 1977. By 1976 the total number of women in the armed forces had jumped to 5.2 percent with 16.1 percent of those females being African American.[61] While on the surface this may seem a simple parallel to women joining the workforce more generally, and a success in the eyes of liberal feminism, as I have demonstrated in this chapter the military has previously been a *specifically gendered terrain*, with specific economic rewards for masculinity, and until very recently only *white* heterosexual masculinity.[62]

The percentage of African American women in the military had risen dramatically between 1967 and 1980—most dramatically as enlistees, since 90 percent of the officer rank jobs went to white women. African American women's numbers in the forces increased over this period from 8.5 percent to 24.9 percent. Reasons for African American women's advances are tied to the promise of technological education and subsequent career opportunities that are much harder to come by in the civilian job market. African American women still remained restrained by their entry as enlistees as opposed to white women's more common entry through the military academies and into the officer ranks in the 1990s. "White" (European American) women soldiers at 90.4 percent of officer rankings, far outstripped their peers of color. "Hispanic" women were 4.0 percent of enlisted women and 1.2 percent of women officers, "Asian Pacific Islander" women were 2.1 percent of enlisted women and 1.0 percent women officers, "American Indian or Alaska Native" women were 1.0 percent of enlisted women and 0.4 percent of women officers, and "Other" women (an undifferentiated category) were 1.4 percent of enlisted women and 1.7 percent of women officers.[63] By 1980 African American women were 6.2 percent of all women officers and 23 percent of all women enlistees.[64]

In 1977 the Army had approved co-educational basic training; in 1978 the Congress voted to end the separate status of the Women's Army Corps, and the Army closed the WAC Training Center and School on 21 March 1979. The regular Army absorbed the Women's Army Corps. In the late 1970s Congress recognized the Women's Auxiliary Army Corps as a veterans' organization, and rewarded the women with access to veterans' benefits comparable to their male counterparts. By the end of the 1970s ROTC was a primary source for the training of women officers.[65] Ironically, ROTC was simultaneously under siege at United States universities by campus antiwar organizations. They attacked ROTC as a military institution, and attacked the universities and high schools where ROTC recruited for granting legitimacy to the forces. When ROTC would come to my high school (1973–76) on "Career Days" we set up pickets and tried to pressure the administration to cancel their invitation.

As of 1991, and the Persian Gulf War, women comprised 11 percent of the forces, with an ethnic distribution of 62 percent white, 30 percent African American, 4 percent Hispanic, and 4 percent "other." The United States armed forces deployed thirty-five thousand women for the Persian Gulf War, roughly 11 percent of the U.S. presence and an accurate representation of their numbers in the forces overall.[66] It is important to note that the number of women in the forces, has remained below 15 percent throughout the period and to the present. With this number in mind, ironically, the importance of women's entry to the highest ranks and the combat specialties is emphatically stated. Such a small percentage of women are interested in the forces, yet the struggles over whether they should be there, and in what capacity, are enormous. This is because of what women's entry to the military represents to the culture.

By September 1995[67] women comprised 12.7 percent of all active duty forces. Female officers were 13.2 percent of all officers. White women officers were 78.6 percent of all female officers and 55.1 percent of enlisted women. African American women were 13.2 percent of all female officers and 34.0 percent of enlisted women. Thus by the middle 1990s African American women had begun to be a stronger presence in the officer ranks. Hispanic women (no breakdown in report of what ethnic Latin origin) were 2.9 percent of female officers and 5.8 percent enlisted women. A category called "Other Unknown" reports 5.4 percent female officers and 5.0 percent of enlisted women. Overall, between fiscal year 1990 and fiscal year 1995, active duty women's numbers have decreased. In counts of thousands FY (Fiscal Year) 1990 showed numbers of women at 2043.7. By FY 1995 those numbers (again in counts of thousands) were 1533.7.[68] These reductions are due to downsizing more generally.

Brenda Moore (1991) demonstrated that while the armed forces are typically touted as a success story for equal opportunity employment

> there is another aspect to the participation of black women in the American armed services that is not so positive. Black women are heavily concentrated in a low technical organization, namely the Army, and in low technical occupations, namely those categorized as administrative and support. Thus while their participation in the armed services is likely to bring strength to military organizations and individual successes in the short term, it may also entrap them into military occupations that will soon be phased out.[69]

What these kinds of downsizing practices will look like over the coming decade is still unknown. Women are entering the military to reap economic and political citizenship rewards during a time when the military mission is also changing. So far, the discussion has been mainly led by women career soldiers and women's organizations promoting institutional equity, including in the forces.

Regular Pay Military Compensation, which includes pay, quarters, and a non-taxable subsistence allowance is the same at each grade for male or female servicemembers. This, coupled with the training and education packages, makes military employment highly competitive with private-sector employment for women. However, while their inclusion in the armed forces' pay scale meant that women and men would receive equal pay for the same work, women are consistently kept back from combat billets that are key to rank advancement, and as already mentioned, African American women remain concentrated in the least technically advanced jobs,[70] and tracked into administrative and support positions. Thus the downside for the combat pilots who today enjoy access to high rank, combat-exposed—and thus benefited—jobs is a race segregation that accrues from disparate opportunities coming up through the ranks, including access to the academies.

Democratizing Citizenship

The twentieth century witnessed major shifts in public understandings of and democratizations of citizenship. African American civil rights activisms came to fruition in great earnest and public reception beginning in the 1950s.[71] This civil rights activism was taken up by other groups fighting for civil rights: by oppressed racial and ethnic groups of men and women activists, by women's rights activists, and by lesbian, bisexual, and gay activists over the subsequent decades.[72] These activist struggles were, and continue to be, critical to expanding democratic citizenship by definition and practice. For examples: the Civil Rights Acts, beginning in 1964, that served to open access to enfranchisement, education, and the political process generally; the effects of the Equal Rights Amendment on political and court decision making for women's rights; and the recent struggles over extending rights of marriage and its benefits to lesbian or gay couples. Each of these civil rights activisms has contributed to understandings of, fueled public debate about, and challenged the military structure with varying degrees of democratizing effect on policy. For instance, the inclusion of women in the military at higher ranks, which occurred precisely in the political environment of expanding women's rights, and the Clinton administration's "Don't Ask, Don't Tell, Don't Pursue" policy attempting (however, failing) to make good on the campaign promise to address the presence of lesbian and gay soldiers, which was a direct result of pressure from lesbian and gay rights activists, and then counterpressure from conservative opponents.

In public discussion of women's roles in the military, the civil rights and specifically women's rights activism since the 1970s has had great influence on what Major Lorry Fenner demonstrated was a largely and repeatedly forgotten debate, from the 1940s to the 1970s, about women's roles in the military. She suggests that, "assumed public anxiety around gender roles encouraged press accounts and military restrictions to be constructed in a way that 'contained' military women within traditional notions of femininity, heterosexuality, and morality."[73] Since the 1970s, there has been a shift, precisely what this study aims to display, in the terms of the debate and the possibilities for women. Even in Fenner's terms, the amnesia is lifting insofar as published histories with a long-term perspective are stabilizing the presence of women in the forces, to some extent. This means that there are openings for scholars like Fenner and myself to develop analyses of the way women's histories in the forces are being written, to contribute to shaping the terms of debate about the ways women will continue to be incorporated, and to raise the crucial questions about the relationship of martial service to citizenship.

To raise these questions and suggest ways of understanding them, I look at some of the debates over women's proper place in the armed forces from the 1970s through the 1990s. Many of these debates have either directly or indirectly referred to definitions and expectations of women's citizenship. These debates are concurrent with the wide-ranging debates over women's place in United States political culture. I chose the debates because they serve to highlight the key points of struggle in the contest over citizenship rights in terms of race, ethnicity, class, and gender (and in varying overlays) in the context of the United States military. These struggles are the gateway to far-reaching economic changes, strategies for political activism, and democratic processes.

I view the debates through the discursive fields of civil rights and women's liberation. I address several political moments regarding women and the armed forces from both the public policy and the women's movements' activities. These moments include: the debates over the ERA and combat, which occurred simultaneous to, and linked to, the lifting of women's quotas in the forces and the initiation of the All Volunteer Forces; the feminist antimilitarist/antinuclear activism burgeoning in the late 1970s and early 1980s; and the 1980 attempt to reinstate the draft, including women, that failed and thus revived the

Rostker[74] case challenging the draft as an infringement on *men's* right to due process; the Reagan Era, which began with an attempted "Woman-pause" in the forces and left its legacy as the largest defense appropriations build-up in equipment and personnel in our history, including unprecedented numbers of women; and finally the Persian Gulf War, the Tailhook convention sex abuse scandal, the Congressional vote to allow women combat flyers, and the Presidential Commission on the Assignment of Women in the Armed Forces. All of these events raise and revisit and still leave seriously unanswered the question of first-class citizenship for women. I will highlight the ways that citizenship claims shaped the debates, and how a focus on the citizenship claims might serve to untangle the web of women and militarism.

The pageants of public and congressional debate over women's proper roles, and the political activisms, parallel and not, of feminists spark my interest. Through writing about these moments I am acknowledging the multiple voices shaping change through the pressures of bodies and language that make up political history. I take up these particular moments because they are watersheds for evaluating the effectiveness and progress of approaches to women's equal citizenship to men. By pushing these different agendas together I also reproach assumptions that women should necessarily aspire to the status quo of men's citizenship, when it is possible that a citizenship authored by feminists might yield more democratic practice after all. These historical moments in which the woman-citizenship-martial sacrifice pageant has played out were embedded in the political and social context and imperatives of their time. It is possible to imagine that a citizenship redefined altogether by feminist antimilitarism might have no military component. Nevertheless, the challenges to what counts as citizenship (e.g., the antinuclear activists' claim that they do not want a piece of a carcinogenic pie) and the struggles to expand citizenship rights have been odd discussants and not centered in this process.

I read this story as a struggle over the meaning of first-class citizenship in the United States, and a question about the ways women will insist on access to that citizenship. Because it is a story about citizenship, it continues to be influenced by the ways that class and racial locations designate citizenship possibilities. I uncover the less-than-stellar opportunities afforded to military recruits and in creating a nuanced, critically astute study of the ways that, reflecting the political culture within which the forces are embedded, race and class and gender markings organize the type of access recruits can expect.

Conclusion

At the beginning of the 1960s serious questions about how women, and which women, would be integrated in the forces were growing in importance. The erosion of WASIA restrictions meant that challenges to the masculinism of the forces and the masculine domination within the forces would have to be policed in other ways, or abolished. The first stage of this new policing was a renewed routing of lesbians by the witch hunts. These were geared especially to break up the power of previously acceptable all-female work ghettoes in the forces. If the forces were going to integrate sexually, the pressure was on to make sure they were heterosexed. Simultaneously, and little discussed even in current accounts of the history of women's integration in the forces, was the struggle over racism in the women's ranks. In this chapter I mentioned a series of demonstrations against racism that occurred in the Women's Army Corps Training Center of Fort McClellan that have received little by way of note or analysis. Brenda Moore has written of the concentration of African American women in the Army, which is the least technologically advanced branch of the forces. This leaves African American women and other women of color outside of the prestigious, and less vulnerable to downsizing, ranks of high-tech officers and inside the occupations most vulnerable to downsizing in the 1990s.

In this chapter, I have linked the procession of women's inclusion in the armed forces, and their expressed interests in the continued expansion of that inclusion, to the legacy of political meaning attached to martial service. This linkage demonstrates the rhetorical and practical power of martial service as a signpost of citizenship, and the more subtle linkage between political and economic access to citizenship that martial service represents.

Beginning in the early 1970s, with the coalescing of significant parts of the women's movements around the revival of the Equal Rights Amendment, and the federal government's decision to recruit women to the All Volunteer Forces, debates about women's equality and women's rights and responsibilities therein were inevitably articulated to, and ultimately foundered on, the questions of women and the draft, and women and combat. In the next chapter, I take up the nodal points of discourse, left and right, about women and the military in the 1970s regarding the Equal Rights Amendment.

| F O U R |

Legislating Equality

*The Equal Rights Amendment, the Courts,
and the All Volunteer Armed Forces*

I turn now to a closer look at the broad-ranging debates linking women's interests in women's proper role in the forces[1] with the women's liberation movement and its use of the ERA to showcase demands for women's rights. The struggles over giving women "equal rights" presented a broad opportunity for changing the terms of women's participation in the economy and culture. Resistance to those changes formed around a mixed bag of rights and responsibilities that not everyone wanted; the question of women in the forces raised deep internal conflict for women's rights advocates, many of whom had cut their activist teeth in the antiwar movement.

This historic shift was a product of the growing women's liberation movement and the proliferation of arenas into which it exerted its influence, as well as the demographic need created by the Vietnam Syndrome and its resultant drop in male recruits. I highlight the Equal Rights Amendment and the equal protection court cases as critical moments in shaping the discursive and practical transformations of the period. The struggles over the ERA are a significant piece of the story because of the public nature of the debates, the prominence of the question/threat of women being drafted and placed in combat, and the significance of the ERA's potential role in changing the legal parameters of equality and civil rights for women. The court cases themselves were both inspired by and redundant to the ERA.

The challenges to the forces' masculinist culture have come from several directions. The armed forces themselves needed to extend eligibility to women to compensate for not drafting men, and began to do so with the 1967 abolition of the 2 percent quota for women. The quota's removal anticipated the adoption of the All Volunteer Forces after the Vietnam War—and the projected need for women to fill ranks that men, particularly white men, were shying away from. The subsequent opening of the military academies to women, and the Supreme Court rulings that began to find in favor of women's equal rights, were all issued in the context of a developing women's liberation movement. Decades of civil rights activism set the stage for this movement, and informed its strategic approaches. The women's liberation movement was especially reliant on the ERA to set the tone for a wide range of legal and political openings for women as a class. Yet while the ERA's anticipated approval and ratification was the impetus for many of these changes, the ERA's downfall in the process of state-by-state ratification can be at least partially laid at the doorstep of the New Right's successful playing-up of fears about the potential changes in women's social status, not the least of which was the specter of women drafted and in combat.

In this chapter I focus on the ways that the women in combat debate began to take shape around fears of unisex everything in political and social life, and fears of the loss of traditional social "support" and structure for women. This debate took some of its urgency from the growing interest among women to take advantage of the relatively equal opportunity in education and employment the forces promised through their marketing to a generation of volunteer recruits. The forces were stepping up their campaigns to recruit women, and women and their advocates were working through the courts to improve working and living conditions for women in the forces.

Phyllis Schlafly's STOP ERA campaign illustrated the potent fears that women would transgress prescribed gender role boundaries. These were potent fears because with only three states left for ratification, Schlafly managed to organize a fledgling New Right into an effective roadblock that carried the day. Moreover, the impulse of Schlafly's STOP ERA movement resonated in 1992 in the Presidential Commission on the Assignment of Women in the Armed Forces, which I discuss at length in chapter 7.

All Volunteer Forces and the ERA

Passage of the Equal Rights Amendment by Congress in 1972 helped to redefine the relationship of women to the tenets of equal protection and due process under the law, and was a strong influence over the expansion of women's roles in the armed forces by presenting a packaged justification for opening the armed forces more completely to women through the All Volunteer Forces. Expectations of the amendment's sure ratification (later proven false) shaped many sex classification decisions in the forces and through the courts. The armed forces used the pending ERA ratification as part of its justification to call on women volunteers, to create co-ed basic training, and to open up more military career opportunities for women, thus further encouraging them to join the forces. Several Supreme Court cases were litigated anticipating the ERA's clarification of equal protection. The ERA also, in concert with women's rights activisms that preceded it and ushered it through the Congress, provided the impetus to establish women's rights legislation, directly and indirectly, through the Equal Employment Opportunity Act of 1972 and the Equal Credit Opportunity Act of 1974. These all, of course, owe a measure of their success to Representative Howard Smith (D-VA) for his attempt to quash the Civil Rights Act of 1964 by adding "sex" to the list of characteristics against which it would become unlawful to discriminate.

The ERA

Section I: Equality of rights under the law shall not be denied or abridged by the United States or by any State on account of sex. Section II: The Congress shall have the power to enforce, by appropriate legislation, the provisions of this article. Section III: This amendment shall take effect two years after the date of ratification.

The Equal Rights Amendment was first introduced in the early 1920s by the National Women's Party and defeated in Congress repeatedly until March 22, 1972. The ERA has always been opposed by arguments to maintain traditional family structures, the primacy of the male breadwinner role, and the fear of losing female-oriented labor protection laws.[2] The 91st Congress held joint House hearings on the ERA in May

1970. This was the first hearing on the ERA since 1955 and forty-two witnesses testified. From 1970 through 1972 both the House and the Senate Subcommittees on Constitutional Amendments considered the Equal Rights Amendment and its wording. Congressmen authored many provisions for explicitly or implicitly excluding women from the draft. Internal congressional pressures, and pressure from women's rights groups to keep the amendment as originally written to insure that its meaning not be diluted by exceptions, defeated these modifications each time.

The House passed the original text ERA, 354 to 23, in the spring of 1971. In the Senate debate on the Equal Rights Amendment, Senator Sam Ervin proposed two modifications. Ervin, Chair of the Subcommittee on Constitutional Amendments, was joined by a small cadre of right-wing activists. The first of his proposed modifications was to add a section to the ERA that would read: "This article shall not impact the validity, however, of any laws of the United States or any State which exempt women from service in combat units of the Armed Forces." The second modification was to exempt women from the draft. Interestingly, there is no law on the books that specifies that women are exempt from the draft; *the ERA was understood to mandate the drafting of women.*[3]

The Senate defeated the first modification, to exclude women from combat, by a vote of 71 to 18. The Senate defeated the second modification by a vote of 73 to 18. On March 22, 1972, the Senate approved the ERA in a vote of 84 to 8, minus Ervin's amendments. This occurred much to the dismay of Senator Ervin and the right-wing constituency that was beginning to coalesce around the struggle to keep women out of combat and away from the draft. The next step was to prevent the ERA from achieving state ratification via a minimum of two-thirds of the states' approval and thus prevent the ERA from becoming the Twenty-seventh Amendment to the Constitution.

Immediately after the Senate vote, Hawaii weighed in as the first state to ratify the ERA. By the end of 1973, thirty states had ratified the ERA with little opposition, followed by three in 1974, one in 1975, and one in 1977. To become the Twenty-seventh Amendment to the United States Constitution, the ERA needed to be ratified in thirty-eight states by March 22, 1979. Equal Rights Amendment activists pressured the Congress to extend this timeline until June 30, 1982, because of the stall in ratification in the years 1978 and 1979. Three more states needed to ratify to meet the requirements and Schlafly's campaign had garnered widespread support and an erosion of confidence that the ERA would succeed.

Right-wing activists opposed to the ERA and what they saw as a link between the ERA and the 1973 Supreme Court decision in *Roe v. Wade*, fought the ERA in the Southern and Mormon states that had yet to ratify the amendment. They also targeted Illinois with its rules for a three-fifths majority to approve constitutional amendments.[4] Contrary to the received wisdom about the liberal middle-class white versus working-class and black splits over the value of the ERA, according to polls surveyed by Jane Mansbridge, "the working class and Blacks were at least as likely to support the ERA as the middle class and whites." Instead, as Mansbridge documents, the split was between the mainstream and the growing constituency of the New Right.[5] The New Right coverged on the woman question (ERA, abortion, homosexuality, and women combatants) facilitated by spokeswoman for the Positive Woman, Phyllis Schlafly.[6]

In Schlafly's capable hands the ERA became a mandate for wide-ranging social change for women and not an end in itself. The complexities of ERA legal interpretation,[7] meant that a fair amount of time would be spent in the courts working through the reach of the amendment and its interface with other constitutional rights, especially the right to privacy.

Unfortunately, there were lessons not learned from previous attempts at top-down Constitutional amendments, such as child labor laws and temperance. Neither of these pieces of legislation came from the states and neither had been able to combat a grassroots opposition. The ability to organize against, and field, opposition at each source was denied these amendment seekers because of ratification time limits and strategic focus, as well as the ease with which they passed through Congress. The opposition caught ERA supporters off guard, and it proved nearly impossible to go back to the grassroots and hash out the opposition's arguments.[8]

Women who worked in support of the ERA in the state ratification process were not prepared for the sudden and deadly response of the right wing. The generalized statements of equality of the sexes opened a major fight over the meaning of femaleness. The New Right was able to harness a number of potent themes: the deterioration of the family, the dissolution of gender distinctions, the loss of protection (via supposed reverence) for housewives and for female workers' reproductive organs, the general decay of "moral" culture, co-ed bathrooms, and women in combat.[9]

What was initially a statement that "equality under the law shall not be denied or abridged . . . on account of sex" became a condensed symbol[10] for the long-standing battle between liberals and conservatives over federal and state power and over the role of men and women as gendered beings. The ERA became the symbol of choice for the right-wing Moral Majority movement to work against liberal and feminist liberal activism. Anxieties over the challenges to gender norming presented by growing lesbian and gay activism also shaped the fears on the right. The same groups who had been arguing against communism and for an increasing militarism—often to the extreme of becoming disreputable on the right—found a crusade that, cloaked in the seeming grassroots mobilization of mothers and homemakers, actually covered the same battleground as before. It was then easy to link the threat of the ERA to deterioration of the family to subsequent deterioration of the patriarchal state, which, by right-wing logic, also meant the arrival of the antifamily, chaotic, communist state.

In October of 1972, Phyllis Schlafly founded the organization STOP ERA. The John Birch Society and Schlafly's newsletter, *Phyllis Schlafly Report* (previously devoted to a hawkish analysis of defense issues), flagged the ERA as "a major new political target." The December 1974 issue of the *Report* sported a headline reading: "ERA means abortion and Population Shrinkage."[11] The issue detailed, in classic rambling Schlafly style, the multiple ways that the ERA would destroy the American way of home life and war.

The Republican Party supported the ERA in Congress until the party was targeted by the John Birch Society, Schlafly's STOP ERA campaign, and the American Party. Schlafly had a huge right-wing mailing network in place through her newsletter, through her contacts with the Birch Society, and through the American Party. The American Party, with Wallace as its presidential nominee in 1968, had as part of its platform a plank "denounc[ing] the ERA as a 'socialistic plan to destroy the home.'"[12]

Jacqui Davison started another anti-ERA organization, Happiness of Womanhood. Many small-town affiliates of STOP ERA and Happiness of Womanhood were started under different names and created the appearance of a spontaneous uprising. Although they appeared as strong grassroots organizations, "many of their individual members, especially the leaders, were also members [or wives of members] of previously existing national organizations on record as opposed to the amendment." These groups were typically long-established right-wing groups considered to be on the fringe of mainstream right-wing ideology at the time, and although they provided the structural framework (e.g., Richard Viguerie's mailing list, Schlafly's mailing list, and the Fundamentalist Church), and the ideological framework, for the anti-ERA movement, they "apparently recognized that the public reputations of these established groups were not an asset."[13]

Profiles of the anti-ERA activists confirm, especially at the level of leadership, the direct but often unnamed ties to the older right-wing organizations.[14] These connections were also apparent at the local levels where anti-ERA activists tended to be religious, middle-aged, middle-class, and likely to be members of the John Birch Society, Daughters of the American Revolution, and the Eagle Forum—a Schlafly organization/newsletter (Berry, 1986).

Placed at the front of the movement were the middle-class housewives. They seemed to respond to the threat against their lifestyles; however, Schlafly and other "principal pro-family activists, such as Connaught (Connie) Marshner, chairman of the Pro-Family Coalition, and Onalee McGraw of the Heritage Foundation, had long time ties to right wing political groups."[15] Richard Viguerie, the direct mail king of the New Right, openly praised the Reverend Jerry Falwell for his role in defeating the ERA in Virginia.

The New Right activists used the ERA to indicate the threat of looming disruptions to the "American way" and to refuel Cold War paranoia about internal and external enemies. "The anti [ERA activists] spoke globally about a catastrophic move to socialism, chaos, loss of privacy, loss of financial security, and even the loss of civilization as we know it. They were nebulous, however, in explaining how these catastrophes could result from ERA ratification."[16] The antis only needed to appeal to a particular constituency that was already largely receptive to the threat and conspiracy theories of communist plots and moral decay. They only needed to frame ERA in these recognizable terms to excite and mobilize their ranks. The anti-ERA groups argued for the rights of motherhood and the preservation of traditional family structures. The arguments against the ERA were made on behalf of mothers and wives, not women as individuals.[17] In this way, the issue of women as equal citizens with men was made irrelevant, because women were defined in relationship to men and the family as, precisely, a different kind of citizen—a legacy of the post–World War II gender politics in the United States.

The New Right argued that too much government, chaotic society, homosexual marriage, and the general unraveling of the American family and the American military with women drafted and in combat, would be the result of passage of the ERA, while also maintaining a long-heard cry from the right: ERA was a communist plot. This was a curious accusation since the Communist Party USA was opposed to the ERA on record before the right wing picked up the banner. The Communist Party felt that energies for organizing should privilege class inequities and the ERA was merely a vehicle for middle-class women. Nevertheless, this piece of the picture disappeared inside the reactionary agenda and rhetoric, and the edges between the destruction of the family and the onslaught of communism were repeatedly blurred.

Schlafly argued for women's natural and superior rights as mothers and housewives and she did speak to the fears of middle-class housewives who had no wage-earning skills or desires to leave the economic security of a male-supported household. She warned them of their husbands' ability to leave them flat. In her book, *The Power of the Positive Woman*, Schlafly discusses the question of male support, with an admittedly less-than-altruistic tone for this most "natural" of social arrangements:

> Some ERA proponents argue that husbands support their wives only because of love, not because of the law. But a relationship that is based exclusively on love or on sexual compatibility, is not apt to survive all those years.... Love is a concept that may embrace many relationships with many different persons. Duty is essential to marriage. The moral, social, and legal evil of ERA is that it proclaims as a constitutional mandate that the husband no longer has the primary duty to support his wife and children.[18]

Schlafly argued for the protection of women, conceiving of womanhood as a sexual class in need of protection. The anti-ERA argument was that women needed to maintain their protected status from and through men (differently articulated depending on the thing from which women needed protection). ERA supporters were also arguing that women needed protection: the protection of the constitutional mandate for equal rights. Feminists also argued that the "protections" Schlafly was insisting women would lose were never there in the first place.[19] Citing the lack of protections in marriage and divorce, child support laws, and so forth, ERA activists countered Schlafly at each turn. The fact that there was no draft did not deter supposition about how one would potentially catch women in it. The counterargument, here articulated by Ginny Hildebrand in *The Militant*, is quite interesting, and demonstrates the strong antiwar strain in pro-ERA positions at the time:

> It's true that future draft laws could not discriminate on the basis of sex. But the current reality is that *no one* is being drafted. A massive anti-Vietnam War movement forced the draft to shut down. And much to the chagrin of Phyllis Schlafly, if Congress ever again tries to draft men or women, it will be confronted by an even more massive and powerful antiwar and antidraft movement—probably led by women.[20]

The argument that women working outside the home would destroy the family, and the treatment of this prospect as a specter of horror by anti-ERA activists, had a very specific appeal. Women who, by necessity or choice, had combined wage work and house (unwaged) work for quite some time stood to gain from the ERA. The only actual threat of change was for housewives. Schlafly argued that economic chaos, through high unemployment, would result from women flooding the wage labor market. Interestingly, Bush, as President in the late 1980s, made the same argument against downsizing the volunteer forces, suggesting that we did not want to let loose thousands of unemployed young people onto the streets.

Right-wing anti-ERA activists had the advantage of catching the pro-ERA movement off-guard. The ease of Congressional approval of the amendment and the rapidity of women's gains had left pro-ERA activists overly confident and loosely organized. Thirty-five states were already ratified with only three more needed when Schlafly's campaign got off the ground. STOP ERA swiftly mobilized in states where the New Right already enjoyed wide support. The anti-ERA forces needed to control less ground than the liberal activists, and they already had significant organizational structure at their disposal.

While the ERA was moving through the states, a major transformation was occurring in the courts through equal rights legislation. The mandate of the congressional vote enabled the courts to consider a number of cases regarding the unequal treatment or classification of the sexes in a new light.

ERA: The Courts and the Question of Equality

The public and political pressures to include women more systematically were bolstered by court decisions, not always on women's behalf, that clarified and solidified women's claims to legal equality with men. Heavily contested, and not nearly complete, they nevertheless began to shift the possible. Pushing along parallel fronts with the civil rights movements for African Americans and riding on the civil rights legal arguments, women's movement legal activists sought to convince the courts that women were not receiving equal treatment on many fronts.

Frontiero v. Richardson (411 U.S. 677, 1973) cleared the Supreme Court in 1973, requiring that the spouse of a female member of the forces be considered her dependent for obtaining housing and health benefits. At issue in *Frontiero*, for armed forces' women, were the differences in proof of dependent requirements for the armed forces to recognize a male or female spouse of a servicemember. This system of benefit allotment reinforced women's less-than-equal opportunity in the forces. This difference in disclosure requirements was found unconstitutional by the Supreme Court because it violated the Due Process Clause of the Fifth Amendment. The Supreme Court's decision reversed a lower court's finding and struck the separate rules for servicewomen. This ruling allowed Sharon Frontiero, and all servicewomen, to claim their spouses as dependents under the same rules as servicemen. However, *Frontiero* had wider significance in the context of the ERA ratification process and the struggle through the courts to establish sex classification as requiring strict scrutiny akin to race in discrimination lawsuits.

Four of the Justices in the case—Brennan, Douglas, White, and Marshall—issued their opinion in concurrence with the ERA's section 1 in stating that "we can only conclude that classifications based on sex, like classifications based upon race, alienage, or national origin, are inherently suspect, and must therefore be subjected to strict judicial scrutiny." However, Justices Stewart, Powell, and Blackmun, while concurring in reversing the statute, argued that it should be done on the basis of the *Reed* (404 U.S. 71, 1971) decision that sex is a category which should be subject to special scrutiny, but not to strict scrutiny under the Fourteenth Amendment framework. They also based their decision in deferment to the "Equal Rights Amendment, which if adopted will resolve the substance of this precise question . . . the Court has assumed a decisional responsibility at the very time when state legislatures, functioning within the traditional democratic process, are debating the proposed Amendment." The one dissenting voice was the newly appointed Justice Rehnquist.

Thus, the legal question of equal treatment for women in the armed forces, and in society more generally, stopped short of requiring the strictest scrutiny in contestation over equal treatment. The issue of the level of scrutiny afforded to cases of gender discrimination was revisited in *Craig v. Boren* (429 U.S. 190, 1976), where the doctrine of intermediate scrutiny was developed to apply to women and reenters this story in a discussion about the draft in the next chapter.

In 1975, the Department of Defense ended its policy of involuntary discharge for pregnancy. The individual services fought to keep the pregnancy discharge policy until the Second Circuit Court issued its decision in *Crawford v. Cushman*.[21] This decision held that Marine Corps regulations allowing the discharge of pregnant women to insure troop readiness did not meet the test of important government interest under the Fifth Amendment's rules, to justify gender-based discrimination. This change was supported when, according to Jeanne Holm,

[i]n 1977, a comprehensive DoD study of lost time for service members concluded that the differences in lost time for men and women were not significant because men lost much more duty time on average than did women for absence without leave, desertion, alcohol/drug abuse, and confinement. . . . The Army did know that some five hundred men a year

were given twelve-week deferments from overseas assignments because their civilian wives were in an advanced stage of pregnancy (a practice common to all the services). By comparison, the average time lost by military women during pregnancy was only eleven weeks.[22]

During this period, a concerted effort by equal rights activists continued the all points pressure to open up service ranks for women. The National Coalition for Women in Defense was formed out of the following organizations: National Organization for Women, Women's Equity Action League, National Council of Jewish Women, League of Women Voters, Girl Scouts, American Civil Liberties Union, and the Women in the Military Project. This coalition lobbied successfully for the opening of nontraditional assignments to women in the Military Occupational Specialties, and for veterans' status for Women's Air Service pilots of World War II. They also lobbied for women in combat and for women's equal responsibility to registration and conscription, but were not successful here.[23] Nevertheless, liberal advocacy for women's equal treatment in the forces continued to be bolstered by the seeming progress of the ERA and by the armed forces' need for women personnel.

Owens v. Brown[24] was decided in 1978, allowing women to serve on Navy ships, albeit not on designated battleships. The case was heard during a period of Congressional testimony on allowing women to serve on auxiliary ships. *Owens* was a class action suit against the Navy charging that section 6015 of the WASIA, which excluded women from serving aboard ship, was sexual discrimination. Judge Sirica ruled that 6015 did indeed deny Navy women equal protection under the Fifth Amendment.

It was only a matter of time before the precedent to grant women equal access to various billets in the forces would come up against the question of combat.

The Military Academies and Combat

The military academies, a major source of commissioned officers, were another hot button spot for debates on women in combat. The Pentagon did not support the sex integration of the academies and the Congress took the lead in opening the military academies to women. Two cases were brought before the courts to win a place for women in the academies, *Edwards v. Schlesinger* (377 F. Supp. 1091, 1974) and *Waldie v. Schlesinger* (377 F. Supp. 1901, 1974). Both class action suits challenged the exclusion of women from the academies as unequal protection of a group by sex classification.

When the Congress took up the question in 1975 the debate shifted tone. At issue was the presumption that the academies' function was to produce the highest skilled combatants:

> The issue of whether women should be cadets at West Point is tied directly to the basic question of whether Americans are prepared to commit their daughters to combat. . . . The Military Academy has, indeed, the distinctive and necessary mission of educating and training [and] preparing . . . officers for combat roles.[25]

This basic question of whether women should be cadets was, at least, resolved in terms of women's general training as military officers, if not in terms of committing daughters to combat.

The subsequent vote in the House (303 to 96), and in the Senate, to admit women to the academies was indicative of growing support for women to have expanded opportunity in the forces, and for some to consider moving women toward combat roles. President Ford signed Public Law 94-106 in 1975, and women competed with men for entry to the military academies beginning in the 1976 school year.

Contrary to this opening of the academies' doors for women, what women found inside was not nearly as opportune. Until the 1990s, marching cadences contained demeaning references to women, and a routine salute for women as well as men was "I am an American fighting man." A controversial account of the cadences from Annapolis by Carol Burke, a former English professor at the Naval Academy, is retold in Jean Zimmerman's book, *Tailspin*.[26] Burke wrote an article for the *New Republic* detailing the misogynist cadences that students and faculty were sending to her. She wrote "[t]hey brought me jokes scribbled on sheets of lined paper; lyrics to bawdy marching chants; latrinalia; legends; accounts of pranks, rituals, and rites of passage; stories of Academy anti-heroes; and personal narratives of life among the Brigade of Midshipmen." Typical cadences included: "Rape, Maim, Kill Babies. Rape, Maim, Kill Babies, Oorah!" and a parody of the song "Candy man": "Who can take a chain saw / Cut the bitch in two / Fuck the bottom half / And give the upper half to you / The S & M man, the S & M man, / The S & M man 'cause he mixes it with love / and makes the hurt feel good." Zimmerman recounts that "[s]tudents and faculty alike were bitter about what they perceived as Burke's distortion of the school's culture through deliberate inaccuracies and exaggeration." She also notes that "the academy made a specific effort in the aftermath of Burke's *New Republic* article to clean up the cadence calls used by the mids."[27] Carol Barkalow had written about this hostile environment in her autobigraphy of her years at West Point, a confirmation of Burke's observations. The long-standing traditions of demeaning women to create a bonding spirit for young cadets was in need of adjustment to the new era. Even in the 1990s, one of the high-anxiety issues of integrating the martial tradition private schools had to do with losing that sharp boundary within which misogyny is a defining characteristic of cadet ritual.

The opening of the military academies to women did not affect the private military-style schools until well into the 1990s. Challenges to these military-style schools were sparked by the acceptance of a woman (accidentally) into the Citadel and her subsequent battle to stay. These state-funded schools, such as the Citadel in South Carolina and the Virginia Military Institute, were sucessfully challenged on their admission practices under Title IX of the 1972 Education Act Amendments, which protects equal access to federally funded education. Before *U.S. v. Virginia* (976, F.Sd. 890, 1992) came up for review at the Supreme Court in January of 1996, Justices O'Connor and Ginsberg were reportedly unhappy with the VMI lawyers' assertion that the presense of women would disrupt the education of the men and make them "nervous." On June 26, 1996, the Supreme Court, with Justice Ruth Bader Ginsberg presiding, issued a far-reaching ruling in the case against the Virginia Military Institute. The court found that the provision of a "separate but equal" school for women was not met by the program at Mary Baldwin College (the purported women's equivalent school), and that to maintain its eligibility for state funding the Virginia Military Institute would have to admit qualified women to its program. This ruling had equal bearing on the Citadel. At least women will not be excluded from the benefits of such schooling, at most it will be a landmark ruling for women's rights more generally speaking in providing stronger ground against sex classification discrimination. It remains to be seen how the decision will be read in other cases of sex-based classifications. Although neither of these military-style schools is a federal armed forces academy, both are part of the long-standing tradition of martial-based education, receive federal funding, and have particular purchase in fields that validate that kind of training, including the forces, which draw officers from both schools. They are frequently discussed in the same breath as the forces when the subject is women's appropriate place in martial culture.[28] Especially informative in this regard is the heated debate over Shannon Faulkner's withdrawal from the Citadel after winning a case against the school's exclusion of females.[29]

The issues for the courts in these cases are based on federal and state adherence to equal access to educational opportunities funded by the federal government as legislated by Title IX of the 1972 Education Act Amendments. However, of particular interest here is that such schools defend their culture of masculinity and reveal an extraordinary bias toward conformity as the bedrock of their curricula. They stand almost as caricatures of the more nuanced resistances and invitations to women in the armed forces' institutions.[30]

In the meantime, women's movement activists interested in the development of policy supporting women were working to ratify the Equal Rights Amendment and to respond both to the cacophony of voices and interests emerging inside the movement and the opposition to the movement's goals, especially in the form of the ERA. In 1977 there was a major gathering of women's movement activists in Texas, with the agenda of hashing out the positions and strategies for the movement's next steps.

The National Women's Conference

From November 18–21, 1977, the first National Women's Conference convened in Houston. Sponsored by the federal government, it was intended by the Carter administration to quell the more radical wing of the women's movement by coopting and mainstreaming the quest for women's rights into the moderate liberal agenda. Zillah Eisenstein has argued elsewhere that the agenda of the state in sponsoring the conference was "to attend to the growing instability created by the conflict between feminist demands and the New Right."[31] The conference members generated a political platform for women's rights that far surpassed the constraining hopes of the government. Several points included in the conference's National Plan of Action related to women and the forces, although their stronger and more sustained interest and discussion pertained to the issues of disarmament, the arms race, and the neutron bomb. In the plank on employment they stated that the Veteran's Preference Act be "amended . . . so that veteran's preference is used on a one time only basis . . . except for disabled veterans."[32] In their plank on employment they also state that, given the low numbers of women veterans, the Veteran's Preference Act is discriminatory against women in the job market.

By the time of the Conference, thirty-five states had ratified the ERA, and it needed only three more to pass. In the plank on the ERA the conference issued a statement about women and the forces, suggesting that the ERA's adoption would give women equal access to military advancement. In this section of their broader statement on the ERA they emphasized:

> ERA will NOT require that there be as many women as men in combat roles in the military service, but it will give women equal access to the skills, training, education, and other benefits that military services provide. There is no draft now, but if a national emergency requires one in the future or if it is reinstated for any reason, women would be subjected to the draft just as men would be, under a system that would undoubtedly provide for exemptions for specific categories, e.g., parents with dependent children, persons with physical, mental, or emotional illness, conscientious objectors, and others. . . . The military services would have the same right to assign women as they have to assign men, but this does not mean that they would be automatically assigned to combat, unless they volunteered for such duties. As a matter of fact, in modern warfare a very small percentage of men in the armed services actually serve in combat, and the decision as to who is best equipped for combat is up to the commanders. Meanwhile, *to deny women the opportunity to freely enter the military services today is to deny them an equal expression of patriotism as well as career, educational, and job opportunities* [italics mine].[33]

The statements above reflected, on the one hand, the small numbers of women already in the forces, as this was just the beginning of the surge of women recruits. On the other hand, the writers were responding to the growing political pressures to stop the ERA precisely because of fears that it would mean sending women into combat, a fear that was becoming more prominent in public debates, as I will discuss in the next section of this chapter. The plank also addressed a number of the other points of anti-ERA fervor such as dissolution of the family, abortion rights, co-ed bathrooms, and so-called increasing federal power. Anti-ERA arguments, especially Schlafly's, suggested that "ERA represents a grab for power at the federal level. A section of the Amendment will take out of the hands of the states and send to Washington control over areas that the Federal Government hasn't yet got its fingers into—marriage laws, divorce, child custody, prison regulations, insurance rates."[34] The writers penned along the fine line between advocating the changes and reassuring that the ERA would not cause any disruptions to the status quo. Under their plank on sexual preferences the writers made a statement against the discrimination against lesbians in the Armed Forces and other government jobs especially pertaining to security clearances. Overall they stated that, "[h]omosexuals are entitled to the same civil rights as are other American citizens."[35]

ERA: Women in Combat—Equal Rights or Extra Responsibilities

Women in combat was the red herring raised by anti-ERA activists—more potent than co-ed bathrooms. The debates about women in combat roles in the context of the ERA were won to the side of arguments that women were socially unfit to the demands of warring, that they would not be capable of killing, and that they were physiologically unable to "man" the equipment. Schlafly argued, with a strong following, that women had the right to be protected by men. Feminist women, witness the National Conference, publicly supported women having access to the forces if they wanted it, but, tied as they often were to the peace movement, shied away from fully encouraging women in the forces. Right-wing assaults on the ERA regularly spoke to women's "right" to be a homemaker, to be elevated onto a pedestal, and to stand by her man.[36]

Especially potent were the arguments by anti-ERA groups, Concerned Women for America and Eagle Forum, that helped to highlight the specter of women being drafted as a key reason to defeat the ERA: the distinctions between men and women would finally be destroyed, and "one has to be kidding to call it a step up for women to make them subject to involuntary military conscription and assignment to combat duty."[37] Of course, this statement is an interesting counterpoint to Schafly's otherwise hawkish stance. This was the key note of right-wing litanies against women in the armed forces, a theme most particularly resonant in the armed forces because of its structured masculinity. As Republican Presidential candidate Ronald Reagan proclaimed: "I do not want to see sex and sexual differences treated as casually and amorally as dogs and other beasts treat them. I believe this can happen under the ERA."[38]

All fifty states did not ratify the ERA before the June 30, 1982 deadline. Gallop polls in June 1982 showed that 58 percent of the (mixed-gender) public supported ratification and only 24 percent of those polled opposed it. The common understanding of ERA's defeat is a combination of the fears that it would mean that the armed forces would become gender integrated and that women would be sent to combat, and the effective work of Phyllis Schlafly's organizational network, STOP ERA, to defeat it state by state.[39] This strategy was relatively easy as her rhetoric was well received in the traditionally conservative states that had not ratified by 1976.

Alongside the struggle over the ERA and its eventual demise, the legal and political institutions were moving forward in justifying women's gradual inclusion in the armed forces in jobs and benefits. In 1976, a Brookings Institute study entitled *Women in the Military* promoted the inclusion and more extensive utilization of women in the forces.[40] This study, utilized by the Department of Defense, suggested that women be more systematically included in armed forces' recruiting, especially considering two major factors: the congressional approval of the Equal Rights Amendment and the ending of conscription. As Binkin and Bach suggest in their introduction, "under pressure from the women's movement, on the one hand, and facing possible shortages of male volunteers, on the other, the Pentagon decided in 1972 that the scope of women's participation had to be expanded and the many sources of sex discrimination removed."[41] The authors' argument for the necessity of including women centered on the ease with which women could be incorporated in the many noncombat oriented roles. They suggested that the inclusion of women in combat roles be studied in more depth and they suggested some trial methods. There were sufficient data demonstrating that women could perform well in noncombat jobs; however, there was not yet a set of performance data on women in combat situations.[42] They suggested some ways to work through this problem while cautioning policy makers that

> [t]he question [of women in combat] is extremely complex, involving a crosscut of social and military factors. Two powerful social forces are in collision: the push for women's equal rights is in conflict with deeply rooted traditions that question the propriety of women under arms. . . . Also at odds are two more practical issues related to national security: the budgetary advantages of recruiting more women are at variance with perceived risks to the U.S. national interest. Were women to constitute a larger proportion of the military establishment, it is clear that personnel quality (measured by educational level and general intelligence and aptitude) would improve. Less certain, however, are the overall implications for military effectiveness. Little is known about how women will perform combat tasks, and even less about how they will affect combat unit performance.[43]

Conclusion

By the time the Equal Rights Amendment was foundering, many protections for women's expanded role in the armed forces were in place. The nation had ratified the ERA indirectly through the courts, the Congress, public opinion, and by nearly two-thirds of the states. There remains a great deal to be gained by the specificity and depth of guarantee in the ERA. However, women have seen many advances despite the ERA's failure to secure ratification.

The fear of women in combat that helped the ERA to falter and the military academies to hesitate in admitting women (but admit them nonetheless), were all acted out on a template of what kind of citizens women should, or could, be. These points of resistance to women's full inclusion in United States political life have in common a fear of gender norms being disrupted, and highlight long-standing expectations of women as citizen-mothers and not as citizen-soldiers. This reaffirms the gendered division of citizenship itself, and by its very nature of exclusion suggests a hierarchy of claims to citizenship, with martial service remaining at the pinnacle.

In various arenas since that time, and partly a result of the default that women did sign up in higher numbers as recruits, entered the academies, and trained as soldiers, women have become increasingly critical to the humanpower of the armed forces organizations. In this way, the 1980s became a kind of sleeper decade for what would become at the end of that decade and the beginning of the next a major wave of public and policy oriented process around the woman citizen-mother as soldier.

Following Eisenstein's (1981) argument that the government-sponsored National Women's Conference was intended to shore up support for women as necessary wage earners, I suggest that women's access to soldiering, as supported by the Binkin and Bach report, without access to the defining practice of soldiering, namely combat, preserves the numbers increase needed for the forces without challenging the core of masculinist militarism. This works in two important ways. One, it defuses the demand for women in ground combat roles (although, as we know now, that did not last forever). Two, it discredits the feminist antimilitarists, because they were clearly out of touch with what some American women wanted. Thus, encouraging the liberalist inclusion of women in the workforce and the military without challenging the glass ceiling inequities keeps the system running, co-opts challenges to its core assumptions, and discredits the radical opposition on both sides!

In the next chapter I turn to the rapid growth of the armed forces through the 1980s and the contradictory effects of an incoming conservative administration on the development of a stable and expanded set of opportunities for women in the forces. This story sets out the legacy from which the more recent military actions raised the important questions of what kinds of working roles are appropriate for women in the forces. The rapid expansion of the forces, and of women's jobs within them, led to a sharp increase in women's visibility in the forces. This visibility culminated in women soldiers' persistent and gradually effective efforts to access the fullest privileges and responsibilities of martial service: work as combatants.

FIVE

Women's Actions
and Womanpause

President Carter has stabbed American womanhood in
the back in a cowardly surrender to women's lib. We are
not going to send our daughters to do a man's job.
— Phyllis Schlafly (Holm 1982)

No man with gumption wants a woman to fight his
battles.
— General William Westmoreland (Holm 1982)

Rostker, Women, and the Draft

The combined influence of the Binkin and Bach report, Department of
Defense studies and hearings comparing women and men's deployability rates, and pressure from organized egalitarian feminists effecting ERA
mandates in the variety of ways outlined in the prior chapter all worked
to impress upon President Carter the appropriateness of including
women in the draft. Whether or not there was a priori knowledge that it
would be a lost battle, this public move to include women in the draft
was a nod to the mainstream egalitarian feminists, and in keeping with
Defense Department think tanks' research that indicated women were
indeed necessary to maintain force quality.

In January of 1980, Carter responded to the Soviet Union's war with
Afghanistan by proposing the reinstitution of draft registration for the
United States. He did so with two proposals to Congress: one requested
reinstatement of the Selective Service Act, and a second stipulated draft

eligibility should include women. Carter acted in seemingly reasonable concurrence with the legal interpretations of sexual equality emergent from the courts, women's expanding access to the forces afforded by re-defining soldiers' benefits, the opening of the military academies, and the All Volunteer Forces' mandate to recruit women. Most of all, the de-bates about the Equal Rights Amendment, which I have described in the preceding chapter, highlighted that gender was unspecified in the Pen-tagon's draft policies. Therefore, including women in the draft was a log-ical progression. At the same time, the comic hit of the year 1980, in the United States, was Goldie Hawn in *Private Benjamin*, from Paramount Pictures. The film suggested that even a spoiled rich white (Jewish) girl could find true empowerment and direction for her life through the mil-itary. The message in the film was that women could be shaped in posi-tive ways by boot camp and learn more about themselves and life through the kind of disciplined hierarchical training afforded by the new equal opportunity military. Wendy Chapkis and Mary Wings analyzed the film as "a dangerous piece of propaganda worthy of more critical at-tention than it has received by antimilitarists and feminists. It is the first post-Vietnam film about the US Army that has absolutely nothing to say about war. It is the first film with a marginally feminist gloss that explic-itly argues for the armed forces as a path to women's liberation."[1] They point out the ways that the film carefully remarks heterosexist boundaries (the wicked commanding officer is a lesbian) and works to entice young women with images of female power and achievement. It presented racialized stereotypes of the characters as well, not the least of which is Hawn as the spoiled Jewish American princess. Private Benjamin was an inspiring though comical woman-as-soldier. It is unclear what effect the film had on the recruitment of women. What it does do is present women's soldiering as an effective way to discipline the "liberated woman" as long as she remains clearly within her appropriate gender role. Volunteer women soldiers looking for meaning in their lives was one thing, drafting women was another story.

Put to the test, the public (by the gauge of opinion polls) and the Congress sharply disagreed with Carter on the appropriateness of draft-ing women. A Gallup poll[2] showed 39 percent of males and 50 percent of females opposed drafting women. The poll also indicated that 53 per-cent of males and 56 percent of females opposed women in combat. The

Senate's Armed Services Committee Chair, John Stennis, publicly opposed the inclusion of women in the draft call. Stennis appointed the Senate Manpower and Personnel Subcommittee of the Senate Armed Services Committee, chaired by Senator Sam Nunn, to study the issue. The subcommittee's report, not surprisingly, recommended a vote against women being conscripted. The report concluded that a draft of women

> would place unprecedented strains on family life . . . *A decision which would result in a young mother being drafted and a young father remaining home with the family in a time of national emergency cannot be taken lightly,* nor its broader implications ignored. The committee is strongly of the view that such a result, which would occur if women were registered and inducted under the administration plan, is unwise and unacceptable to a large majority of our people [italics mine].[3]

Clearly, the committee and the Congress saw the threat to appropriate gender roles as too great to risk drafting women.

The Congress as a whole concurred and activated the Selective Service Act (50 U.S.C. App. Section 451), earmarking funds specifically for male registration. Two members of the subcommittee were in dissent from the vote. Senator Cohen went on record stating that the decision not to draft women was

> fatally flawed because they erroneously focus on the assignment of women to combat and fail to address the improved plans for the use of women to meet 'non-combat mobilization requirements.' The assignment of women to combat roles is an issue that unnecessarily clouds the central issue of how a nation can best meet its personnel requirements in times of mobilization.[4]

Feminist response was mixed. This was in part because of the fact that feminist activism had its roots in nonviolent civil rights and antiwar movements, and thus had largely avoided or minimized comment on women in the forces. NOW issued a formal statement opposing the draft altogether when Carter first proposed the change, insisting that if there were to be a draft, men and women must share in it equally. In a document entitled "Opposition to Draft and Registration" of January 1980, NOW stated that they oppose[d] the reinstatement of registration and draft for both men and women. NOW's primary focus on this issue is on opposition to registration and draft. However, if we cannot stop the return to registration and draft, we also cannot choose between sisters and brothers. We oppose any registration or draft that excludes women as an unconstitutional denial of rights to both young men and women. And we continue to oppose all sex discrimination by the volunteer armed services.[5]

This debate and the decision in the Congress were simultaneous with the stunning reversal of fortune for the ERA. Its once assured state ratification process was being stopped dead in its tracks by Phyllis Schlafly's organizations. The drafting of women and the specter of women in combat were the twin demons on which the anti-ERA movement was flying.

By 1980, the draft and combat had become, along with abortion, Schlafly's central themes. All the earlier issues—unisex toilets, wives' right to support from their husbands, and homosexual marriages—took a distinctly subordinate role. As the ERA deadline neared, Schlafly became fond of posing for publicity photographs holding a pamphlet on women and combat.[6] Moreover, the recurring theme of combat as the necessary result of drafting women was a key holding point for both sides. Those right-wing activists against women being drafted, or in prior years against women being allowed into the ranks, were sure that women would end up in combat and were clearly opposed. Those who fought for women to have access to the draft and the ranks were constantly reassuring their opposition that women would not be in combat. The National Women's Conference was an exception here in that, as I discussed in chapter 4, they accepted that some women might volunteer for combat duty, but not that a draft would require women to be combatants.

The struggle to define women's military roles rested on questions of equality and difference between women and men. A number of cases[7] had gone to the courts, in the late 1960s and early 1970s, to challenge the Selective Service Act (SSA). The cases by and large were issued by men looking to challenge the unequal protection of men enacted by the male-only draft. Most notable thus far had been *U.S. v. St. Clair* (291 F. Supp. 122, 1968) which was heard in the United States District Court, Southern District of New York. The District Court decided against James St. Clair's challenge to the constitutionality of the Selective Service Act's (SSA) exclusion of women. The court found that the SSA did not violate St. Clair's constitutional right to due process under the Fifth Amendment. The court stated that

> [i]n the Act and its predecessors, Congress made a legislative judgement that men should be subject to involuntary induction but that women, presumably because they are "still regarded as the center of home and family life" (*Hoyt v. State of Florida*) . . . should not. . . . In providing for involuntary service for men and voluntary service for women, *Congress followed the teachings of history that if a nation is to survive, men must provide the first line of defense while women keep the home fires burning.* Moreover, Congress recognized that in modern times there are certain duties in the armed forces which may be performed by women volunteers. For these reasons, the distinction between men and women in the armed forces is not arbitrary, unreasonable or capricious [italics mine].[8]

The courts consistently found that conscription of men only was legitimate because men were eligible (capable) for combat and women were not. As Deborah Rhode, a feminist legal scholar, pointed out: "[e]ven if one assumed the legitimacy of excluding women from combat, their exclusion from registration did not follow."[9] This is true because there are many noncombat positions that women could have been drafted to do, just as they were doing them as volunteer recruits. However, the primacy of combat eligibility is not only the mystique of martial service, it is its linchpin. And the argument that only men were appropriately combatants sealed the case.

The renewal of the Selective Service Act in 1980, and its reinforcement of targeting males only, revived *Rostker v. Goldberg*. This was a court case first brought in 1971 by several young men resisting the draft to the Vietnam War, and it languished as the war and conscription ended. In the meantime, in *Craig v. Boren* (429 U.S. 190, 1976), the courts had developed the legal category of intermediate scrutiny under the Equal Protection Clause of the Fourteenth Amendment. The contest in this case was over whether males, 18 to 20 years old, were receiving unequal protection. These males were subject to an Oklahoma law restricting them from buying "low-alcohol" beer. Females were able to purchase the "beer." The Supreme Court found that their right to equal protection under the Fourteenth Amendment was violated. The juridical distinction of *Craig* was that the Court used it to clarify the terms under which sex discrimination cases were assessed. The Court affirmed its earlier reading in *Reed v. Reed* where it had established that sex classification was a category that deserved special scrutiny. In *Craig*, the Court established the level of intermediate scrutiny as that which requires the government to prove substantial interest in sex-based classifications to justify their use. This fell short of the much stronger burden of proof, strict scrutiny, issued on the government in the case of racial discrimination as set forth in the *Korematsu* decision in 1944.

The *Craig* ruling meant that *Rostker v. Goldberg* (453 U.S. 57, 1981) would be heard with different emphasis. *Rostker v. Goldberg* began in 1971 as an antiwar protest. Goldberg filed a class action suit with the intention of challenging the draft as a violation of draft-eligible males' equal protection rights under the Due Process Clause of the Fifth Amendment, because the draft exempted women, and as a case of involuntary servitude. Rostker was the director of the Selective Service System. The District Court in Philadelphia heard the case first, in 1971, and quickly dismissed it as irrelevant. The Third Circuit Court of Appeals revived the case in 1974. The Appeals Court decided to consider the case in terms of the question of unequal protection, and remanded the case to the lower court for a decision. The ending of the draft in 1974 rendered the case moot.

Carter's decision to reinstate the draft and the failure of his proposal to include women revived the case in the U.S. District Court for the Eastern District of Pennsylvania, which issued its opinion on July 18, 1980. The District Court found that the Military Selective Service Act (MSSA) was unconstitutional by applying the instructions of the *Craig* decision. The court found that the Act violated equal protection in the Fifth, and while clearly marking that it was only considering registration and not combat, the court enjoined the Selective Service System from initiating registration. Rostker won a stay of injunction from Justice Brennan, and registration began on schedule. The case was appealed to the Supreme Court.

The Rostker case carried the weight of conflicting mandates: the Senate Report and congressional vote to allocate funds for a male-only draft, the recent Court precedents instructing the use of intermediate scrutiny in cases of sex classification through equal protection arguments, and the mixed commentary from women activists. On the one hand there was Schlafly's organization, vocally and visibly opposed to the ERA and women in draft or combat. On the other hand, feminists issued mixed responses to being potentially equal for a draft, but rapidly losing ground on their attempts to be equal under the law due to the demise of the ERA.

Thus, as the ERA was losing it final state mandates, NOW was issuing an *amicus curiae* to the Supreme Court regarding *Rostker* stating that "compulsory universal military service is central to the concept of citizenship in a democracy."[10] They also filed statements in the Senate for the hearings on the "Reinstatement of Procedures for Registration Under the Military Selective Service Act" before the Subcommittee on Manpower and Personnel of the Senate Committee on Armed Service in the spring and summer of 1979. The NOW national staff continued to assert their antimilitarism while, according to Jennifer Tiffany,[11] succumbing to the linkage of militarism and citizenship. Thus from mainstream women's rights groups, the argument for getting first-class citizenship was based precisely on what Schlafly raised as the warning flag. Women would take on men's worlds on men's terms!

The final Supreme Court decision in *Rostker*, with Justice Rehnquist presiding, declared that Fifth Amendment concerns of equal protection were overruled by strong government interest: discrimination to have a combat-ready military was acceptable under the constraints of constitutional law. Moreover, the Court was fully supported by the decisions reached in Congress through its Senate Report. Thus, Justice Rehnquist wrote: "Congress' decision to authorize the registration of only men, therefore, does not violate the Due Process Clause. The exemption of women from registration is not only sufficiently but closely related to Congress' purpose in authorizing registration." The Court took up the mandate of the congressional decision, citing its own prior cases regarding women and the draft and finding that

it is apparent that Congress was fully aware not merely of the many facts and figures presented to it by witnesses who testified before its committees, but of the current thinking as to the place of women in the Armed Services. In such a case, we cannot ignore Congress' broad authority conferred by the Constitution to raise and support armies when we are urged

to declare unconstitutional its studied choice of one alternative in preference to another for furthering that goal. . . . Congress' determination that
the need would be for combat troops if a draft took place was sufficiently
supported by testimony adduced at the hearings so that the courts are not
free to make their own judgment on the question.[12]

Wendy Williams wrote a particularly cogent response to the Court's
decision in *Rostker*. She said, "[t]o me *Rostker* never posed the question
of whether women should be forced as men now are to fight wars, but
whether we, like them, must take the responsibility for deciding whether
or not to fight."[13] By Williams' reckoning, women are precisely called
upon to take that citizenship responsibility alongside men. In the several
years that followed the Court's conclusion, liberal feminists argued that
women needed to take on equal responsibility to men in the military in
order to enact that citizenship. This is the period in which Stiehm begins
to study the dynamic of nonparticipation and its costs via *Women and
Men's Wars*. As I suggested above, the mainstream liberal feminist advocacy groups followed suit. In short, Private Benjamin and her sisters—
few of whom were young women from privileged backgrounds—should
be heralded as first-class citizens. In the future, the decision to include
women in the draft will have to be argued on the grounds that women
must be able to assume the same citizenship responsibilities as men until
martial service is not defined as a mark of full citizenship.

Feminist Antimilitarists in Action

At the same time, in the early 1980s the feminist-influenced antinuclear
direct action movement was in full swing. Inspired by civil rights strategies of nonviolent resistance, these actions and activists fought back
against nuclear power, nuclear armaments, and militarism. These activists, as I detailed in the first chapter, were intent on analyzing the connections between racism, sexism, and militarism. At the Women's Pentagon Actions, the Seneca Falls Peace Encampment, and at Greenham
Common in England, feminist antimilitarists were arguing that war was
a "white dick thing," at the same time that the National Organization for
Women was arguing that military service equaled first-class citizenship.
Feminist antimilitarists were focused on fighting militarism as a mas-

culinist institution without noticing the ways that women were, not only hurt by, but also implicated in, militarism through its cultural replications and firepower effects.[14] This left the field of negotiations over women's attraction to the promise of first-class economic and political citizenship the military recruiters offered up unchallenged by feminist antimilitarist savvy. Although Chapkis and Wings (1981) make a plea for feminist antimilitarists to look at the ways that masculinist militarism is reinscribed through women's recruitment as per *Private Benjamin*, the activist community continued to talk about militarism as a dick thing and assume women (and enlightened men) would thus be repelled from it.

The split between these feminist groups is intriguing to track. First of all, in 1980, NOW President Eleanor Smeal was arguing, while the SALT II negotiations were under way, that "peace is not a feminist issue." This was in response and dire contrast to the framework for feminist antimilitarism being developed in the women's actions I cited above and the anthologies and other feminist antimilitarist writings I discussed in the first chapter. Mainstream feminist groups like NOW worried that feminist antimilitarisms reified the gendered divisions of labor they were struggling to dismantle, and that feminist antimilitarist actions were discrediting mainstream (read legitimate) egalitarian agenda.

Some feminists, and especially antimilitarist feminists, critiqued the NOW approach. Kathleen Jones argued that "the reduction of demands for a new system of public policy priorities to demands for an agenda of nondiscriminatory opportunities within the existing framework bears all the markings of cooptation. . . . The assumption is that access to the state's legitimate use of force is necessary in order to redefine the values in defense of which that force is currently employed."[15] In movement circles people were saying "we don't want to fight for a piece of your carcinogenic pie!" Jones' critique centered on the observation that while liberal feminists concerned themselves with accessing for women "objective distribution of existing 'public goods' and responsibilities on a nonexclusionary basis,"[16] they avoided the question of what was to be distributed. NOW was not moved by such a critique, but rather interested in wresting full equal "objective" access.

Feminist antimilitarists and their actions developed critiques of militarism that were dependent on their masculinist tropes: missiles and penises, hierarchies of power, and so forth. This placed feminist antimilitarism in a gendered bind even though the tropes were literally allowed to be bent, such as the "Mothers for Peace" affinity group at the Mothers and Others Day Action in 1987 where men and women were costumed as pregnant mothers. Feminist antimilitarism nevertheless was open to criticism that it hearkened back to a traditional framework for peace that was absolutist and left no room for a more nuanced rendition of the nation's proclivities toward war. Elshtain argued,"[u]ntil such absolutist constructions are challenged, not in opposition to but in the name of a critical and ironic feminism, peace will remain a problem."[17]

Womanpause and the Reagan Administration

By the early 1980s, under the influence of the Reagan administration's outspoken interest in conservative family values and against the ERA, the Department of Defense attempted to reverse course and downsize the women's ranks. The "womanpause," the Defense Department's cheeky name for a strategy of pushing women back out of the forces by lowering recruitment targets for women and redefining many jobs as combat-related, was a short-lived strategy of the Air Force and Army. Nonetheless, by its very name it indicated the strong tinge of antiwoman feeling in the Defense Department and the unmistakable referencing to women's reproductive cycle, and indeed its marked endpoint in menopause. This strategy was defeated by Secretary of Defense Casper Weinberger's memorandum to the forces on January 14, 1982, stating "[w]omen in the military are a very important part of our total force capability. . . . This administration desires to increase the role of women in the military. . . . This Department must aggressively break down those remaining barriers that prevent us from making the fullest use of the capabilities of women in providing for our national defense." On July 19, 1983, the Secretary of Defense sent a memorandum to all the Department Secretaries "calling for full utilization of women consistent with existing combat exclusion laws and related policy."[18]

The attempt to phase out women's increased participation may have been a strategy to justify the need for a male draft in the pro-militarization environment of the Reagan era, according to Holm (1982).[19] A womanpause strategy also contradicted the logic in the Binkin and Bach research (1977) that was otherwise heavily relied upon to formulate policy about women in the forces. Binkin and Bach demonstrated that, without a draft, women recruits were needed to keep the personnel numbers up and the quality at its highest; this was the Department of Defense's position and the administration's strategy up to that point. There are undocumented arguments that a particularly racial argument may also have played a role here, in that if more (white) women would sign up the forces would not become a forces of color. The Reagan mandate was for expanding the armed forces, but focused especially in terms of the technologies (such as Star Wars) and implementing the Rapid Deployment Force. The contradiction of the armed forces trying to cut back on women recruits at the same time they were attempting to expand the forces looked suspicious to Senators and to the Administration as evidenced by Weinberger's statement above.[20] It also, in hindsight, resonates with numerous analyses of the threat women were posing to the forces' masculinist culture. In congressional hearings, General Robert Barrow could say, "War is man's work. . . . [The man] wants to think that he's fighting for that woman somewhere behind, not up there in the same foxhole. . . . It tramples the male ego. When you get right down to it, you have to protect the manliness of war."[21] Nevertheless, the Department of Defense ultimately expanded its roster of jobs for which women could be eligible. By the middle 1980s, women instructors had begun training men for combat-based Military Occupational Specialties (MOSs). Women were still restricted from combat duty.

Women made up 10 percent of the All Volunteer Forces by 1985, and African American women, at 11 percent of the United States population, comprised 26.5 percent of those women. Overall, 32.5 percent of All Volunteer Forces women were women of color in that year.[22] By 1989 the number of African American women in the forces had risen to 33.7 percent.[23] The increase in African American women's numbers in the forces indicates on the one hand their ready acceptance into the institution, as well as their eagerness to join the forces. However, a closer look reveals that the majority of these women remain in the lower ranks with the lowest paying jobs and least opportunity for advancement. All women of color are overrepresented in the enlisted ranks. By 1994, across the forces, African American women constituted 34 percent of the enlisted women and only 13 percent of women officers, Latinas constituted 5 percent of enlisted women and 2 percent of officers, and European American women constituted 57 percent of enlisted women and 80 percent of the officers, although this number was down from figures in 1980. The officers are the class from whose ranks come the flyer groups—the groups receiving the benefit of the opening of combat positions.[24] Clearly, a privileging of white female members of the forces is occurring even as the forces are "opened up" to the less than 15 percent of American women who are choosing to join.

The armed forces has the earliest and best record of equal opportunity among government and private sector employment, which is still not very good. The forces, though racism has been formally deinstitutionalized, are still shaped by the broad effects of a culture historically structured on racism. The 103d Congress held hearings to obtain general information about racial discrimination in the forces and published their findings on December 30, 1994. Entitled *An Assessment of Racial Discrimination in the Military: A Global Perspective*,[25] the report was submitted by the House Armed Services Committee. It details various allegations of racial discrimination. It is not comprehensive, and it vaguely alludes to the need for further studies. In December 1995, a commission was convened to research the recurrence of racism in the forces and especially the presence of racist hate groups, because of the recent murder of an African American couple by two white soldiers in Georgia.

Come Out, Come Out Wherever You Are

Interestingly enough, at the same time that women were being recruited more heavily, the mechanisms for policing those women's sexuality and for containing their achievements were being reinforced. In 1981 the Department of Defense declared that it would renew enforcement of the Uniform Code of Military Justice, Article 133: "forbidding conduct unbefitting an officer and a gentleman," conduct that includes homosexuality, and Article 125, which specifically outlaws sodomy. Long on the books, but erratically enforced, these policies of excluding lesbians and gays from armed service were approached with renewed vigor, although with a slightly different tenor of punishment. Of course, the "gentleman" part of the article needs some revisiting in the sex-integrated military. Outgoing Pentagonian W. Graham Claytor, Jr., sent a memorandum to the branches and the Secretary of Defense modifying Department of Defense Directive 1332.14, the Enlisted Administrative Separations Code, to provide explicit rules for the expulsion of homosexuals from the forces. The memorandum softened the punishment in the code, allowing honorable discharge. However, as Randy Shilts explains it, officers demonstrated a marked reluctance to enforce the policy. In the All Volunteer Forces a range of rules, plans, and responses can be tracked that at first glance seem utterly contradictory. In fact, they function to map the contradictory needs of the forces. On the one hand, a military that still needs human operators needs to keep enough bodies available (whatever their sex or sexual practices). On the other hand, the military needs to police its cultural boundaries as it becomes flexible in recruitment practices, in order to maintain the institution's stature as a masculinist proving ground.

The 1980s were characterized, according to Shilts, by acceptance among military personnel of their gay (male) compatriots. Not so readily accepted were lesbian soldiers, who were often targeted by the increasing numbers of heterosexual women coming into the services.[26] Until this time, the military, as a nontraditional job environment for women, attracted women who did not fit cultural norms. The armed forces had been known as a place where lesbians might find one another.[27] As the forces "professionalized," becoming more of a reasonable (read mainstream) career track for women, the numbers of lesbian enlistees compared to heterosexual enlistees seemed to decrease. Because of the official ban on lesbian and gay persons in the forces, figures are more hearsay than "fact." However, Shilts remarked that "[w]hile military lesbians estimated that homosexual women comprised perhaps as many as 35 percent of the females in uniform during the early 1980s, they calculated that by the late 1980s the percentage had dropped to 25."[28]

In 1987, at over 10 percent of all armed forces personnel, the percentage of women members in each of the forces were as follows: Air Force 12 percent, Army 10.3 percent, Navy/Marines 8.2 percent. The highest concentration of women officers were in the medical fields, at 40 percent of women officer totals. The second highest numbers were in administration. Women still ranked highest in the traditionally female and more particularly non–battle-related positions (the Risk Rule facilitated this division, keeping women out of combat turf). Of the officer women on active duty, 82 percent were white, 12 percent were African American, 2 percent were Hispanic, and 4 percent were in the category Asian/Pacific Islander, American Indian/Native Alaskan, and unknown. In the enlisted category, white women comprised 62 percent of all enlisted women, African American women were 32 percent, Hispanic women were 4 percent, and Asian/Pacific Islander, American Indian/Native Alaskan, and "unknown" women were 2 percent of the total.[29] Job profiles of the enlisted women showed the highest percentages were in administrative jobs. Thus in both categories, officers and enlisted women in 1987 continued to be predominantly represented in the realm of traditional female occupations: health and administration. Moreover, in 1988, "the greatest proportion of European-American women [was] concentrated in the Air Force (38.8 percent), the largest proportion of African-American women [was] in the Army (53.6 percent) and the largest proportion of Spanish-American women is in the Navy (38.6 percent). Like Black women, African-American men are also heavily concentrated in the Army. Because the Army is less a technical force than the other branches of service, the heavy concentrations of blacks in this branch raises concerns about the type of occupations they are trained for and assigned in."[30]

Under pressure from the DACOWITS to assure the quality and consistency of women's experiences in and between the forces, the Secretary of Defense formed a task force on September 16, 1987 to review the status of women in the armed forces and make recommendations to the Secretary of Defense. Dr. David Armor, Principal Deputy Assistant Secretary of Defense for Forces Management and Personnel, was appointed Chair. The Task Force on Women in the Military issued its report in January of 1988.[31] The report took up a variety of issues regarding women's status in the forces. These issues were the treatment of women and their morale in the forces, the consistent application of the combat exclusions, and the impact of force management policy on women's military careers.[32] The Task Force recommended, in Section I, that sexual harassment policies be affirmed, that better support systems—social and medical—which acknowledged women's minority presence be created, and that DoD policies "for on-base entertainment be changed to incorporate more explicit and well-defined standards of good taste."[33] This policy has apparently not been applied throughout the ranks, according to Judith Merkinson of GABRIELA, as evidenced by the fact that when seven thousand United States' soldiers were due to be stationed at Subic Bay during the recent conflict between China and Taiwan, bar owners around the base sent out notice to their female employees to come to work prepared to dance naked. As the DACOWITS reported in 1987 from their fact-finding mission in the Pacific Rim, the incidence of female prostitution and female nude dancing in base clubs was overwhelming. This item was one of the key points then addressed by the Task Force.

Utilizing the DACOWITS findings the Department of Defense readily conformed, in discussion at least, to the standard notions of propriety, decency, acceptable sexuality and sexual expression, in general adopting the moralizing tone of the DACOWITS findings. In practice, of course, it continued to be quite another matter, with base-sponsored sex work through the bars fully active and known.[34] During this same period, feminist antimilitarists and feminist antipornography activists were stepping up parallel claims against the horror of men's, and especially military men's, sexual behaviors' explicit connections to violence. Pornography and prostitution, it was argued, were forms of violence against women.[35] Feminist antimilitarists were arguing that patriarchy, violence, and masculinism were intertwined. The men's movement was arising to reclaim a masculine power from the supposed ashes of its feminist-ignited demise. While this set of sex-centered "moral" dilemmas was being sorted through, the United States was waking up to the worst sexually transmitted disease epidemic in our history; instead of framing AIDs as a question of public health, the powers that be were focused on the supposed immorality of the most afflicted population, gay men.

Section II, on Combat Exclusion, addressed the inconsistent application of the risk criteria between the forces which in effect closed many more positions to women than necessary by definition. The Task Force recommended that the Risk Rule be specified such that "noncombat units can also be closed to women on grounds of risk of exposure to direct combat, hostile fire, or capture, provided that the type, degree, and duration of risk is equal to or greater than that experienced by associated combat units (of similar land, sea or air type) in the same theaters of operation."[36] This ruling affected women's positions across the forces with a more broadly cast net of "combat" risk, while the universalizing of criteria for combat risk jobs also resulted in the opening of some previously closed positions such as certain Navy aircraft and mobile construction battalions, Marine Corps Security Guard and Security Forces, and Air Force Red Horse and Aerial Port Squadrons. One of the main concerns of the Task Force was

> whether changing war fighting doctrine, emerging technologies, and global strategies justify the use of risk of harm or capture alone as a primary criterion for identifying assignments precluded because of the combat exclusion, at least without some clear connection to combat. Women are currently utilized in units or theaters of operation in which they will be exposed to substantial risk of hostile fire or capture, depending on specific wartime scenarios.[37]

Thus the Task Force responded to the changing technological production of warfare and to the military build-up of the 1980s, both of which took women to new levels of engagement and further challenged the organization of the forces in relation to women. The terms of this inclusion still rested on exclusion from direct combat, but by the Task Force's admission this line of combat was becoming increasingly blurred. They relied on the geographic location of military personnel to try to solidify the differently situated female soldier, indicating that signal and intelligence jobs often placed women, unrestricted from those jobs, in the line of combat fire ahead of the combat troops. Thus the new Risk Rule provided for women's exclusion from those jobs to maintain consistency in combat exclusion and uniformly, across the services, open the similarly situated noncombat risked jobs to women.

The final section of the Report recommended that each of the services develop strong programs to encourage women's leadership and career aspirations. The Task Force found that men were still having difficulty accepting women in leadership roles and that "the Services must ensure that the career progression patterns established for women officers include leadership and management development positions that will equip these officers with the skills necessary to lead and manage at the highest levels in both joint and in-Service positions."[38]

From October 1987 through February 1988, hearings on "Women in the Military" (HASC 100-52) were held to research portions of House bill HR 2719. The House bill, sponsored by William Dickenson (ranking Minority member of the House Armed Services Committee), proposed to expand the types of jobs available to military women outside of direct combat, namely consistent opening of combat support assignments to women and an assurance that all services be consistent in applying the combat exclusion for "equitable" access to climbing the ranks. Led by Chairperson Rep. Beverly Byron (D-MD) of the House Armed Services Committee Military Personnel and Compensation Subcommittee, the hearings addressed the current status of women in the forces and were sympathetic to the earlier Department of Defense Task Force Report. Focused on the uniform development and maintenance of opportunities for women in the forces contained by combat exclusions, the hearings and the subsequent Defense Authorizations Act for the following fiscal year supported women's presence and affirmed the general terms of the Task Force.

The hearings included DACOWITS testimony from their fact-finding tour of the Philippines in 1987. The DACOWITS report in the Philippines was the original impetus for Defense Secretary Casper Weinberger to establish the Task Force, which shared its findings at the hearings. Dr. Jacqueline Davis compiled the WestPac Report summarizing DACOWITS findings at Cubi Point and Subic Bay. Judith Gibson, Vice Chairman [*sic*] of Public Relations for DACOWITS, gave a statement from their findings to the Military Personnel and Compensation Subcommittee Hearings. Gibson stated that "[w]ith respect to Cubi Point/Subic Bay in the Philippines in particular, I believe that the types of entertainment described by Navy women and apparently condoned are inappropriate and unacceptable on a United States government installation. The resultant environment is demeaning to the military woman, the military family, and the female employee."[39] Mrs. Sydney Hickey, Director of Government Relations for the Military Family Association, testified that "it is inconceivable that wives and children would be allowed, even encouraged to accompany their military sponsors in orders of the United States government to an area where open prostitution, near-nude waitresses, and burlesque shows were officially sanctioned in military clubs."[40] Several issues are raised by this report that do not appear within it. Stepping aside for the moment from the assumption in this statement that the problem with such armed forces-sponsored sex work is that wives and children will see it, it is crucial to mark here the discontinuity between the push for families (in this case women and children) to go base hopping with their spousal soldiers and the continued support of a base centered sex work culture. This perspective, offered by the Military Family Association, does not address the trouble of this military-sponsored sex work environment for straight or lesbian women soldiers, for gay soldiers, or for monogamously heterosexual soldiers, none of whom are beneficiaries of this overseas perk. Saundra Pollack Sturdevant and Brenda Stoltzfus have written an excellent documentary book exposing the connections between the U.S. military and Asian prostitution, which covers the Phillipines, South Korea, and Okinawa. It provides portraits of some prostitutes' lives and general analysis of the dynamic employment relationship between the U.S. military and the prostitution business as coordinated through the military clubs and private clubs around the bases.[41] Moreover, the official and unofficial sponsorship of this kind of entertainment for soldiers creates a hostile working environment for the women soldiers, just as nude calendars in the boss' office would in corporate life. Nothing is said in the governmental reports regarding the harm done to the prostitute women themselves. The reliance of the military on base culture that constructs rest and relaxation (R&R) as sex for a fee is not criticized and far from discouraged.[42]

This report about government-sponsored female sex work was compiled with information from the 1986 DACOWITS report concerning sexual harassment at Army bases in England and West Germany. The response by the DoD came in the form of reiteration of sexual harassment policies, reiteration of support for military families and support for military spouses who were being forced to relocate disrupting their own careers,[43] reiteration of what would count as appropriate "entertainment" (i.e., no nude dancing in the base clubs), and most importantly for questions of women and combat, a redefinition of the Risk Rule to assure women's distance from combat zones in military operations. This last measure indicated the Task Force's concern with continuing to manage women's access to higher ranks and their perks. The use of the Task Force to study both the social climate for women soldiers via sexual harassment and base entertainment, *and* the Risk Rule underscores the need to manage both women's relationship to and the very awkward contradictions inherent in, incorporating women to a masculinist military system.

Also in 1986, the blockbuster hit *Top Gun* appeared on screen to demonstrate the sexy masculinist world of the Navy Top Guns. This film incorporated a woman in a powerful role, of course with brains and conventional beauty combined. In fact, she is first seen as a beauty in the bar and only later do we discover that she is "Charlie," the civilian specialist with top security clearance and a PhD in Astrophysics. As the Top Gun trainees learn about their curriculum in dog fighting, one turns to another and whispers, "This gives me hard on." His companion whispers back, "Don't tease me." Maverick's (Tom Cruise's) arrogant statement that he thinks he will be on the plaque of the best pilots pleases the instructor, who says arrogance is the most valued attribute in a pilot. As the new pilots leave the training room one jokes, "The plaque for the alternates is in the ladies' room," and they all laugh hysterically at this. Numerous interactions among the men can be read as homoerotic/homophobic nodal points. As I watch them I feel intrigued at their intimacy with one another, yet they are clearly mocking the relationships. This is especially apparent as the scene shift from the dialog I described above to show them entering a Navy bar full of women in skimpy clothing fawning over the uniformed men. It is never clear if these women are prostitutes or partying singles; however, their collective body language makes it clear to the viewer that they are ready for sex. The film is a constant dance between fast planes and sex. As they enter the room Maverick says to his pal Goose, "Now this is what I call a target rich environment." The next day, after he has unsuccessfully hit on Charlotte Blackwood ("Charlie" the Ph.D.), he discovers that she is the civilian instructor. Their banter resumes with electrifying heterosexual play, interspersed by the constant homoerotic banter between Maverick and Goose, and for that matter, the other male couples (pilot/copilot buddie sets). I don't want to overread the homoerotics of this portrayal because it is clearly a film presenting a certain kind of male bonding and heterosexist masculine power. The parallels between this film's homoerotic and misogynist relations and the hazing rituals in the forces that I discussed earlier certainly beg the question of more intensive study of the construction of sexuality and power in the forces overall.

After Maverick and Charlie one-up each other a few times, she comes after him in the hall. He separates from Goose to talk with her, but first Goose says, "OK, well don't be late again," and straightening Maverick's collar he continues, "You look great." Maverick gets the last word for this encounter telling Charlie that if she wants information on the MiG he encountered she can "read about it" through her top security clearance. He is the pilot with the real story. She is the civilian who can read the report about his authentic experience.

This film excited many young men to aspire to Navy training during a decade far removed from the Vietnam syndrome, far removed from a sense of real "war," and untouched by the antimilitarist movements that circulated just off screen. It was seen as a very successful recruitment tool and the Navy happily consulted in the technical aspect and lent footage of fighter pilots and their jets airborne. It crafted a version of the military quite similar to Private Benjamin's, with no real association to battle, but rather geared toward the excitement and benefits that could be gained by participation in the forces. These films present, by absenting real war, a vision of all of the pleasure and none of the pain of military reality. *Private Benjamin* was a film company's construction, whereas *Top Gun* producers consulted with the Navy to develop the film. Both operated as personnel recruitment tools during the 1980s.

Conclusion

The 1980s was a period of unprecedented military expansion. Women were increasingly present and visible, although only 10 percent of the overall personnel numbers. Individual lesbian and gay soldiers were fighting for their civil rights to be recognized by the forces through legal means. This period was characterized by deepening resistance to these twin challenges to the forces' historic stance as a masculinist enterprise. With the concomitant efforts to build up women's presence in the forces, the Reagan administration was at least confused about what role women should play in the expanded forces and at most determined to keep women filling the support roles so the men could be available for combat. This drama was exacerbated by the sharp divisions foregrounded with New Right rhetoric on proper roles for women and men, giving more public air time to the likes of Schlafly, Westmoreland,

George Gilder, and David Horowitz to voice their concerns over the (potential) loss of masculinist martial distinction in the sexually integrating forces. This period was simultaneous with efforts to stage the most massive military build-up in United States history, and resulted in the deepest national debt to date.

This period was also one of heightened antiwar, anti-intervention, and antinuclear activism. As I detailed in chapter 1 this activism, especially in the antinuclear movement, was shaped by feminist analyses of militarism and a starkly antipatriarchal focus. The antinuclear activism located war as a dick thing and sought to demonstrate the ways that people and the other inhabitants of the world were endangered by the practices of militarism. This took the form of analyzing the comparative costs of military over social spending as in Lourdes Beneria and Rebecca Blank's article in *Rocking the Ship of State* (Harris and King 1989), and in the charts in action flyers and handbooks, as well as in the speeches and actions themselves detailing the ways that military spending forfeited social programs, military research produced toxic wastes that were destroying the planet, and military masculinism was destroying the possibilities for peace.[44] What these analyses did not do was to develop analytical linkages to the predicament of women's growing numbers in the military.

The challenges to the armed forces' culture of masculinity were widespread. Changes in public perception of the forces after the Vietnam War and a drop in the numbers of eligible males willing to volunteer for enlistment were the first salvo. In a context of emergent and strong women's rights activism, and a history of expanding legal civil rights due to the civil rights movements' street and juridical approaches, the armed forces were both invited and by legislation forced to open the ranks to women and at least place a veneer of a culture of professionalism over the culture of masculinism.

The Defense Department was also reevaluating the nature of the Military Occupational Specialties and their relevant proximity to combat. Always, the backdrop and haunting question for these points of expansion was the issue of women as combatants. Could women co-exist with men in the forces and have their achievements marked with the same valor as men's without martial sacrifice? Could women and men be deployed in fighting units together? Unit cohesion, unbridled sexual activity,[45] and a breakdown of the traditional roles for men and women were questions unresolved and often bigger than life. All these issues brewed quietly within the military and liberal feminist advocacy circles until a series of armed interventions brought women's presence in the forces to the arena of public debate at a level unmatched since the battle over the ERA a decade before.

| SIX |

Mothers and Others for
Peace Meet Women Soldiers

The symbolic discourse of webs, witches, and rituals of
exorcism outside the gates of military facilities should
be understood as a critique of the fatal intertwining of
postindustrial technology, patriarchy, militarism, and
commodity culture specific to late capitalism.

—Noël Sturgeon (1991)

Feminist antimilitarism enacted a theory of and practice of opposition to
masculinist militarism that was unable to account for women's increased
visibility in the forces of the late 1980s and early 1990s. In some sense,
both the military and the antimilitarists were taken by surprise at how integral to the forces women had become by the late 1980s. While the
Reagan administration created a build-up in armed force and provided
an opening, albeit not fully visible to the public, for women to increase
their presence and position in the forces, extensive, and highly visible,
antinuclear and antimilitarist direct action formed a significant counterpoint. This activism was grounded in feminist paradigms that took their
shape from a range of discourses over time: the earliest proclamations
about women as the peaceful sex and mothers as pacifist protectresses
from the 1800s, to the second-wave feminists' critiques of patriarchy as
the *raison d'être* of militarism, especially realized in the antinuclear movement. These paradigms shaped antimilitarist activism of the 1970s and
1980s, where I was schooled as an activist. They also unintentionally created an analytical void when attending to the phenomenon of women
soldiers.

In this chapter I discuss the appearance of women on the battlefield at first incidentally, and then officially, as fighting soldiers. Regardless of their actual "jobs" on the battlefield, their presence set off a gender tremor in the United States. This tremor propelled us as a nation to grapple with the possible transformation of soldiering as masculinist culture to a realm of soldiering as ungendered professional work. It also raised the gender tremor of women and men in their appropriate cultural roles, of the claims on citizenship and legitimate bodies using force for the national security. Women as soldiers raised a series of important questions that had been brewing on the back burner for some time. First of all, what were women doing so close to the actual combat zones? The public was much less aware of their presence than was the Pentagon. The military budget and personnel build-ups in the 1980s had allowed the women who took advantage of openings in academy and enlisted training in the late 1970s to take their place among the deployable ranks. What this meant to the public was that suddenly, with our interventions in Grenada, Panama, and finally the Persian Gulf War, women were seen as soldiers. The surprise also caught the forces, not specifically trained in accepting women's presence as soldiers, off-guard. A second, and related, question was, could women be effective in combat, and where exactly was the combat line? There was no U.S. study of women's performance in combat, although women had crossed that line, off the record, many times.

> For example, during the 1983 invasion of Grenada, female C-141 transport pilots were told after take off that they had received waivers to fly combat missions. . . . They would do the work and be subject to combat conditions (the risk) without the benefit of specific combat training, reward, or recognition. . . . In the 1986 Libya raid, KC-135 aerial refueling crews would have been eligible for Combat Air Medals, but since women served in the flight crews the missions were classified as "non-combat" and no one received the medals which are important to promotion and, therefore, pay[1]

Women's patriotic participation was no longer confined to the risks taken by women nurses in military hospitals (hospitals which of course were near and sometimes casualties of battle). Now we were seeing women soldiers in communications vans at the front lines, or on refueling missions for the fighter jets, or in med-evac helicopters all within the wide-ranging contemporary battlefield.

The series of military interventions from the late 1980s through the Persian Gulf War, and now with ongoing U.S. military presence in the Gulf and Yugoslavia/Kosovo, have each raised the visibility of women as soldiers for the United States civilian public, and have each likewise raised the expectations and skill levels of women as combatants. I focus in this chapter on the moments when women became visible to the public as soldiers in battle and the repercussions of that visibility. I then step back to look at how the women were being incorporated and which women were being incorporated to what. I present this material simultaneous to the response by antimilitarist activists, especially the large numbers in opposition to the Persian Gulf War.

Panama

In December of 1989 Operation Just Cause, an armed intervention by United States troops to capture President Manuel Noriega of Panama, included seven hundred women participants. Although women were present and active in the Grenada invasion, this was the first time the combat line was so publicly blurred. The blurring happened when Captain Linda Bray led her company to "liberate" a dog kennel. Her unit was caught in a firefight because Noriega supporters held the kennel. "Bray had troops under fire in three different locations on the night of the invasion and she was proud of them. The story she wanted to tell was how well all of them performed. 'But that's not what came out,' she says. 'It came out Women in combat. And it came out in the glare of super-hype.'"[2]

Bray was not supported by her colleagues who grew weary of the media attention and hype surrounding her role as a combatant, albeit an unofficial one. Her male colleagues vilified her. She said, "It became pretty rough to just continue on a day to day basis without the soldiers fighting or morale dropping." The Army also investigated her unit because a Panamanian soldier alleged that they shot all the dogs in the kennel. The investigation, after lasting two years cleared Bray and company.[3]

For the American public, struggling over women's appropriate roles in society and the forces, she stood as an icon and a question mark for women and combat. Her job description did not include combat. However, her company's actual experience in the battlefield was indistinguishable from combat experience while not *distinguished* with the same honors and promotions. This was precisely the point that Jehn raised in the 1988 hearings on women in the military. Instead, as Bray describes it, "It was like they [her fellow (male) officers] ganged up on me to prove that I wasn't anything special, or I hadn't accomplished anything special, and I was a nobody. . . . I came home crying almost every night."[4]

In January of 1990, a *New York Times*/CBS News poll found that 72 percent of the people surveyed thought that women should be allowed to serve in combat units. Women's advancement to a variety of non-stereotyped roles in the broader society, through the work of equal rights activists and the changing job market, enabled this public acceptance of women in combat. What is important to remember here, is that the right-wing activists had repeatedly raised the specter of women and combat since the early 1970s, and most extensively in the debates over the Equal Rights Amendment. These earlier debates had broken enough ground, and the legislative sophistication of the terms of sexual equality during the period were clear enough to bode well for a change in the terms of the debate, at least within egalitarian circles.

On March 20, 1990, the Committee on Armed Services Military Personnel and Compensation Subcommittee held a hearing on Women in the Military. This hearing was intended to update the Subcommittee on the status of women since the policy changes of the 1988 Task Force Report. The primary results of the earlier hearings were that women had enjoyed the opening of additional noncombat positions and of clarified and strengthened sexual harassment procedures within the military.[5] This is true procedurally speaking, though of course the Aberdeen court martial and other sexual harassment cases into the 1990s have proven that the issues are far from resolved in the forces, or for that matter in other institutions of government and private industry. The committee incorporated testimony from women at Fort Bragg regarding their recent experiences in the Panama invasion, and furthermore, the broad context of the hearing was the expected drawdown in the forces for the 1990s, with a clear understanding by committee members that women's positions, generally subordinate to men's, left them more vulnerable to the cutbacks. I would remark here that as Brenda Moore (1990) pointed out, the women most vulnerable to the downsizing cuts were the enlisted and low-tech workers, the majority of whom were women of color. This means, simultaneous to the celebrated increase in women's access to the specialty career ranks, women in the enlisted and low-technology positions were being downsized out of the services.

Representative Patricia Schroeder (D-CO) testified in support of her bill to direct a four-year test of women in the Army taking up combat arms. DACOWITS proposed this bill on the strategic assumption that, since the Army did not have a policy excluding women from taking up combat arms, there would be no legal block to the test. Schroeder explained a deeper impulse to the committee:

> Anybody who has seen the latest Army recruiting commercial, has seen a female solider operating a "non-combat" communications van during field maneuvers. I think all of us know that if you were in a real battle, the first person you usually try to hit is the person running the communications van. So it appears that women can be the first to be killed, but they are not allowed at the front line and supposedly in the battle. I think it really shows you how tenuous some of these classifications really are. Looking at those commercials, I think, really brings it all home.

The committee looked to Christopher Jehn, Assistant Secretary of Defense, Force Management and Personnel, to describe changes in women's positions in the forces, overall women's role in the Panama invasion, and clarify the impact of the women's combat engagement there. He informed the Committee that the Task Force recommendations had resulted in "over 30,000 noncombat support positions to women," and that changes in education and assignment plans, and ship berthing arrangements were all under way.

Jehn then turned to what he characterized as a misperception by the American people that women were serving in combat in Panama:

> Female servicemembers are not absolutely prohibited by law or policy from taking part in hostilities. In accordance with the combat exclusion statutes and related Army policy, women are not assigned direct combat roles; the support and service units to which they are assigned, however, may still encounter hostilities to varying degrees in the performance of required missions. All members of such organizations are trained to operate and employ weapons issued under unit tables of organization and

equipment. Accordingly military women are authorized and expected, if necessary, to use assigned weapons in self-defense, to protect the lives of others, or in the line of duty (e.g., military police, sentries). The female soldiers in Panama were not members of combat units; they performed combat support duties. Thus no combat laws or policies were violated. The women in Panama performed the duties expected of them, and they performed them quite well.[6]

Jehn's statement suggests that women will bear arms as MPs, such as Linda Bray above. He is careful to note that women are not technically assigned combat, rather they might encounter it by accident. Surely the parameters of ground combat support need revisiting here.

The women soldiers who testified were asked if they thought women would like to be assigned combat jobs. Representative Lancaster (R-NC) was fervent in his attempts to get both representatives from the highest ranks and enlisted witnesses to project their impressions of the numbers of women in their units who would volunteer for combat duty. He pressed for a response to reflect on the advisability of implementing Schroeder's proposal for a test case on the Army as mentioned above. Asking Master Sergeant Diane Cahill, USAF, to respond, he first exhorted her with the comment that the male brass he had queried had said that they thought 90 percent of the women would say no. Cahill responded:

> Sir, I find it really difficult to venture a guess. I have not really discussed it with any other female members on whether we would go to combat. We are just there at work. During our exercises we are in the situation and we handle it. *I think it is kind of odd that we are asking for females to see if they would like to go into a combat situation. I would like to see a survey of a percentage of men that would like to go. I do not think it would be any different* [italics mine].[7]

Several other witnesses concurred with Cahill's statement. One woman even recounted that the men in her unit were surprised that no one asked them if they wanted to go into combat![8] Major Kucharczyk testified that

> Nobody defined combat. . . . As far as I am concerned, those of us who maintain aircraft, the fighters who are going to fly those missions, we may

not be on the very leading edge on the ground; but in the modern warfare era that we are in today, the leading edge is not up there necessarily at
the front. So we are all in combat. We are all capable of being in combat.
. . . I swore the same oath that everybody else who is in the military did.
It is not by exception, it is not by exclusion. I swore to defend the country, my country and my Constitution.[9]

In response to questions from the committee as to whether women
had equal opportunities for advancement with men given their inability
to take the combat MOSs Captain Conley said:

> I cannot sit here and say that I will not advance because I am female. How-
> ever, *it is very true that combat experience is something that is valued by our
> services. In fact, it is the core value of our profession.* To be excluded from
> that cannot help but slow our people in their advancement to the senior
> ranks to colonel and on to general. So while combat leadership is proba-
> bly not necessary even to be a Wing Commander in the military airlift
> command, it is necessary in the long run. I would hope that women will
> be flying fighter aircraft in our country very soon [italics mine].[10]

This testimony by women servicemembers remarked the lack of genuine boundaries between combat and noncombat billets, and thus the
unofficial combat experience each had accrued. Their testimony further
illuminated the importance of official recognition of combat experience
in terms of promotion in the forces that are, after all, based on ability to
mount a fighting force. This kind of testimony about women's capability, earnestness in participating as martial citizens to the capacity of their
skills, and the already frequent proximity of women to battlefields and
thus combat, was not a new phenomenon, yet as women did progress to
the armed forces' glass (brass) ceiling in greater numbers, the collective
testimony grew louder and stronger.

In the early 1990s the steadiest increase in women soldiers and the
highest percentages overall were among the women of color. Even considering their increasing numbers overall, all women still were only 12
percent of the armed forces' personnel. In this group, 38 percent of all
active-duty women are minority: 30 percent African American (as compared to 11 percent in civilian employ), 4 percent Spanish, and 4 percent
Other. Minority representation is greater among females than males in
the forces. For example, there are 30 percent African American females

in the forces, compared to 19 percent African American males.[11] So the "be all you can be" educational and vocational training marketing of the armed forces for women was working along the lines that Binkin and Bach had projected. Women's training opportunities in the forces were quite attractive, especially for women of color who were doubly discriminated against in high skilled work. This was not quite the equal opportunity it seemed as these entry-level workers were more often than not confined to the enlisted ranks and not typically making it to the career path of officers and those from the academies.

Another Mother for War? The Persian Gulf War, the Woman Soldier, and the Feminist Antimilitarist

In August of 1990 Iraq invaded Kuwait in a dispute over oil fields that straddled the border of their two countries. The United States and the United Nations responded to this "threat to world oil markets" by mobilizing Desert Shield. On January 16, 1991, after months of threatening mobilization of United States and United Nations troops, testimony before Congress (some notorious now for its fabrication, such as the incubator babies story),[12] and massive street demonstrations against U.S. involvement, Desert Shield became Desert Storm, or the Persian Gulf War. In February 1991 air assaults wiped out the remaining Iraqi forces in Kuwait, much of the civilian infrastructure of Iraq, and massive numbers of civilians. By this time 37,000 military women were in the Gulf. The official report from the Department of Defense, *Conduct of the Persian Gulf War*,[13] lists 26,000 Army, 3,700 Navy, 2,200 Marine, and 5,300 Air Force women deployed to the Persian Gulf. U.S. women on active duty in the Gulf were 12 percent of the overall forces. Estimates ranged that over 40 percent of these women were African American.[14]

The Persian Gulf War,[15] and the largely Defense Department-controlled media coverage of the war and the women deployed, generated a great deal of concern in the United States—a concern at times approaching national obsession—regarding the roles and numbers of women in the military. This public visibility of women in the military opened a broad field of inquiry and panic. On February 24, 1991, the Associated Press polls showed a slim majority approving of women in combat, while 64 percent said mothers should not be deployed. In the first weeks of the war a number of amendments and proposals were introduced on the floor of the United States Congress, each designed to "protect" women from war by virtue of their child-producing duties. Some targeted women directly, and others worked toward managing any military family where deployment would mean no parent at home. The actual numbers of military parents were low; however, the sign of parent in the "moms' war" meant women and that meant problems for a military bent on preserving its masculinism.

Polls taken prior to the development of Operation Desert Shield into Operation Desert Storm (the euphemistic labeling of troop deployment and troops into combat in the Persian Gulf War) showed a huge gender gap, with women overwhelmingly supporting noncombat solutions. That gap closed significantly when the war was under way, with women falling into line supporting the fighters. There is, of course, nothing naturally female about loathing war, and nothing naturally keeping women from supporting war when it is under way.

The media quickly dubbed the Gulf War the "moms' war" and regaled us with images of women soldiers on the nightly news, as the cover story of *Time*, *Newsweek*, and in the daily press. A media study by the University of Southern California's Women, Men, and Media Project looked at eleven of the major national newspapers and found that "85 percent of front page news and 70 percent of local first page news was devoted to men. . . . There were few stories about female soldiers and those that did appear were centered on women's parental status. . . . Editorials and news stories about the war's impact on families were critical of mothers for going to war. . . . There was not one article or editorial on the impact of a father leaving his children to go to war."[16] Of course, in reality, some men were left home as single parents and the press was woebegotten about how those temporarily single fathers would manage. One would suspect about as well as single mothers always do. While I did not do a cross media analysis of the coverage, I did find a number of images of women marching, cleaning their guns, and loading missiles and supplies.

Male (I have not found an account of any women publicly admitting the same) U.S. soldiers popularized an unusual "pin-up girl": Jacqueline Phillips Guibord, a fully clothed, married, Mormon woman who was an undercover cop busting narcotics and prostitution rings. She posed for a

Wrangler jeans ad, leaning against the hood of her police car in a jean jacket, rifle by her side. The picture, published in *People, Rolling Stone, Equus*, and *Horse and Rider* found its way to the Persian Gulf and into the hands of the Marines. Two Marine Sergeants wrote to Guibord through Wrangler Jeans Company and requested copies. Their letter said: "We are in a country where women are treated differently than in the States, and are not near as beautiful. Your picture is a constant reminder why we are here. If you have any similar pictures, please send a few to this office for distribution." Guibord sent the pictures signed, "Semper Fi, Jackie." Among the responses she received to being a pin-up for the War she said she had "gotten a lot of positive feedback from females who were delighted that a fully clothed woman could be considered beautiful."[17] How should we understand this new pin-up? Is it a product of the Saudi Arabian restrictions on racier models? A sign of the transformation of masculine desire to include women who show their firepower instead of their nakedness? She was certainly projecting a "wholesome" image of women. On the other hand, she was not marketed for that target audience, but rather for a more general one. Of course, those soldiers emerge from that general audience as well.

Fully clothed pin-up girls, women soldiers cleaning their guns and loading bombs, flying supply jets: these were the images of United States women in the Gulf War. The jarring and largely unanticipated transgression of gender boundaries through images of women soldiers in the Persian Gulf War contributed to a widespread reevaluation of the relationship of women to soldiering, combat, and parenting. Enloe (1992) suggests to us that those images of women were produced to affirm the status of the "professionalized women soldiers."

In the Persian Gulf War, U.S. military women became the objects of a confused iconography of soldier, good/bad mother, and sex object. Constructing all the women soldiers as moms, or potential moms, served to domesticate the war and diminish its true visage as a ghastly event. Due to the presumptions about sexuality in American culture, showing the soldier women as moms, often waving to the babes in their fathers' arms, labeled the women soldiers as heterosexual and mothers, relieving, for the moment, the classic anxieties about soldier women being dykes or whores. This method of containing the meaning of women's presence also worked as a way of coping with

United States public distaste for battle, thus simultaneously distancing, othering, and screening the situation, effects, and conditions of the war. Intended on the one hand to naturalize the presence of (heterosexual) women in the forces, it also provoked unanticipated questions. How could women be fighting to protect our women and children? What horrors awaited the female POW?[18] How quaint, strange, unimaginable it was, according to the running documentary on the evening news and again in the many cover stories about "moms at war," to see some of those women soldiers' husbands at "home" struggling with the double burden of wage and family work?! (Why is the struggle with what feminists know as the "double burden" not documented and interesting when women are doing it?)

April 11, 1991, was the official cease-fire; the war was over, although the United States unofficial goal of capturing Saddam Hussein was not achieved. As United States soldiers returned—by press accounts—"victorious" to their "wives, newborn babies, and families," where were those women and men who do not have "wives, newborns and families" of the sort implied? What about the lesbians, gays, and bisexuals who, if they dared to out themselves, or were forcibly outed by others, were swiftly discharged upon their return?[19]

Although the new (publicly speaking) women soldiers responded with enthusiasm to the call to "be all that you can be in the army," instead of meteoric ascent through the ranks they came home to congressional battles over a new "mommy track" through pending legislation designed to "protect" women—as potentially occupied wombs—from actual battle-field deployment. In economic terms, unlike the post–World War II U.S. economy which saw a rise in prosperity lasting into the early 1970s, the domestic crisis which was smoke-screened by the war had an enormous impact on the government's ability to fulfill its promise to returning soldiers to help them "be all that they can be." After the war, Congress cut back veterans' benefits. Social welfare, school funding, and living wage employment opportunities have all dwindled over the last decades. In short, the domestic economic crises in the United States that temporarily receded from view through the war came back to haunt us. As is always the case, the downsizing and domestic economic downturning were borne on the backs of the underprivileged men and women who were so intensely overrepresented in this war's troops.

"War Is a Dick Thing!"

As it became apparent that the United States was going to war with Iraq over the disputed oil fields with Kuwait, activist projects against the war swung into gear. Through my work teaching a course on women and politics and through my organizing work with the community setting up rallies, teaching nonviolence preparations, and attending various meetings to strategize our antiwar response, I participated in both analytic and strategic conversations about the war and its various implications. Many of the people I worked with were quick to apply the feminist analyses of militarism to this latest incursion of U.S. foreign policy making. We had tools from other movement projects that showed us the ways that masculinism and militarism were entwined and the ways that this war could be seen as an activation of patriarchal greed.

When the Desert Shield turned to Desert Storm I and my colleagues were, I think, shocked to find the United States actually engaged in a war. We were used to and had histories of fighting against the hidden wars, the Low Intensity Conflicts of the post-Vietnam period. This was another story altogether. Bush's line in the sand had actually become a high-intensity hot war. We were ready with our organizing networks in place and huge demonstrations against the war graced the city streets and clogged the city centers. Analyses of the war ranged from the usual U.S. imperialism to the attachment of the United States and other western nations to subsidized oil from predictable governments, and the irony of our on-again off-again engagement with Hussein was not lost on folks. Feminist approaches brought with them the analytical tools developed in the antinuclear movement, strongest in the prior decade, that made the interconnections of phallic symbols and phallic desire nested in the drive to military dominance as the social equivalent of sexual dominance of the patriarchal kind.[20] Feminists also paid attention to the status of Saudi, Kuwaiti, and Iraqi women and children as the participants in and victims of the war.

As the images of the war came back at us it became clear to me that we were experiencing a shift in the visage of war and would need to account for it in our antiwar projects. Women soldiers were participants in the war, as I have been discussing at length. This meant that the slogans and easy connections between patriarchy and war would need extensive rethinking. We would need to account for women's presence; and more precisely for those of us who paid scant attention to women as soldiers in the first place would need to think about the reasons why we were able or compelled to do so. What does it say to us as feminist antimilitarists that we did not know about the women soldiers? Is this a distraction, given their small numbers overall? Can we still say: "war is a dick thing"? These are the questions that animate this book. They arose in the context of actions against the Persian Gulf War.

Gender Trouble in the Forces

The crisis of meaning in the military over the intrusion of women in combat positions and the increased visibility of lesbian and gay soldiers, both voluntarily and involuntarily outed, continued to generate serious controversy and backlash during the early 1990s. This backlash has taken the form of numerous rapes, harassment, and an ever more vigilant resistance to the presence of lesbian service people.[21] According to the General Accounting Office, the discharge numbers for homosexuality generally had gone down between 1980 and 1992; however, women were still discharged at nearly three times the rate of men for suspected homosexuality: in 1980, 213.8 women out of 100,000 were discharged compared to 74.5 out of 100,000 men, and by 1992, 80.7 women out of 100,000 were discharged compared to 34.1 out of 100,000 men.[22] Numbers for women are considerably higher, in part because the accusation against women rests often on male discomfort with women excelling at traditional men's work in the forces. For instance, in 1990, Vice Admiral of the Atlantic Fleet, Joseph S. Donnell, issued a memorandum to facilitate targeting and expelling lesbian service women. He said in the memo that they could be identified by their appearance as "hardworking, career-oriented, willing to put in long hours in the job and [being] among the command's top professionals."[23] What kind of bind does this put women service members in? Clearly women are pressed to achieve in the terms that any career professional will seek, yet they are forced to "manage their gender" as Melissa Herbert (1998) tells us and may suffer the consequences of their success as being the telltale "sign" of their unacceptable homosexuality (Bennecke and Dodge 1990).

The August 27, 1991, issue of the *Advocate* contained an essay by the (in)famous Michelangelo Signorile entitled "The Outing of Assistant Secretary of Defense Pete Williams." In this essay he outed the Assistant Secretary, particularly, as his editors wrote in introducing the piece, because of Williams' work with Secretary of Defense Dick Cheney in engineering the ouster of

> 700 gay and lesbian soldiers who fought in the Gulf War . . . *The Wall Street Journal* reported in January and again in July that their superiors had full knowledge of their homosexuality prior to their fighting in the Persian Gulf. The military's message is clear: It's ok for gays and lesbians to risk their lives for our country, and it's ok for the Department of Defense to then ruin the lives of these Desert Storm troopers.

The *Philadelphia Inquirer* noted on February 14, 1993, that, "[w]omen represent 9.8% of the total military force, but they accounted for 23% of the homosexuals dismissed from the service between 1980 and 1990—3,897 of 16,919."[24] This reminds us that women's behavior as it conforms to traditional martial valor is not acceptably feminine and thus successful women soldiers must be homosexual. Although the military is marketed as a place where women can also "be all that they can be," they are only sanctioned beings within particular behavioral confines. They cannot be the best spitfighter, the most stern and efficacious commander, and so forth, because these are especially sanctioned as men's roles.[25]

After the Gulf War: Drunken Sailors and Masculine Privilege

It doesn't make sense when women at Tailhook, who couldn't defend themselves against drunks would be sent out to fight against Serbs and Iraqis. . . . Didn't your mother ever tell you not to hang around drunken sailors? Why did the women go there?[26]

The policing of male martial culture's boundaries is accomplished by a severe benefit-ranking system and nurtured by rituals of fraternal hazing and sexual debasement fraught with contradictions and deliciously messy boundary crossings of homoerotic desire and condemnation. A shipmate's first crossing of the equator in Naval tradition is a key ritual of hazing. Jean Zimmerman discusses these line-crossing, or shellback, rituals in her book *Tailspin*.[27] One of the rituals is "sucking the cherry"—where a recruit is to suck a cherry or other small object out of the greased navel of a shellback, or initiated Navy man. A variety of other rituals involve shoving recruits' heads in latrines full of applesauce, tricks, games, and in the most horrific of domination rituals: raping newcomers.[28]

The Tailhook scandal was a watershed in the history of the Navy and presented the American public with a close-up view of just how well entrenched sexism in the Navy was. In the years since the 1991 Tailhook convention numerous hearings on sexual harassment have occurred on Capitol Hill illuminating the harassment in each of the branches and suggesting ways to reeducate military personnel. After the Tailhook Investigation Reports were issued, the Military Personnel and Compensation Subcommittee and the Defense Policy Panel of the Committee on Armed Services in the House of Representatives held hearings to develop a model for working through claims of sexual harassment and for creating prevention programs modeled after their drug use prevention programs.[29]

There is something tragic and comical about drunken sailors and masculinity. The intrusion of women, lesbian, and gay soldiers' rights activism on the homoerotic/homoparanoic environment of the forces challenges one of the forces' major cultural foundations. The misogynistic "safety net" around shellback rituals in the Navy, and other forms of hazing in the other branches of the forces, stands as a sharp reminder of the nature of the male-bonding in the military and its centrality to the combat unit's cohesion and efficacy. The presence of real gay men, real lesbian women, and real straight women as members of the forces, who more often than not have to outperform their straight male counterparts just to survive the scrutiny over their difference, threatens to demystify, resolve, and remove this splendid martial tension.

Brutal Responsibilities and Second-Class Citizens

To argue either that women's difference from men ensures women's inclusion in the forces will transform the forces' brutality,[30] or that women should be excluded from the forces because they will not be able to be brutal enough, or to argue that women are the essential peacemakers and thus the natural opposition to war, is to reify women as the gendered, beautiful souls. This damage comes from the antifeminist militarists whose assaults on the inclusion of women in the forces are deeply connected to and reinforced by a more general right-wing assault on women's rights and grounded in a reification of women's traditional role as reproducing nurturer.[31] This damage also comes from feminist antimilitarists who demonstrate for women as peacemakers by social or biological construction and against the patriarchal war machine as a masculinist project. As I suggested earlier, this latter position effected an oversimplified representation of the force behind the Persian Gulf War. How then to insist women have equal access to the institutions that bestow power and economic privilege, such as the armed forces, and still argue that armed force is not the way to resolve international crises? How then to maintain that women's socialization as caregivers makes them ideally suited to understand the repulsiveness of militarism? How then to hold that feminism is a visionary practice of yearning toward justice and peace that somehow must also embrace the struggles—wherever they are—for women's equal treatment as citizens?

Citizenship and Combat

In struggles to increase women's access to jobs in the military, the focal area is access to combat. It is this way because of our earliest constructions of first-class citizenship that point to martial valor as keynote. This defining characteristic of first-class citizenship from the development of U.S. notions of patriotism constructs the woman citizen as not first class. Allowing women to engage in combat alongside their male comrades presents at least the possibility of women being considered as first-class citizens under this definition. The combination of women and combat represents an interconnected set of political struggles around sexual role and access boundaries, harassment, camaraderie, physical capacity, racial and gendered homogeneity, and class politics in the armed forces. This tangle resolves differently depending on one's position regarding women's roles in United States society. For those resistant to women in the forces, fears of disruption in the traditional social order are paramount.[32] The belief is that the degendering of the forces will lead to a degeneration of the forces' spiritual sense of mission. Who will they be fighting to protect? More specifically located, and deeply akin to this perspective, is the assertion that women in the forces, and especially in combat, will lead to a degeneration of the forces' combat ability (compatibility?) and jeopardize national security. This is the place where fear of officially allowing lesbian and gay soldiers to serve also rears its ugly head. The same arguments about loss of troop cohesion and combat ability were launched in resistance to the racial integration of the forces post–World War II.[33] Fears of the loss of masculine distinction in the forces are widespread, especially as the forces' missions diversify to include more base cleanups, humanitarian aid, and peacekeeping missions under the United Nations.[34] Despite numerous studies displaying women's combat capabilities, many opposed to women in combat insist that women cannot perform, physically or psychically, the rigors of combat.

In the early 1990s a series of legislation opened all combat jobs to women, with the exception of Special Forces, Navy submarines, artillery and Army infantry—areas deemed too closely tied to hand-to-hand combat (or in the case of submarines, too difficult to refit with women's quarters). This means that women who train as flyers are eligible to compete for combat billets. The legislation does not open combat jobs for all women since flyers will be officers and the officer ranks are largely peopled by white females (80–90 percent depending on field), recruited through the military academies. The armed interventions between the 1980s and early 1990s played a significant role in raising the visibility of women already in the forces: the invasion of Grenada, the invasion of Panama, and the Persian Gulf War. It also began the process of recognition that women in the forces were being re-envisioned as the "professional soldier women"[35] that they indeed had always been in practice. This was not an easy transition. In all three military actions, the public shock that women were in the forces and could be present in combat situations forever changed the terms of the debate over women in the forces.

These military actions highlighted and fueled the growing tension over women soldiers' appropriate place. They demonstrated the meaninglessness of the distinction of combat versus noncombat job assignment as a result of women soldiers being caught in firefights and the crossfire in supposed noncombat assignments. One distinction remained between the men's and women's experience of the combat theater: pay and promotability. Women officers were training men to fly the combat aircraft. Clearly capable of operating the machinery of war and of teaching strategies for fighting, these women were quite capable of handling the combat billets. Without a draft the armed forces had become an institution that recruited people into a profession. The impulse to join rested more squarely on expectations of career opportunities. Women joined their male counterparts in taking seriously the advertised encouragement to "be all that you can be." Ending the combat exclusion was the next logical step for women to achieve the respect and rank necessary for a successful career in the forces.

The Fall of the Combat Exclusion for Women Flyers

Representative Patricia Schroeder (D-CO) had been trying to get an amendment into the House Defense Authorizations Bill to remove the combat exemption on women for several years without success. United States experience in the Persian Gulf War changed the terms of the debate. The Hill-Thomas hearings in the fall of 1991 helped to raise the awareness of sexual harassment and discrimination as well as to put the pressure on for other areas of women's remaining inequalities. Unknown yet to the public (and to remain so until July 1992), the tenor of the changes emboldened Paula Coughlin to complain to her superior in the Navy about her horrifying experience at the Tailhook convention that prior fall.[36]

In the debate over fiscal 1992's bill, which occurred at the end of the war, Schroeder again proposed the amendment to allow female Air Force pilots to be assigned to combat billets, and while she worked the amendment, a group of female pilots worked the halls, including Mimi Finch, who was later assigned to the Presidential Commission and a voice in dissent from the commission's findings.[37] Representative Beverly Byron (D-MD), Chair of the House Armed Services Subcommittee on Military Personnel, was a long-time supporter of women in the forces, yet historically less than enthusiastic about women in combat. Representative Byron moved that the amendment be expanded to include pilots in the Navy and Marines. Finally the instruction in the bill was to repeal the combat exclusion on Navy and Air Force flyers (the Army does not have a specific law excluding women) by amending 10 U.S.C. 6015 to read, where amended:

> women may not be assigned to duty on vessels engaged in combat missions *other than as aviation officers as part of an air wing or other element assigned to such a vessel* nor may they be assigned to other than temporary duty on *other* vessels of the Navy except hospital ships, transports, and vessels of a similar classification not expected to be assigned combat missions.[38]

The instruction followed to repeal 10 U.S.C. 8549 which is the code restricting Air Force women from piloting in combat. The bill passed the House unopposed.

As Linda Grant De Pauw, a military historian, pointed out: "Politically, the focus on flyers was ideal. Flyers are all officers, they do not fight in the 'mud,' they are all volunteers, and in all the services combined only about a thousand women would be affected."[39] It bears emphasis here that, as De Pauw notes, these women were volunteers and their training was rigorous (to understate the case). Therefore, the question of their capability was redundant at best. It would seem to have been a shoe-in, easy, not controversial. Instead, it touched the depth of anxiety for some in Congress and in the broader political community around the forces about the changed possibilities and visions of women's work in the boldly gendered world of the forces. It did not get by so easily in the Senate, or in the bill's final version as public law.

The Senate version of the Defense Appropriations Act passed 69 to 30. It included an amendment repealing restrictions on women flyers paralleling the House's, called the Kennedy-Roth amendment. Senator Edward Kennedy (D-MA) and Senator William Roth (R-DE) sponsored this amendment. The Chair of the Senate Armed Services Committee, Sam Nunn (D-GA), along with Senators John McCain (R-AZ), ranking Minority member of the Senate ASC, John Warner (R-VA), and John Glenn (D-OH), modified the Senate Defense Appropriations Bill with a second amendment regarding women and combat, section 541–560 of the final law. This second amendment called for the formation of the Presidential Commission on the Assignment of Women in the Armed Forces. It directed that removal of the women flyers' combat exclusion be delayed until this special commission studied and made recommendations about the impact of women soldiers in combat jobs on military readiness and on society. As McCain expressed it on the floor of the Senate, "We will find the best way to both defend this nation's national security interests and provide equality for women in all ranks and military specialties" (Presidential Commission 1992: iii).[40] President George Bush signed the Defense Authorizations Act of the 102nd Congress (Public Law 102-190 for fiscal year 1992) into law on December 5, 1991. It was one of his last acts as president.

The opening of certain combat jobs to women signifies a major cultural shift in the forces and in broader cultural debates about women's roles, specifically in the United States, yet with international influence.[41] The debates leading up to the opening of combat jobs to women are a fascinating site for viewing the shifting constructions of gender and the continued salience of the category of race in United States culture. The opening of specific, officer-eligible combat roles leaves those women at the intersection and co-construction of racial and gender oppression at a continued disadvantage, albeit largely unspoken in the debates. Instead, the focus of congressional debate on women in combat has been centered on the disruption of male-bonding in combat performance and an appeal to traditional women's roles on the one hand, and on the other, the time-tested conviction that women could handle flight-based combat billets and had performed well in Desert Storm.

The formation of the Presidential Commission on the Assignment of Women in the Armed Forces effectively circumvented the Pentagon's Defense Advisory Committee on Women in the Services (DACOWITS), which had already recommended to the Pentagon at its spring 1991 meeting that all combat exclusion statutes be repealed. They did this based in part on the testimony of women veterans of the Persian Gulf War.[42] DACOWITS has served as the advisory arm for the Congress and Pentagon on issues pertaining to women in the forces since its founding in 1952. DACOWITS has frequently been a key player in all congressional hearings on women in the forces. For example it was pressure from DACOWITS' 1987 report about the status of women in the armed forces that prompted the Secretary of Defense to form a Task Force to review and make recommendations for policy change resulting in the uniform-across-the-forces re-classification of jobs in 1988. DACOWITS was not the Congressional choice for reviewing the historic amendment to PL 102-190, having already positioned itself in favor of women as combatants through its original proposals that women in the Army test out for combat positions in a four year trial. (The Army had no specific rules against women in combat jobs, although women were not assigned to them.) This proposal was the basis for Schroeder's first submission of an amendment to the Defense Authorizations Bill. DACOWITS had continually come out publicly in support of women testing for combat MOSs.

The Congress acted in response to public support of women and their performance in the Gulf War, to the widespread outrage over the Tailhook scandal, and to the transformation of the actual demographics, if not yet the culture, of martial citizenship. The Congress also acted, in the passage of the modified amendment calling for the Presidential Commission to slow and ponder the changes, in response to right-wing pressures to contain the intrusion of women into the forces and the growing perception after the Gulf War that women could do whatever men could do—even in the forces. Strong voices for the preservation of masculinity that had prevailed at other historic moments such as the ERA debates of the late 1970s were heard again.

The removal of the combat exclusion on flyer women promised a more ready access to the career ranks. However, this removal, as I explained above, would only benefit those few who were flyers and not the many other women in the forces for whom combat assignments still remained out of reach, and with them the highest recognition and benefits of martial citizenship. I turn now to the formation of the Commission, the revisited debate over combat for women soldiers, and the resolution of the combat exclusion laws.

SEVEN

Can Women Kill?

> I also believe an element of why men assume the com-
> batant role is that, contrary to the opinions of some
> women, men take on that brutal responsibility out of
> self-sacrifice; it is because they do respect, and truly care
> for women. It is the ultimate act of love and self-sacri-
> fice to lay down one's life for another. Along with mil-
> lions of other women, I am grateful for the roles men
> selflessly assume. In no way do we consider ourselves
> second class citizens, or of less value to society, just be-
> cause we do not participate as combatants in our Na-
> tion's wars.   —Sarah White (1992)

The Presidential Commission on the Assignment of Women in the
Armed Forces convened in early 1992 to discuss the feasibility and propriety of women being allowed to fly combat missions, and, more generally, to assess their participation in the forces. As I discussed in the prior
chapter, the Presidential Commission's formation was a compromise and
stall on the enforcement of Public Law 102-190, which allowed women
to train and serve as fighter pilots. The empaneling of the commission
occurred in March 1992, after the Persian Gulf War and the Hill-
Thomas hearings, and spanned the sexual harassment investigations of
the "Tailhook Convention, 1991." The commission had the advantage
of actual wartime evidence to draw upon in terms of women's general
service, although not in terms of official combat performance. It was also
shaped by multiple public pressures of the two powerful sexual harassment cases.

There was, to date, no official evidence of women's combat duty performance for a study of women's roles in combat to draw upon. This meant that women's physical and mental capacities for combat abilities were tested clinically, and known by unofficial anecdote. A variety of testing, as I indicated in the prior chapter, demonstrated women's greater capacity for mental acuity in flight and on computerized projects.[1] Skill requirements for combat are changing as war planning becomes increasingly reliant on computerized warfare and air-launched combat. Discussions of women's capacities as combatants, as evidenced in the commission's report, were preoccupied by assumptions and presumptions of women's and men's appropriate social roles.

The Presidential Commission's final report (herein cited as PCR) was shaped by general rationales for excluding women from combat jobs, and perhaps the military, and rested on the logic of "traditional family values." Concerns about restoring traditional family values—women are mothers and not warriors—are deeply embedded in the Presidential Commission Report, and several of the members of the commission have histories with organizations promoting "family values." In the report, there is a convergence of some of the language of antimilitarism with the language of social conservatism. This intersection carefully reinscribes the differences between women's and men's social roles: men are warriors, women are peacemakers, men are self-sacrificers protecting the women and children, women are homemakers and reproducers. The thread of "family values" ties together my interests in the struggles over women and combat with the struggles over of color and lesbian and gay soldiers openly serving in the forces. This is because the presumptive family in this scheme is one organized around particular models of family: namely, the Cleaver[2] model.

The commission's report is concerned largely with the question of combat, through which the report presents a picture of the struggle over women's traditional roles, anxieties over women's availability as mothers (constructed as *the* proper caregivers for children), and over women's capabilities at work while pregnant. The report also highlighted the struggle over the meaning of equal opportunity and the proper martial citizen, and inadvertently displayed the potential cracks in patriarchal practice in armed forces' culture. Scholars of military culture[3] have argued that the armed forces possess a unique culture of masculinity. The pages of the Presidential Commission Report illuminate some of what is at stake for this masculinist culture through attention to several of the commissioners' and their witnesses' testimony of their opposition to women in combat. This opposition rested early and often on their concerns that radical feminists were challenging military culture and would ruin the armed forces.

The interesting tension here is that self-proclaimed feminists were nowhere near the debates. On the one hand, the two outspoken congresswomen on behalf of the expansion of women soldiers' billets to combat duty had authored the bill with the testimony of women veterans and others to back them up. These voices were not accounted for in the commission's research, nor did they stand as vocal outsiders. Feminists outside the beltway had little to say either. Feminist antimilitarists were largely unaware of the proceedings. This can be explained, I think, by two phenomena. First of all, looking back to the NOW convention in the 1970s where the question of women and combat was addressed by feminists, we can recall the strong sentiment that women should not be asked to take on the responsibility of warring without also receiving the full benefits of citizenship—a sentiment that resonates to this day. Secondly, the depth and breadth of the recent and strongly feminist opposition to the Persian Gulf War was replete with intensely gendered rhetoric: "Read My Labia: No War for Oil", "War Is a Dick Thing," and so forth, which left little to no room for a considered and particularly feminist antimilitarist response to women actually lobbying Congress for combat positions.

The commission's report was published and sent to President Bush on November 15, 1992, in the wake of his loss of the presidential election and a shift of the Presidency to the Democratic Party for the first time in twelve years. Because of the timing of this political shift, the Presidential Commission Report did not force the reversal of the policy changes in the Defense Authorizations Act (PL 102-190) regarding women and combat. Instead, the report stands as a record of the deep divisions and obstacles remaining for women in integrating themselves into the forces. Testimony for and against women in combat roles and, indeed, in the forces, is on the record from within the forces and from the forces' intellectual pundits. Through its silences, as effectively as its articulations, the Presidential Commission Report underscored the crude assumptions about sex roles and racial/ethnic roles in mainstream debates about the parameters of United States citizenship. I will spend some time on the report here, discussing it in content and context, and in relation to the commission members themselves.

Structure, Instruction, and Disintegration of the Commission

My method of reading the commission's work through this report is to work through the authors' presentation of the material.[4] The material presented in the report itself is not the detail of each hearing they held and each fact-finding mission, but rather an orchestrated (and sometimes negotiated as evidenced by the appearance of oppositional voices) display of their conclusions. The hearings held by the commission around the country at bases and training centers were to take on somewhat of a media circus atmosphere. Similar to the witch hunts of the McCarthy era[5] they had a kind of surreal inquisitional quality to them. Walkouts by the conservative members when they did not approve of certain testimony, conservative members' dismissal of such testimony as coerced by a few ambitious career military women, and most astounding of all a scene where Elaine Donnelly, during one of the fact-finding missions, gave a press conference. She constructed a tower of Jenga™ children's building blocks on the table before her. To illustrate the way that increasing women's presence in the forces would destroy the structural integrity of the forces, she pulled random blocks out of the tower. On live TV the tower refused to fall.[6] This proved to be an ominous foreshadowing of Donnelly's inability to stop the legislation of women's access to combat jobs in the forces.

According to the instruction in Public Law 102-190, section 541, the commission was to be appointed by the president, George Bush, and composed of fifteen members "who have distinguished themselves in the public or private sector and who have had significant experience (as determined by the president) with one or more of the following matters..." Section 541 goes on to list research and policy making regarding social and cultural matters in the forces, the law, experience with combat job qualifications, combat service, military personnel management, "experiences of women in the military gained through service as a female service member, a manager of an organization with a representative presence of women, or a member of an organization with responsibility of policy review, advice, or oversight of the status of women in the military," and finally "experience with women's issues in American society."[7] This last category was addressed by the appointment of one current member of the organization Concerned Women for America (CWA). Concerned Women for America is one of a myriad of traditional "family values" organizations that have worked to curtail the advancement of women's political and social rights since the fights over the Equal Rights Amendment in the 1970s. CWA is connected to Phyllis Schlafly's Eagle Forum.

Section 542 of the law describes the duties of the commission as the following: "assess the laws and policies restricting the assignment of female service members and . . . make findings on such matters." Commissioned studies were to consider the implications of women in combat for combat readiness, the public attitudes in the United States on the use of women in the military, legal and policy implications of voluntary or involuntary assignment of women to combat, to the draft, and the need and costs of facility and vessel modifications, and finally "the implications of restrictions on the assignment of women in the recruitment, retention, use, and promotion of qualified personnel in the Armed Forces." The Bush administration appointed a number of commissioners who were already outspoken in their opposition to women in the armed forces, especially in combat.[8] Among the fifteen commissioners there were six women. Three of these women were outspoken opponents of women in combat: Elaine Donnelly, a protégé of Phyllis Schlafly, former DACOWITS member and Executive Director of the Coalition for Military Readiness; Kate Walsh O'Beirne, Vice President of Government Relations at the Heritage Foundation, contributing editor for the *National Review,* and wife of a retired career infantry officer; and Sarah F. White, Master Sergeant in the U.S. Air Force Reserve in the Intelligence Command, and legislative analyst for Concerned Women for America. These three women plus Brigadier General Samuel Cockerham, USA (ret.) and Ronald Ray, attorney at law and former first Deputy Assistant Secretary of Defense for Guard/Reserve Readiness and Training, were the authors of "Section II: Alternative Views." There, as I discuss further in the chapter, they interpreted the findings of the commission to state that women do not belong in combat situations of any sort.

The other commissioners expressed disaffection with their service on a commission in which many of the members were decidedly set in their opinions about women's capabilities before the commission even convened its first hearings. Captain Mary (Mimi) Finch, USA wrote about her experience on the commission in *Minerva*, noting her exasperation with commission members who walked out on hearings that did not fit with their beliefs and with those members' clearly prejudiced views.[9] Mary E. Clarke, Major General, USA (ret.) and the last commander of the Women's Army Corps, submitted a separate commissioner's statement in the report in which she recounts:

> Early on in the deliberations, it became clear that a number of the Commissioners had come with a set agenda and no amount of facts or testimony would change their minds for expanding opportunities for women in the military. This was evident in their questioning techniques of those whose testimony they thought might support women in combat, absenting themselves when they knew testimony would not support their views, and their insistence upon using equal opportunity as a red herring rather than recognizing women's capabilities and contributions to the military services. . . . [T]hey constantly used the words 'degradation of the mission' when discussing women in the military, even though testimony from commanders of mixed-gender units in all of the services disputed their assumptions. . . . One of the most disturbing aspects of their assertions was that many of the active duty military personnel who testified in support of women in combat were unduly influenced by internal and external forces and therefore were not speaking their own minds out of fear of the impact on their careers. I find this insulting to our professional officers and non-commissioned officers.[10]

Clarke is referring to the accusations made by several committee members, and political pundits such as David Horowitz, that the repeal of the combat exclusion was simply about appeasing women because of Tailhook, bowing to radical feminists (women's rights advocates), and being pressured by a small group of aggressive, career-minded women soldiers (the flyers who lobbied Congress for the repeal). The epigraph for this chapter by Sarah White is a strong example of the way that the issue was framed, even in the serious taxpayer-funded research and findings by the commission. Women are only seeking to be combatants out of their selfish career aspirations, and are only an aberrant few, while to the contrary, "millions of other women [are] grateful for the roles men selflessly assume."

The report has a complex structure that is important to grasp in order to decipher its meanings. I will attend to that structure here to generate a backdrop for my discussion of the findings in the report itself. The report is an official document of the United States government, issued in print by the U.S. Government Printing Office. The report begins with a cover letter to then President Bush, to whom it was to be directly submitted. It follows with an introduction to the issue of women and combat, including reference to the Public Law which called for the commission and a description of its intended methodological approach. It was to be a fact-finding series of hearings, research groups, and surveys. These introductory remarks are followed by several key sections that I will outline below and then examine in more detail by topic.

Section I, "Issues and Recommendations," presents each of the seventeen issues the commission determined to bear on the congressional mandate. The subsections of Section I contain the question as formulated by the commission, the text of their recommendation, a summary of what appears to be the majority view (although in each case it is toned down in comparison to the statements issued in groups or individually later in the report), a breakdown of the vote without the names of the voters attached, and a list of relevant findings indexed to the appendices and culled from the commission records on the topic to operate as a series of support notes for the position voted up in that subsection.

Section II contains a statement entitled "Alternative Views." It is signed by the group of commissioners who were completely opposed to women in any combat situations, some of whom, like Donnelly, had been on record as being opposed before being appointed to the commission. This statement is thirty-eight pages long, and its purpose is to argue against Public Law 102-190 and insist that women do not have what it takes to be in combat situations in the forces. The interesting thing about this section is that the commission votes recommended against women in combat situations with the exception of their presence on seafaring combat vessels. Nevertheless, the commissioners who formed a block against women in combat submitted this section to the final report. It fully details their opposition to women in combat.

Section III contains various commissioner statements, singly and jointly in response to particular votes, and regarding their experiences on the commission. Section IV's subsections are the appendices and contain the variety of data culled from the hearings they conducted to represent their findings and support the recommendations. The appendices also contain a copy of the sections of PL 102-190 that initiated the commission, Roper survey results, and catalogs of the fact-finding missions, trips, meetings, a list of statements submitted for the record, bibliographies of material for the issues, and finally, commissioner biographies.

Based on the congressional mandate, the commission determined seventeen issues to bear on the decision over whether women should be allowed access to, or conscripted to, combat jobs. These were: quotas and goals, voluntary versus involuntary duty, fitness/wellness standards, occupational physical requirements, basic training standards, pre-commissioning standards, gender-related occupational standards, parental and family leave policies, pregnancy and deployability policies, combat roles for women, ground combat, combat aircraft, combat vessels, Special Forces, Risk Rule, transition process, and conscription. Each of these issues was explored in smaller panels of commissioners, through hearings and written materials, with the findings intended to be reviewed and voted on by the whole group, although there were a number of occasions when members chose to be absent for certain parts of the hearings in protest to the particular testimony.

Combat Votes and the Armed Forces as Social Welfare

The votes on combat are interesting to look at for their display of the stakes involved in unmarking gender boundaries for particular occupations. Seven of the seventeen issues considered combat directly, and I will focus on them here. The first, issue J, asked generally if there are any circumstances where women should be assigned to combat. Of the fifteen commissioners, eight voted yes, one no, and one abstained. Five commissioners did not vote. These five are the signers of the "Alternative Views" section that argues that women should not be assigned to any combat roles. I will come back to that section of the

Presidential Commission Report and address it in more depth further in this chapter. In issue K, the ground combat exclusion, a majority of ten commissioners voted for the exclusion, two abstained, and three females issued a statement in dissent: Clarke, Finch, and Neizer. Issue L concerned combat aircraft and in it the commission took up the specific congressional approval of repealing these restrictions on women's work in the Forces. The commission voted, by a one-vote (8 to 7) majority, to recommend that the amendment in Public Law 102-190 which repealed restrictions on women aviators be removed and the prior restrictions reinstated. This was the decision of the conservative commission members.

Rather than acknowledge the actual changes in training and expertise which were the groundwork for repealing the combat exclusions, those opposed sought to demean the policy shift, insisting that women's full inclusion could only result from lowered standards. In the "Alternative Views" section, Secretary of Defense Richard Cheney was quoted saying, "We're not a social welfare agency"(PCR, 43). In Cheney's statement is the irksome accusation that to allow women in the forces to work in roles that they are now often training men for is tantamount to "social welfare." In other words, Cheney is saying women cannot cut it and the armed forces are not going to contribute to the delusions of women who claim expertise and entitlement in these areas. The accusation by a Secretary of Defense that allowing women to be assigned to combat roles is a form of social welfare is irresponsible at the very least. In its clearly derisive use it demonstrates a lack of sensitivity to actual welfare recipients, and raises the mark of the "undeserving poor" often read as women and especially African American women. Thus, Cheney is arguing that women allowed access to combat roles are actually "undeserving women" and will not be tolerated in this man's army.

Sarah White is convinced that men assume combat roles out of self-sacrifice and their deep abiding respect and care for women (see epigraph). Martial sacrifice is held up by White and other conservative panel members in their dissent to indicate men's valiant martial citizenship as unique and inherently heterosexually masculine. This is the traditional perspective of the circumscribed role for both men and women in martial service. Even with the process of structural change that has brought women into the armed forces in greater numbers, by the mandate of the

Pentagon and its web of think tanks, and the supposed cultural changes resulting from women's movement pressures, the belief that martial service is a guy thing is still quite strong in certain quarters of political power.

The irony of appeals to men's valiant qualifications and self-sacrifice to protect women from the ravages of war are highlighted by stories of Tailhook, from which, as Schlafly tells us, the women should have known to stay away, and by accounts from the Persian Gulf War itself where there were a number of accounts of women being raped or harassed by "friendly fire." Neither of these sets of incidents betraying the idea of men's valiant self-sacrifice were addressed in the Commission's Report. Nor, for that matter, was the Department of Defense's final report to the Congress, entitled *Conduct of the Persian Gulf War,* accountable for the personal conduct of the department's soldiers. To be fair, the incidents of harassment were typically emerging after the war was over. However, the provision of the *Princess Cunard* was known to the department arguably ahead of time since it provided transportation for the prostitutes! There is nothing in the report to Congress, coded or otherwise, to indicate this perk. The Gulf War shoreleave party was the *Princess Cunard,* an international cruise ship outfitted with beer, hamburgers, and Filipina prostitutes.[11] This shoreleave perk is a manly tradition richly embued with the valor of conquest for male soldiers, and complexly orchestrated in the Gulf War where the local women were not available for prostitution. Clearly, having sex for hire was deemed important by the coordinators of R&R if they went to the trouble of bringing in Filipina prostitutes. How did the U.S. women soldiers relieve their sexual tension, and what role does that sexual tension play in their acts of martial sacrifice? In a fully sexually (including orientation) integrated armed forces, who would be hired to sexually service whom? The complications are astounding. Would the force of the forces be as potent if sexual conquest were not part of the benefits package?

Accusations by commission members that the forces' masculinity was being challenged by the inclusion of women in the battlefield abound in the report. First of all, this nervousness that the masculinity of the forces was being challenged is a good sign for those of us wishing to disabuse the forces of such a limited appeal. However, the several accusations that feminism, and especially something that David Horowitz called "radical feminism," was the (mis)guiding force behind putting women in combat, rings decidedly false. The irony here, and a critical function of this book, was that "radical feminists"—feminists who would call for an overthrow of patriarchy and at least the military—were not even participating in the debates.

The depth of anxiety over women and other "non-masculine" soldiers intruding, violating, defiling real men's (so fragile?) space provides a remarkable insight into the actual fragility of patriarchal social power. This, of course, does not diminish the horrific force—economic, social, and political—of patriarchy and especially does not mean that patriarchal practice does not continue to be harmful. Nor, as we have seen in the several years since the commission's report, does it mean that patriarchal practices are not operating in the forces anymore. A look at recent revelations of extensive and systematic sexual harassment and violence toward women in the forces gives sobering testimony to the contrary. However, the task of this project is to point up the genuine anxieties and weaknesses in the patriarchal code. My hope is that by doing so I can contribute to the construction of freedom projects looking to break the patriarchal code. I think that feminist antimilitarists can have a lot to say in this regard. We need to account for women's roles in the armed forces accurately, from their points of view, and with consistent yearning for justice and peace.

A statement of dissent from the recommendation to repeal the opening of combat assignments for women was submitted by Herres, Clarke, Draude, Finch, Hogg, Minow, and Neizer. Their statement emphasized that there was no empirical evidence demonstrating women's incapacity to perform well in combat aviation and that women have been flying the aircraft and teaching the aircraft to male pilots for ten years already.[12] "In the absence of evidence that important governmental interests would be detrimentally affected, we should not deny women the opportunity to serve their country in the field of combat aviation. The proponents of the Commission's recommendation have never provided such evidence" (PCR, 80).

In issue M, regarding combat (Naval) vessels, the commissioners who were supportive of the congressional passage of PL 102-190, recommended by an 8 to 6 majority, with one abstention, to recommend that the portion of 10 USC 6015 which excludes all women except those attached to an air wing be repealed and women be allowed "to serve on combatant vessels except submarines and amphibious vessels" (PCR, 31). These commissioners felt that the "current Navy law governing the assignment of servicewomen is inconsistent because it allows women to serve as aviation officers aboard Navy ships, but prohibits their assignment to combatant ships in any other capacity" (PCR, 31).

Fourteen of the commissioners agreed that women should not be placed in Special Forces. The Risk Rule, which keeps women out of certain combat situations, by assessment of the likelihood that fighting would occur there, was retained by a 9 to 4 vote with two abstentions. Six of the commissioners issued a statement of their dissent. Eleven of the fifteen commissioners voted against conscription. In response to this vote on the draft, six of the commissioners issued a statement of dissent, arguing that "[y]oung women and men should be required to participate in a universal national service program with civilian and military options. The military option would be consistent with the recommendations of the Commission and not contravene the effectiveness of the All-Volunteer Force."[13]

Physical Capability and Standards of Readiness

The other points of recommendation by the commission are curious for their near but imprecise relationship to combat readiness and thus are informative about the presumptions concerning women under which the commission operated. One set of the recommendations pertained to physical standards and requirements. These were fairly routine questions of women's abilities in training in the various billets, or job assignments. The commission's recommendation on "Fitness and Wellness Standards" was by twelve votes that "[t]he Services should retain gender specific fitness tests and standards to promote the highest level of general fitness and wellness in the Armed Forces . . . provided they do not compromise training or qualification programs for physically demanding combat or combat support MOSs [Military Occupational Specialties]" (PCR, 5). On "Occupational Physical Requirements" the commission was divided with nine voting in agreement that the services adopt specific requirements for strength and endurance testing. The dissent in the "Alternative Views" section was to the effect that women should not need to test for the "strenuous combat MOSs" if they are not deployed to them. In all other cases, most agreed that women should test out relevant to the specialty for which they are applying. A Roper survey cited by the commission indicated that among military personnel 70 percent agreed that "physical standards for each combat assignment should reflect the demands of that assignment on a gender neutral basis"(PCR, appendix D-1). On Basic Training Standards the commission voted 8 to 6 to recommend gender-specific entry-level training. This is built on the assumption that there is a difference between entry-level training and MOS training that needs to be reflected in its gender specifications. In the case of entry-level training the gender categorization plays a role, in this logic, due to the different physical capacities of women and men. In the case of MOSs, the process of training and selection should be "gender-neutral" to achieve screening appropriate for the requirements of the specific billet.

These kinds of specifications on physical capacity as determined by testing for actual skills required, and an actual individual body's capacities for performing them, make sense. A number of the witnesses to the commission testified that women do not face physical exclusion from pilot jobs under these criteria, and have been training in these jobs now since Admiral Zumwalt opened them in the Navy in the mid-1970s. Ronald Ray, one of the commissioners, and a signer to the "Alternative Views" section, testified that the brutality of hand-to-hand combat is potentially present in each combat situation as you "close" with the enemy. In his view, combat of any sort still excludes women. Here the changing conditions of the forces in light of advancing technologies that center on computerized warring make possible many new forms of combat and physiological profiles of combatants.[14]

Parents, Pregnancy, and Childcare (Mothers)

A more controversial set of "Issues and Recommendations" were the two sections dealing with parental policy and the management of soldiers' reproduction. In the commission's recommendations on "Parental and Family Policies" they suggested that the Department of Defense review its current policies and strengthen the application of its Dependent Care Plans, a system of identification of childcare plans for dependents of deployable servicepeople. They recommended further that a system of checks on single-parent deployability, and dual-service parent deployability be developed to ensure that a child is not left without at least one parent. Disallowing the second of two parents to join the military, or making the second parent of a dual-service couple leave the military are several of the alternatives they proposed (PCR, 15). While the commission was fairly circumspect about this issue and developed a series of recommendations which basically asked the Department of Defense to look into the matter and decide how to work the problem, public pressure and media hype presented a different picture. This is in fact an interesting departure between the report's and the public's views. More often the report's recommendations did not fit with poll-based public sentiment, or Pentagon practice for that matter. In this case, however, the media representations of women leaving behind their children were so stunning that perceived widespread "public" concern about mothers in the Gulf War led to several attempts on the House floor, by Representative Barbara Boxer (D-CA) and others to create new policies to allow exemptions from deployment for single parents, for one parent of two-parent families, and for pregnant women. According to the research by the commission, there are "76,000 single parents and 46,000 dual parents on active duty, comprising 6.5 percent of the active force" (PCR, 16). Women represent 34.7 percent of the single-parent troops, and men represent the other 65.3 percent. The number of single-parent women soldiers is remarkably low compared to the percentage of single-parent women in civilian society, which is roughly 80–90 percent of all single parents. Even so, we are talking about 6.5 percent of the forces being parents at all, which is a remarkably low number, and with the majority of these being single father soldiers, it is clearly not simply about women's undeployability. This difference goes unnoticed by the commissioners who instead see this as a serious deployment problem for women. By the numbers it would seem that we should be worrying about male deployability!

Opponents of measures to keep single or second parents ineligible for deployment rightly feared that this would lead to a mommy track in the forces, effectively excluding women from command positions and other deployment-sensitive, higher-paying positions in the forces. The popular framing of this issue as a question of the mom's war, as babies being left behind by their moms, and dads struggling at home to work and care for the children, did not bode well for this issue to turn on gender neutrality. Men represent the higher real numbers of single military parents. Yet, when the spotlight is on female service members and their eligibility to serve, parenting is suddenly a critical category for determining that eligibility. To make this leap of judgment in the forces regarding women's eligibility for service is to reinscribe the notion that women are expected to be the primary caregivers for children. Furthermore, the commission's assignment was to determine if women could serve as combatants, which is several steps removed from questions of general deployability which it would seem should be handled in a different venue.

In the next section on "Pregnancy and Deployability Policies" the commission recommended that the currently enacted rules regarding pregnancy and deployability seemed sufficient, they recommended that a "pregnant servicewoman should not be assigned to or remain in a position with a high probability of deployment. . . . [A] deployment-probability designation coding system could be established to determine which positions have the higher probabilities of deployment and thus would be subject to restrictions under the recommended policy." They went on to suggest, in keeping with their strong attempts to be gender neutral on these issues, that "comparable restrictions should be applied to other servicemembers based on projected amount of time an individual will be unable to fulfill normal duties of his/her position because of injury, etc."[15] The language of the PCR is painstakingly gender neutral— and effectively equates pregnancy with other "injuries" or limiting conditions. This is appropriate. However, the presumptions in these two sections about women's central role in reproduction, especially in childcare work, and their automatic inclusion as questions to be resolved for issues of women's deployability, is problematic. Federal law prohibits reproductive capacity to be considered as an employment factor for job eligibility and/or retention.[16] Certainly the armed forces must use federal law as a guide here when determining the general terms of deployability.

Alternative Views: The Case against Women in Combat

Out of concern that their point of view would be sullied by the overall findings of the report, the group of commissioners who unequivocally opposed women's entry to combat-related work penned a separate section to present their case. This section of the PCR was written by Samuel Cockerham, Elaine Donnelly, Sarah F. White, Kate Walsh O'Beirne, and Ronald Ray. It contains a statement of the absolute opposition of this group of commission members to women in combat, and reviews each "issue" to present their position unmediated. In their introductory letter to then-President George Bush, under the commission's letterhead, they stated that

> After careful consideration of the testimony the Commission heard and the research it conducted, we are pleased to present you with this Alternative View Section of the Commission's report, which outlines the basis for a consistent position opposed to the use of American women in combat. . . . We believe the importance of this issue demands an alternative perspective be presented for your consideration, and we appreciate the opportunity to state our views clearly in this section.[17]

I focus on this section for its remarkable display of bias against women serving in equal standing with their male counterparts in the armed forces. The commission, albeit by a small majority, did recommend that women not participate in combat, going against the passage of the congressional legislation. That small majority and the recommendation to allow women to be assigned to some combatant ships, to modify the law that only allowed women aviation officers to be assigned to the ships (not as combatants), was not won to the No vote that these commissioners felt appropriate. The "Alternative Views" section, for the most part, is redundant, with some instances where it pushes the rollback even farther than the general recommendations did. In its "Executive Summary" subsection they quote then Secretary of Defense Richard Cheney "restate[ing] the focus of the American military" as follows:

> [I]t's important for us to remember that what we are asked to do here in the Department of Defense is to defend the nation. *The only reason we exist is to be prepared to fight and win wars* [emphasis added by authors]. We're not a social welfare agency. We're not an agency that's operated on the basis of what makes sense for some member of Congress' concern back home in the district. This is a military organization. Decisions we make have to be taken based upon those kinds of considerations and only those kinds of considerations.[18]

The commission votes and especially the views of the signers of this section were more deeply influenced by the views of political, social, and spiritual civics on the right than would seem to be the case in this quote.

If the commission were to have gone by the force of this quote, which seems to suggest an approach of "get me the best soldier for the job," logic would suggest that gender does not matter. Even if gender mattered, women are excellent performers in all capacities of military work, and the Gulf War testimony right down to the former prisoners of war proved this out. This, of course, includes the many lesbian service members unidentified as such because of the history of discrimination against their sexual identities. By the gauge of job capability and performance records, the armed forces itself would have to accept, and gradually has been accepting, the trend toward opening the ranks as the best thing for the forces since it became a volunteer and so-called professionally based organization. With appropriate testing for ability in a physical and mental battery of tests which ignore gender and sexual orientation, the armed forces would be able to structure its fighting force in the most optimal manner. However, the commission members signing against women in combat were deeply marked by their predisposition that women do not belong in the combat theater and that the attempt to put them there is a radical feminist plot which will endanger the American way.

The signers of the "Alternative Views: The Case against Combat" section go over each of the commission's recommendations and issue their own evidence and commentary on each. In relationship to Department of Defense goals and quotas, the general commission vote was to encourage the use of eligible servicepeople as qualified. In the "Alternative Views" section this became a more general conservative movement to end "use of gender-related quotas, goals, or set asides."[19] This position reiterates former Defense Secretary Richard Cheney's fear that the armed forces were becoming a social welfare agency by their use of so-called recruitment quotas. The "Alternative Views" commissioners' comment on "Issue H: Parental and Family Policies" confirms what I have described above as the commission's fixed vision about who counts as child-rearers. Their use of testimony from several witnesses regarding the horrors of separation for children and mothers serves to highlight the bias. There is no testimony presented on how separation affects fathers, or children separated from fathers—and again the focus is on the heterosexual, two-parent, nuclear family, or the single-mother family, which is on the rise in the forces from 1980 to 1995. My local paper ran an advertisement of a young, white, woman officer, single mother of two, profiled as the perfect candidate for U.S. Bonds. She is presented in uniform, not with children—only the written text alerts the viewer to her parental status—reinforcing her ability to "stand alone," as it were, with the help of U.S. Bonds and a career in the armed forces.

The authors of the "Alternative Views" section felt the need to reemphasize their vote against women combat flyers and suggest that under no circumstances should women be in combat positions. In their own words they said that "the military must be able to choose those most able to fight and win in battle"(PCR, 44), and that "[f]or the deployed American fighting man, there is no home and family waiting at the end of the day. The home is where the soldier stands to face the enemy. Good order and discipline are crucial for morale, survival and victory in battle" (PCR, 44). What are they saying? As Brigadier General Michael Hall, USAF (ret.) put it in testimony before the commission: "As a commander charged with implementing this [exclusion policy], I cannot acceptively [*sic*] explain to myself or to those I lead why job-qualified women are denied opportunity because of their gender. . . . Job skill qualification for assignment consideration is the only full supportable basis to make decisions."[20] As for the question of home and family waiting at the end of the day, this turn of reasoning does not justify why one sex would be more able than the other. To match the twist of logic one would have to say that men, in traditional models, are more likely than women to expect to "come home" at the end of the day to family, while women's lives are typically constantly entangled with such concerns. This does not even touch the presumption that all soldiers have, or should have, such a thing to yearn for.

The commissioners signing this section acknowledged the fact that women have been assigned combat jobs in Canada, Denmark, and the Netherlands. Women military pilots are also trained in Great Britain and Spain. They do not accept this as a model to draw from but rather decry it because the women have been included for equal opportunity reasons. They support this position by quoting from retired Army General Norman Schwarzkopf: "Decisions on what roles women should play in war must be based on military standards, not women's rights."[21] Yet women have successfully deployed in each of those countries. According to this group of commissioners, the people who are in favor of allowing women to compete with men for the higher-status combat MOSs are wrong because they are simply arguing on equal opportunity grounds—a stand-in for handouts. On the other hand

> Those skeptical about assigning women to combat . . . have primarily focused on the needs of the military and combat effectiveness, as well as *deep-seated cultural and family values millions of Americans hold and are still teaching their children.* As one commissioner put it, those values can be summed up in one simple phrase: Good men respect and defend women [italics mine].[22]

These commissioners relied heavily on a family values argument resonant with right-wing political positions. This claim for women's proper role as nurturer and tender of the homefires creates a serious question—which they do not raise—about women's appropriate place in the forces, since any job is potentially in or near a combat area and men's job is to protect women. The only logical decision reached from this set of beliefs is that women should not be in the forces to begin with, and especially not for equal opportunity/equal rights reasons. This is the starting point for "traditional family values" advocates.

A key component of the group's argument against women in combat is the phrase "Good men respect and defend women." It is repeated on pages 46, 60, and 61 and underpins much of the testimony selected to support the claims in the "Alternative Views" section for excluding women from combat billets. The group cited testimony from several social critics. The tenor of this testimony is best evidenced by this excerpt from David Horowitz, who writes extensively about the feminist attack on the armed forces and other institutions.[23] Horowitz is an ex–New Leftist and current president of the Center for the Study of Popular Culture in Studio City, California. His rhetoric leaves no room for accountability:

> *[W]ithout statistics and without detailed reporting from the field . . .* American ability to wage war has already been seriously weakened by the deployment of relatively large numbers of women troops to an overseas battlefield, even without sending them into combat [italics mine].[24]

Horowitz follows with the example of children being left behind by their mothers who were deployed to the Persian Gulf War. SERE (Survival, Evasion, Resistance, and Escape) trainers also testified with a moderate caveat that the American public would have to be educated to expect that women soldiers could return from wars having been raped as POWs, or killed. Taken as part of the larger picture, of course the public would need to be prepared for this, but why it is any more heinous than men coming home in bodybags or suffering as prisoners of war is never made clear. In fact, both of these things happened in the Persian Gulf War and the public response was mild.

Dissent in the Commission

In Section III "Commissioners' Statements," there are several collective and singly written statements of dissent from the votes to exclude women from combat. They are consistent in pointing to the technical proficiency of women in each of the specialties: combat aviation, ground combat, and work on amphibious vessels and submarines. They assert that the testimony against women in combat never refuted that proficiency. They suggest that the commissioners against women in combat came with preconceptions and heard what they wanted to hear and walked out on the rest. The commissioners in favor of combat generally support the implementation of gender neutral testing for occupational qualifications.

None of the statements in dissent from excluding women mention other aspects of discrimination in the forces.[25] Most noticeably absent is any mention of the concurrent public debate over lesbian and gay service members and the then-President-elect's intention to eliminate the policies which exclude them from service. The question of parallel concerns and parallel logic regarding the exclusion of those who would disrupt the morale of an all-male, heterosexist club would seem worthy of cross consideration by the commissioners who favor women's access to combat jobs. However, when it comes to women and combat, other than the "extreme" and sadly inaccurate accusations of David Horowitz that it was all a feminist conspiracy, the debate rested on the terms of a generic female writ large across the images, on the one hand, of nurturing mother-wife needing and welcoming the protection of the self-sacrificing male and on the other hand, a seeming hand full of self-centered ambitious women seeking to further their careers. The debate never ventured to the deeper waters of challenging the legitimacy of generic sex role typing, of the discriminations faced by women of all colors and more severely by women of nonwhite backgrounds in the forces. The exposure of the events at Tailhook, which were simultaneous to this commission's tenure and served to underline just how pervasive and demeaning discrimination against women in the forces was, served no illuminating purpose in the commission's deliberations.

The final report, already damaged by its press and by its delivery to an outgoing President, was sent to George Herbert Walker Bush on 15 November 1992. There had already been an uprising of debate on the question of lesbian and gay soldiers with Clinton's pledge to lift the ban, given his heavy support from the lesbian and gay communities. The Tailhook investigation was ongoing, and the first Democratic President in twelve years was about to take up residence in the White House.

Women Can Kill

On April 28, 1993, under the new Democratic President, Defense Secretary Les Aspin presented his formal response to the Presidential Commission with his "Memorandum on the Assignment of Women in the Armed Forces." He said, in his press conference: "We know from experience that women can fly our high performance fighter aircraft. We know from experience that they can perform well in assignments at sea. And we know from Operation Desert Storm that women can stand up to the most demanding environments. So we are acting on what we know."[26] In memorandum he cites the post–Cold War need for downsizing and for recruiting and retaining the most qualified personnel. The Secretary instructed that all except for direct ground combat positions be opened to women consistently across the Reserve and Active Forces. He assigned an Implementation Committee to develop clear instruction for implementing the openings and reviewing the relevance of the Risk Rule. The debate over women and combat was temporarily laid to rest, albeit at a new stage of development. In the meantime, Clinton's campaign promise to lift the ban on lesbian and gay service personnel was causing no end of political trouble for the President and his fledgling administration.

Don't Ask, Don't Tell

Only two American institutions stand in the way of the homosexual movement completely accomplishing its goal of equating perversion with normalcy. Those institutions, both currently under siege, are the Boy Scouts of America and the nation's armed forces."[27]

Responding to the fight over allowing lesbians[28] and gays to serve in the armed forces and the promise by President-elect Bill Clinton to lift the ban on their service in the armed forces, Representative Dannemeyer (R-CA) and Representative Cliff Stern (R-FL) formed the Republican Steering Committee on Homosexuals in the Armed Forces, a nine-member conference group for which Dannemeyer made the above statement. Along with former Representative Robert Dornan (R-CA), they heard and gave testimony on December 9, 1992, regarding the perils to the United States of the proposed changes. Nancy Sutton, Executive Director of Family First testified: "Will we have to wait until little boys must abandon playing with Stormin' Norman action figures and instead play with sodomizing GI Joe dolls?" Michael Macaluso, Jr., Chairman of Citizens for a Decent Community, testified that: "Homosexuals have been relentlessly working to establish themselves as a legitimate part of society. If they accomplish their goal, it will be the end of America."[29]

Sam Nunn, as Chair of the Senate Armed Services Committee, not only spearheaded the effort to get the Presidential Commission convened to dampen the vote on women in combat, he was also vocal in his opposition to seeing the ban against lesbians and gays overturned. President-elect Bill Clinton was heavily lobbied by lesbian and gay activists to choose Les Aspin, then chair of the House Armed Services Committee, as his Secretary of Defense. Clinton obliged. The Armed Forces Joint Chiefs did not actually believe Clinton would follow through on his campaign promise to lift the ban (and, after all, they were correct). In January of 1993 Clinton directed Aspin to do research in preparation for an executive order lifting the ban. In response, as Shilts describes it: "Joint Chiefs Chairman General Colin

Powell repeated his earlier antihomosexual position. His statements so precisely mirrored what white generals had said in support of racial segregation a half century earlier that some younger military officers believed he was being facetious. He was not."[30]

The President's promise was severely modified after much hand-wringing and pressuring from the Congress. With the support of the RAND National Defense Research Institute's report, *Sexual Orientation and U.S. Military Personnel Policy: Options and Assessment,*[31] commissioned by Secretary of Defense Les Aspin, the President's attempt at policy change for lesbian and gay soldiers was issued as the well-known "don't ask, don't tell" Executive Order, on July 19, 1993. The changes set in motion by the combination of events at the turn of the nineties kept on rolling to some women's benefit in opening up prestigious jobs in the forces and allowing women to edge closer to martial citizenship, provided that they were sufficiently closeted if lesbian, and white either way.

Changes

On January 13, 1994, in a memorandum to the Joint Chiefs of Staff, Secretary of Defense Les Aspin rescinded the Risk Rule, deeming it inappropriate given the change in combat exclusion laws. The idea that women could be kept away from armed conflict by adherence to the Risk Rule—that is, women only allowed in areas where there is the least likelihood for "hostile fire"—fell apart in the Panama invasion and then again in the Persian Gulf War. There is no area where soldiers in a war are not at risk of being engaged in combat. The memorandum also clarified the "Direct Ground Combat Definition and Assignment Rule" with the instructions that "women shall be excluded from assignment to units below the brigade level whose primary mission is to engage in direct combat on the ground."[32] Both of these changes were to be effective as of October 1, 1994. On July 29, 1994, the new Secretary of Defense, William Perry, announced that the armed forces would open 80,000 new positions to women as of October 1, 1994. In September of 1994, the first gender-integrated enlistees' training began for the Army.

In that same year reports began to emerge about the growing poverty among base families. The general downsizing of the military has had the effect, not just of closing bases and cutting off weapon system development, but of curtailing social services for the lower-ranked soldiers and their families. With roughly 65 percent of servicemembers either married or single parents, the burden to provide social services is high. WIC (Women, Infants, and Children) services, the Air Forces Aid Society, the Navy-Marine Corps Relief Services, and the Army Emergency Relief Grants were put to extensive use to try and support the soldiers and their families.[33] This support is not extended to domestic partnerships of heterosexual, lesbian, or gay couples because of the lack of federal support for these domestic arrangements. Nevertheless, the growing poverty of the soldier family has also meant a drop in new enlistments. All the services reported low enlistments to the Department of Defense in 1994, and the advertising and recruitment budgets were raised for 1995. Congress and Secretary of Defense Perry tried to remedy the situation by announcing an incentive plan to subsidize private construction of base housing, and the Congress addressed the issue in the 1996 Defense Appropriations Bill allocating a 2.4 percent pay raise for active-duty personnel, a 5.2 percent increase in the military housing allowance, and funding to improve barracks and family housing, build childcare centers and set a mandatory minimum personnel level. With attempts to rebuild the social structure of the forces in an era of cutbacks most deeply felt on the personnel levels, the question looms of whether the armed forces are a good career choice. So does the question of the draft.

The changes effected by the public appearances of women soldiers and the equal rights activisms on their behalf resulted in the demise of portions of the "combat exclusion." This public attention to women as soldiers and the changing needs and face of the military answered some questions and raised many others. It is to these I return in the final chapter.

EIGHT

Citizenship Rites

This chapter synthesizes the issues that I have raised in thinking about feminist soldiers and feminist antimilitarists. I raise the unresolved questions and suggest what I think might be fruitful sites for additional work. I suggest ways that I think meanings and practices are currently evolving regarding women in the military and what that might mean for feminist soldiers and feminist antimilitarists. I discuss the technological changes and potential devaluing of foot soldiers, the film representations of women as soldiers, and raise questions and hopes for the present and future.

In examining the several episodes of United States political history where the articulation of a proper role for women as martial citizens took center stage, I have asked the questions of what was at stake for different women, for the armed forces, and for the United States more broadly. I have situated the debates over women's roles in the context of the sea change in United States social and economic politics. I have shown the ways that the debates have worked around femininity attempting to contain women in a traditionally polarized role. More specifically for feminists and for antimilitarists, I demonstrated that the women soldiers are interested subjects, not subjects of false consciousness. In emphasizing the racial composition of the forces' women and the job disparities among those contested high-technology combat ranks for women, I have also worked to re-mark the racial discrimination which still forms the structure of the armed forces. Economic critiques of the forces' actual provision of opportunities hold promise for making the armed forces be all that they can be in terms of women's access to those opportunities. The opportunities alone are not enough to assess the social value of the forces for democratic society.

As a social institution the military has been pushed, especially since the late 1960s, to reevaluate its treatment of and expectations of women, and in due course its expectations of men. Although the openings for women to redefine their relationships to the military have been readied by the armed forces to suit its own purposes of filling ranks vacated by unwilling young white males, the coincident rise in women's rights activism provided incentive and even push to accommodate those changes. I outlined, in chapter 2, the vast transformations in international politics and economy, and the connected changes in the United States politics and economy that have helped push for and make demand for changes in women's participation.

The first part of Enloe's imperative "that the military is too important a social institution to be allowed to perpetuate sexism for the sake of protecting fragile masculine identities" (1993a) is gradually being addressed as women's decades-old struggles for access are realized and increasing numbers of women are achieving high ranks in each of the branches. Again, it is worth noting that we are still talking about an organization where women remain less than 15 percent of the membership. It is also important to realize how that access is limited by race, and is still not complete in terms of jobs available.

Arguments for Feminist Soldiers

Women have fought long and hard for inclusion and respect in the realm of martial citizenship. Until and unless we as a nation move beyond martial politics, women have just as strong a set of rights and responsibilities to bear martial service as do men. Until the résumé of martial service and sacrifice is not an extra set of points for service eligibility in political office, witness the discussions and fights over Clinton's refusal of service and his potential ineffectiveness as the nation's leader, we need, as women, to have access to those responsibilities and achievements in equal measure as men. As Wendy Williams pointed out, we need to be able as women to refuse service and take the consequences, or our citizenship will not be validated in the current regime, and moreover our conscientious objection as feminist antimilitarists will have little clout. If women are entering the military because it has promised access to higher education, and better paying jobs, what will happen when they collectively hit that glass ceiling? And how will the racial and sexuality hierarchies be deployed in this process? And in the meantime, as I have shown in the prior chapters, women's entry to such a powerfully male preserve has effected change in (some of) the rules of the preserve. What we do not know is if the armed forces will respond by reinforcing a segregation of women's work from men's and differently raced women's from one another, as a reflection of and a reinstitution of society more broadly, where "be all you can be" begins with an uneven playing field.

The fact of continued racially marked advantage and disadvantage in the forces must be accounted for in analyses of the forces and their supposed benefits for women. Brenda Moore begins this work for us,[1] but we need to take it on more broadly. Race inequities still exist in the military, reflective of the racial inequities in the culture. Both need to be addressed more fully. Moreover, we need to engage these conditions through and within inquiries and yearnings for a future that does not rely on military solutions.

Taken on their own terms, the questions of women's place inside the military are being resolved gradually to women soldiers' benefit. Women were formally installed to most combat jobs by the middle 1990s. Research is under way in the Army to determine if women could effectively wage ground combat. Taken up from the outsider view, critical of militarism, the events of the 1980s and 1990s were the gradual wake-up call for feminist antimilitarists to engage in projects such as this one, working to understand the various interests at work in placing women in the military, and to anticipate the possible transformation of the military from patriarchal to simply professional, but no less deadly, practice.

Technology and Professional Soldier Girls

United States armed forces' battle plans are increasingly reliant on computerized and automated systems. There is less of a viable argument to restrict the work to men as more women gain the technical skills to assume those jobs. Technological advances are enabling women, regardless of physical condition, to work the same combat machinery as men. This still requires a development in adjustable sizing to fit smaller men and women's bodies. That, however, is a technicality, and not an ability problem. This stage in the professionalization of the forces provides the opportunity to re-imagine the roles of women in the forces altogether. Furthermore, some scholars of the forces suggest that the shift to information technologies for combat mean new structures of command. As Addis, an economist, views it:

> [T]he sophisticated technology of modern weaponry requires an educated personnel and a continuous flow of information between the lower ranks and the decision-makers. This contrasts with the one-way flow of information (orders to the subordinates) of traditional hierarchical ranking. The armed forces may therefore be evolving towards a less authoritarian model of internal behavior. This evolution may change the masculine cultural climate and render them [*sic*] more tolerant of a feminine presence.[2]

Is this professionalization of the armed forces an adequate reconciliation of the "antagonistic images of militarized femininity," which Elisabetta Addis marks as (1) patriotic women (female support net behind martial men), or (2) women fitted to the persona of traditional soldier?[3] It is possible that technological changes are key to shifting hierarchical and patriarchally based military culture, and would in effect shift the relationship of females to the forces more broadly? The underlying assumptions to such a vision are that women are in essence nonhierarchical, and that they are nonsympathetic to patriarchy. The assumptions are also embedded in a modeling that suggests the technologies are ungendered (pure) in and of themselves. This was an analysis dreamed of long ago by Shulamith Firestone[4] envisioning technology as a way out of the material conditions of women's social and economic oppression through reproduction. More recent scholarship on technology from a feminist perspective provides us with a vision for how to bend it but is also cautionary about just how deeply the technology is embued with the valuations of its creators.[5] More to the point, and as Enloe (1992) previously instructed us, we are faced with militarized femininity as in camp followers and patriotic mothers, or now, militarized femininity in the form of professional women citizen-soldiers. Elshtain's (1987) "beautiful souls and just warriors" dichotomy transformed to "beautiful warriors"? Do we want to choose militarized citizenship in the first place?

As the military shifts its superficial and structural cultures to include women formally as various kinds of soldiers, there has been a simultaneous shift toward computerized and cyborgian figures in martial planning.

Gray argues that this cyborgian soldier is the new masculine in martial valor and that the human soldiers, male and female, are feminized in this schema. This is not so hard to imagine when we think back to the naming practices of the bombs in nuclear research, the birthing declarations being "it's a girl" if the bomb did not explode, and "it's a boy" if it did,[6] feminist analyses of gendered militarism more generally also have told this war story.[7] These feminized soldiers, male and female, are rendered dependent on the technologies in order to do their job and one might argue, in order to face their job. It is still difficult for me to hear the first official woman bomber pilot, Kendra Williams, recently deployed with the Gunslingers in "Desert Fox" over Iraq, come back from her mission to a plate of fried chicken and say she had fun and is ready to do it again. I have to think that some of her enthusiasm is bred by the depersonalization of the target humans through distant high-tech bombing. On the other hand, I also see in these women pilots and their desire to be all that they can be as part of their squadrons, precise evidence of one of this book's arguments. Simply because they are women soldiers it does not follow that they will be nice warriors, they are rather female warriors trained like their male counterparts to "do their job." Though they may not be necessarily gendered bombs, they remain, as Cohn (1990) instructed us, "clean bombs."

At the turn of the twentieth century the forces are shifting focus toward technomanagerial roles as evidenced by the following numbers: in the Air Force 60 percent of the officers have Masters or PhDs. In the Army 25 percent of the officers do, and in the Navy it is 50 percent.[8] As the forces become more fully enacted through technologies, the forces become less essentially masculine. As the forces become unmanned, they are opened to various kinds of bodies being articulated to the machinery of war. Gray demonstrates for us that the defense planning reports indicate the increased and accelerated use of computers, bionics, cyborg warriors, satellites, and so forth. He suggests the complicated terrain on which these new strategies must be negotiated. Witness the following:

> Officers, technical specialists, and even the average soldiers to some extent will have to be helped to be innovative and show initiative, two qualities high-tech weapons, in general, and AirLand Battle (ALB), in particular, depend on. Many analysts see such conflicting advice as indicative of the

unrealistic assumptions of ALB, which is probably true. But it also shows that postmodern war calls for more than one kind of soldier. At a minimum there must be those who can perform almost mindlessly under extreme conditions that most humans cannot bear, and at the same time there is a need for experts in management, technical repairs, and the application of weapons systems.[9]

One only need think of the Borg in *Star Trek* to envision the kind of cyborgian developments that enable thinking and acting militarily to be conducted without regard for body type. Various sexes and sexualities can come to be integrated in the system. This means that women, as the forces (and the broader culture) become more technologically integrated, would not necessarily pacify the forces to any meaningful extent with regard to militarized politics. The "clean bombs" of Cohn's description can just as easily be created and/or launched by a woman.[10] Thus, these kinds of present and future developments in the technologies of war point toward a lessening in importance of the more traditional Rambo warrior model. Gray concurs here that postmodern war is rewriting the identities of soldiers through the privileging and masculinization of the machine and the downsizing of the masculine soldier himself. This means that the theater of soldiering itself is open to reinterpretation. We do not yet know if Addis' suggestion that the dependence on information technologies and diffusion will dismantle the hierarchical aspects of military culture is correct. It does, though, seem that control still originates in a command central.

Women are making headway into the forces. Evidence of this abounds in the ways that white women soldiers, and even some women of color soldiers, are ascending the ranks. Books are being written, as I suggested in chapter 1, that celebrate and fuel that headway. Conferences are being convened every two years by the Women's Research and Education Institute (WREI) to discuss women in the military with themes such as: "Women in the Military: Changes at Home, Lessons for Abroad in War and Peacekeeping" (1994); "Conference on Women in Uniform: Strategies for Success in the Military, Police and Fire Fighting Services" (1996); and "Women in Uniform: Exploding the Myths, Exploring the Facts" (1998). These conferences work on primarily feminist egalitarian militarist terms to support women in these traditionally male occupations and as my confidante, Carol Cohn, suggests from her attendance there, they work as a combination of "liberal feminist rejoinder" to arguments that women should not participate and in the form of support for the women waging the struggle. The current and high-profile activism for women in the military from the staff at NOW is also a piece of this action. Lieutenant Colonel Karen Johnson,[11] Vice President of Membership at NOW, has been a primary spokesperson against masculinist rejoinders regarding women's capabilities in the forces.

The professionalization of the forces overall, coupled with the changing face of dominant countries' experiences of war, for instance U.S. casualties as compared to Iraqi casualties, and the sanitization of the Persian Gulf War[12] for U.S. citizens, enables a vision of war as a clean, domesticated, and just act of diplomatic relations. This professionalization and the distanced computer-operated fighting tools, represented for the United States in the Gulf War on television screens as computer games, plays out minus the grit and terror of wars passed, and certainly minus the grit and terror of wars in your own backyard.

Combat

The question of brutal hand-to-hand combat for American troops is one that recedes from salience in the wake of these new technologies. Yet when the debates are about women and combat, the specter of women facing off men in hand-to-hand becomes a central icon for those opposed to formalized inclusion of women to combat arms. Recall the statement by former Representative Patricia Schroeder about the commercial with the woman soldier in the Army communications van as the first person in the line of fire. The problem lies in not recognizing that women in the United States forces face hostile fire because they are in the military. Women should have the same ability to fight back as their male counterparts, and, following suit, the same commendations and promotion benefits.

Draft

The draft is a vehicle for creating and maintaining a combat ready military, according to the benchmark rulings by the Supreme Court. The line between the All Volunteer Force and the draft regarding generating combat readiness is a strange one. Based on the presumption that conscription's sole purpose is to raise a fighting force, the Rostker ruling, with its logic grounded in the need for combat-ready troops, is potentially challenged now with women allowed in most combat roles. It was always challengeable on the grounds that fighters are not the only key participants in battle. In the Department of Defense's report *Conduct of the Persian Gulf War*,[13] beside the many tasks performed by enlistees supporting the fighters, from loading munitions to medical care for the wounded, the writers detail the extensive civilian support for the war, support like food services and administrative tasks, which are not combatant. However, as we saw in the Gulf War through the destruction of the barracks in Saudi Arabia, neither are they immune to attack.

The debates work around the question of difference between allowing volunteer women to fly fighter craft and drafting women—forcing them—to go into combat. This is a key issue about the relationship between combat training as a specialized skill and ground/hand-to-hand combat, which has yet to be adequately resolved. As the law stands now, women are only excluded from ground combat, special forces, submarines, and artillery.[14] All women in the forces, like all men, are trained in the use of guns. If a draft were to be called, the ruling in *Rostker* would need to be revisited as its justification lay in the fact that Congress had the important national interest to be able to call up a fighting force. Women are no longer excluded from most forms of combat, and therefore there should no longer be a technical reason for them to be excluded from a draft call. Women soldiers, like their male counterparts, should be required to perform all tasks which they are physically and/or mentally capable of performing.

Feminist Egalitarian Militarism

Liberal feminists rest their analyses and arguments on democratizing the military in the hopes of making it a more economically and politically just place. Stiehm (1996) argues that the civilian mind needs to pay attention to the military to democratize it. This is in order to develop a military that is infused with democracy, a people's militia, after all. This logically compels us to consider the argument that the military should be peopled by male and female conscription. This would avoid or lessen the desire to have the military be the place where people of color and white women go to be trained in high-end careers and to achieve the first-class economic and political citizenship that the military currently promises and sometimes bestows. Given that there is currently no parallel institution in terms of even the meager advances the military makes in this regard, we have to find a way to move those opportunities into other social institutions and invest them with the same economic and political meanings.

To make conscription a requirement means that all citizens are forced to deal with the fact of the military in society and to understand it either through participation or refusal to participate. As long as we have a military, all citizens need to take responsibility for it. To allow, as Stiehm has argued, some citizens to avoid responsibility and most citizens to accept protection passively is to dilute the potential moral force of democratic decisions about the military. Stiehm further argues for democratizing the military by strengthening the bond between the military and civilians. Her argument suggests that by creating a conscripted rather than voluntary professional force it would necessarily be more fully linked to "civilian mind," her term for the mindset of the citizens who trust and rely on the military to make decisions about its own actions. She suggests that, "Our goal must be to make might and right congruent. That will require civilians and the military to work together, without minds constricted by the narrowness of either 'military' or 'civilian' thinking."[15] On the other hand if we construct the military as a professional institution and hold it fully accountable to the democracy, we have to contend with the problems of the entire "black box" budgets, the secret missions. What we need to figure out is a way to democratize the practices and policies of the military such that as in true democracy there are no secrets, no unagreed-upon actions. Of course this betrays my naiveté regarding military action—how could you successfully fight a designated enemy if all your strategy and technological developments were public knowledge.

We need to wrest the terms of citizenship from their current fastening in the first instance to martial service. Can we envision a nation state that is not constructed out of some form of identity of protection via some form of militia? Do we want ours in effect to be a mercenary militia, one where careers are built on military service, and which serves as the ultimate career base for elite political service? So much disdain is held in our current career military for its civilian leadership. The career military oppose civilian authorized changes by arguing that the civilian leaders are acting out of political expediency and are out of touch with the real needs and functions of the military. How do we attend to this kind of alienation in a military apparatus which is supposed to serve the democracy? Of course, I am taking the "democracy" as a given that we at least aspire to. If we truly want a democracy, as in rule by the people, then what kind of military is compatible with that vision? I do not pretend to answer that question here. First of all, I do not know what that military might look like, but I yearn for it to be small and for it to command a far smaller portion of our national expenditure than it currently does, it is so much less expensive to provide education and social services than to build bombers that it boggles the mind. Second of all, I think and believe that as a nation we need to be able to discuss the shape of the military together. We need to be able to set collective priorities. In the twentieth-century U.S. military we have not done so.

Films and Women Soldiers

Comprehending and acknowledging the incorporation of women and the proliferation of histories and stories of women soldiers remains a critical task for feminist antimilitarists. For instance, there is interesting work to be done in reading the meanings of retrenchment and advance signaled in several recent films with allusions to the Persian Gulf War: the blockbuster *Independence Day,* the less popular (even with Denzel Washington as star) *Courage under Fire*, and finally, *G.I. Jane.* These films, of course, are indications of public sentiment, echoes of public debates, and often magnified in order to capture entertainment value. Indeed, they are symptomatic contributions to the debates with varied levels of impact. Nevertheless, I find them important guides for interpreting domestic United States consciousness and public conscience on the topic.

In the first, *Independence Day,* a future history, the President of the United States is a male Gulf War combat flyer veteran, who eventually dons his flight jacket again to help save the world under United States leadership, and with an African American male pilot hero—Will Smith—from hostile aliens (a story of its own to unpack, but not here). I have been instructed by Kathy Ferguson that her son saw the hero of this film as definitely the African American fighter pilot. One might arguably extrapolate from this that most youngsters percieved the film in that way, especially given Will Smith's rise to stardom.[16] Although women in the "real history" have been incorporated as combat flyers, not a single woman in the film is presented as a flyer. When they desperately need combat pilots to complete the mission, instead of drawing on the historically permissible resource of women pilots, they use a drunken Vietnam veteran pilot who becomes a heroic martyr. In this film, independence (the African American pilot and the Jewish reporter are both independent and valorous) and martial sacrifice (in the form of the proven heroic Persian Gulf War veteran President and the drunken Vietnam veteran) are left to the men. Of the three focus women, none is salvageable as a heroine: Will Smith's girlfriend is a topless dancer; the President's wife dies from being shot down while pursuing her own philanthropic project, leaving husband and daughter to fend for themselves; and the girlfriend of the Jewish reporter becomes his girlfriend again at the end through realizing that she was wrong to criticize his lack of ambition.

In the second film, *Courage under Fire*, the reputation of a woman helicopter medic, played by Meg Ryan, is at stake for the first medal of honor to be awarded to a woman. She is a dead (read safe) heroine, and the story of her actual stellar quality as a heroine is left uncertain. Ryan is redeemed by an African American officer, played by Denzel Washington, with skeletons in his own closet. The center of the film is really Denzel Washington's character (the black male conscience as warrior is the one that really matters) who is throughout the film interrogating his own heroism as he works through his Gulf War experience of causing the "friendly fire" death of some of his soldiers by firing on their tank accidentally in a desert battle. He asks at one point "Did she display any doubt or fear when she had to make decisions?" This directly reflects on his own worries over his decision making and the ways that, more broadly, the feelings of doubt and fear intrude on even the most heroic stories. Interestingly, one of the things that marks her bravery in the retelling of the story of her role as captain, is that after she is shot by one of her soldiers, presumably by accident, another one of them wants to help her and she says, "I gave birth to a nine pound baby, asshole, I think I can handle it." Remarking her heroism and courage in terms of her unique experience (amongst that group) of childbirth is an interesting twist on the essentialism debate over female capacity for warring and enduring potential injury.

In both of these films, the armed forces are being complexly revisioned in the aftermath of the Gulf War. No women combatants is the theme in the future history of *Independence Day*, white women and African American men are tainted, or at least unappreciated, heroes in *Courage under Fire*. The latter gives us some wiggle room for women soldiers as heroines however, in that it actually displays the complexity of heroism itself and brings women's experiences to bear on the definitions of martial valor and combat wits.

"The only thing that scares me are the sexual politics. I'm just not interested in being some poster girl for women's rights." Demi Moore's character, Lieutenant Jordan O'Neal in the movie *G.I. Jane*, emphatically utters these words to her boyfriend in the bath as they discuss her selection for SEALS (Sea Air Land) training. She makes it quite clear in the film that she is no feminist, but is simply doing her job and wants the promotions her lieutenant boyfriend got by "going operational." This film, like *Top Gun* a full decade before it, is riveting with its sexualized excitement. I would argue that *G.I. Jane*'s version was more complex with scenes of O'Neal's workouts and headshaving as gender bending. High power images and music run throughout and I would suspect that it similarly resulted in higher recruitment numbers, although it is not as favorable a picture of the Navy elite as *Top Gun*. In fact, the Navy refused to consult on the film, so hounded was it by the Tailhook debacle and so critical was the film of the retrenched masculinism in the elite corps. The film also runs an unusual trajectory from the first "girl recruit" film: *Private Benjamin*. By the time we reach *G.I. Jane*, the woman soldier is portrayed as a professional. She is more savvy about sexism to the tune of demanding equal treatment, but does not need to associate herself with women's rights, and in fact, distances herself considerably, as evidenced by the above quote. The film presents less caustic lesbians who are merely dangerous by association, rather than being mean and overbearing as they were portrayed in Private Benjamin's life. Benjamin took up the Army to get a life. O'Neal is in Navy Intelligence already and clearly has a life. She no longer needs the door opened for her in any sense of the word.

So what is happening in this film? As our Senator, who looks much like the recent children's film bad gal (Cruela Deville) in *101 Dalmations*[17] zooming around in her big black car and leaning down from high places to talk to people, reminds us in the congressional subcommittee hearings that are the opening shot: "Women are a vital link in the lifeline to combat. If women measure up, then they've got the job." This scene sets the tone for the film, which is about looking for the test case to prove women worthy of ground combat assignments. The hardest training environment is chosen and Demi Moore (O'Neal) is the candidate. She is chosen after a fascinating closed-door review of candidates, the rest of whom were dismissed variously for looking like "the wife of a Russian beet farmer," or for being in need of a "chromosome check." O'Neal is both picturesquely feminine and smart. Our "beautiful warrior" has arrived.

After the Senator's interview of O'Neal confirms that she is "a solvent heterosexual" she is signed up. *G.I. Jane* reaffirms the idea that, as Herbert[18] suggests, women soldiers manage their gender performance to steer clear of accusation and dismissal, and it demonstrates the ease with which a woman can become a full soldier, a first-class professional soldier, and a complete citizen, with sacrifice and merit taking her to the top without challenging the heterosexist force of the forces. On the other hand, *G.I. Jane* raises a significant challenge to what the Master Sergeant calls the tradition of the forces' reliance on masculinism. It does not challenge the racism of the forces, rather it treats the subject as solved, at least at the surface. The one African American male SEAL with her sympathizes about the work it takes to overcome the stereotypes about your people and his presence indicates that he has made it, by inference so will she. The Latino male is the bad guy in this story who seeks to undermine and get rid of O'Neal; he functions as the unreconstructed machismo that used to run the forces, but now looks somewhat outdated in the context of his colleagues' behaviors. The women in this story are all white. All the blacks are men. Where are the brave?

Closing Thoughts Opening Thoughts

Feminist antimilitarists need to use the tools of a complexified picture of the forces, and especially women invested there, to analyze the deep impulse of women's interested presence in the forces. We also need to focus on the meanings of the resistance to women in the forces—through fictional enactments, through sexual harassment and abuse,[19] through the continued government subsidization of prostitution at military bases; it is here that the resilience of masculinism is most apparent. We need to recount the stories from a perspective that the military is too important and too dangerous.

Thus, the second half of Enloe's imperative. I have suggested that a focus on the question of citizenship and the history of martial service as the ultimate exchange for first class citizenship must be a centerpiece for any sustainable critique of the forces. War is no longer just a dick thing, and in order to be taken seriously as opponents of war, feminist antimilitarists will have to develop analyses of the armed forces which reach past the forces' patriarchal history to look at the benefits to which women want access. We need to acknowledge women's accomplishments there while continuing to work toward the separation of militarism and citizenship.

In constructing a feminist antimilitarism that accounts for the conditions I have outlined in this project, a longer conversation with feminist antimilitarist theorizing, both in written work and in direct theory, needs to progress. We need to articulate an approach to dissent from militarism in the reshaped forces of the late twentieth century. This body of work must also be used to explore the role of the armed forces as both civilian and martial employer, a role which has been eroded even while recruitment efforts for volunteers were stepped up in the mid-to-late 1990s.

The military remains entrenched in its culture of masculinity. Feminist antimilitarist critiques of and strategies against the militarization of United States culture can accurately continue to point to its patriarchal underpinnings. The danger is in assuming that because it is a masculinist institution now, it always will be, or that it would be radically altered by women's increased representation therein. It should be evident from the feminist political scholarship that the "man in the house" can be replaced by the "man in the state" and beautiful warriors can and do drop bombs just like their male counterparts. Until women are able to (officially) be all that they are in the military, including lesbians, spitfire fighters, mothers (lesbian or straight) and perform martial sacrifice, and until men are able to be all that they are, including gay or straight, fathers (gay or straight), caregivers, and sensitive, it will be clear that the kernel of truth in the military is its masculinism. This is especially remarked as the Service Members Legal Defense Network's research finds that "in 1996 the armed forces repeatedly excused violations of current law including witch hunts, seizure of personal diaries, and threatening service members with prison unless they accused others as gay—all in an effort to target and ferret out gay men and women who serve our country. The result is that gay discharges have soared to a five-year high at a cost exceeding $25 million in 1996."[20] Thus, after all, it remains a patriarchal institution embedded in a power structure that reifies heterosexist masculinist power. As that changes, and it is changing ever so slowly, feminist anti-militarists can shift our strategies. To be able to do that kind of shifting requires an articulation of the realities of women's uneven and problematic presence in the military to our critiques of its institutionalized sexism and racism.

It is only in combining these views that the armed forces can be assessed by United States citizens interested in the further development of the nation's democratic process. We still need to weave a web of resistance to armed force as a way of politics. This web needs to be woven of a complex analysis of militarism that can function to destabilize notions of gendered armed forces that persist on the right and the left, to account for the economic and environmental repercussions of maintaining a militarized government, and to separate martial service from first-class citizenship rights. In this way, we will realize some of our yearnings for justice and peace.

NOTES

Notes to the Introduction

1. See Feinman (1998).

2. For example, many of the authors write about their military experience and the history of their own branch, detailing the struggles and achievements of integrating women into said branch. See Holm (1982) for what is widely recognized as a definitive history of women in the military, with special emphasis on the Air Force. Ebbert and Hall (1993) have written a major work on the Navy. Also Treadwell (1954) and Morden (1990) have written the official history of women in the Army and their work is published through the Center for Military History's Army Historical Series. A number of other books have been published as (auto)biographies of particular military women, for example, Barkalow (Barkalow with Raab 1990). The central history and analysis of gays and lesbians (less fully) in the military was written by Shilts (1994); see also Humphrey (1990). A tendency to use oral history and autobiography is quite strong in the literature on women in the forces. Several examples of this method are Schneider (1988) and Weber (1993). The majority of these studies are premised on the appropriateness of full incorporation of women to the military. Many more recent books have emerged detailing the histories of women in the military in different branches and times.

3. This is a broad ranging literature. See for example, early works such as, Brownmiller (1975); McAllister, ed. (1982); Puget Sound Women's Peace Camp (1985); Cook and Kirk (1983); Chapkis, ed. (1981); and Enloe (1983). More recent treatments include Addis et al., eds. (1994); Cooke and Woollacott, eds. (1993); Elshtain (1987); Elshtain and Tobias, eds. (1990); Enloe (1992, 1993b). Finally, in the nonacademic press recent books addressing women in the military and the question of war from feminist opposition to militarism include especially, Zimmerman (1995); Francke (1997); and Ehrenreich (1997).

4. Enloe (1983, 1990a). Enloe has also written on the aftermath of the cold war for gender politics, including an analysis of the way women soldiers were represented in the Gulf War (1994).

Notes to Chapter 1

1. Many of the ideas in this chapter were first developed for a talk I gave at the Contemporary Social Movements and Cultural Politics Conference, University of California, Santa Cruz, March 1991, immediately after the Persian Gulf War: conversations with audience members there helped sharpen my analysis and build my confidence that I was on to something! Portions of this chapter have been published as "Reweaving the New World Order: An Ecofeminist Analysis" in Darnovsky et al., eds. (1995) and "Women Warriors/Women Peacemakers: Will the Real Feminists Please Stand Up!" in Lorentzen and Turpin, eds. (1998).

2. For example, some of the signs read: "War Is a Dick Thing," "Fighting for Peace Is Like Fucking for Virginity," "No More Missile Envy Please," "Real Men Pull Out Early," "Read My Labia, No War for Oil." I am indebted to Sonia Alvarez, Giovanna Di Chiro, and Judy Feinman for their lists of the slogans during demonstrations in San Francisco and Santa Cruz, January 1991. In addition, the antiwar meetings I participated in and nonviolence preparations I led were deeply informed by feminist antimilitarist questions and perspectives, with the most common analyses by participants being the direct associations as above, however ironic in intent.

3. For the first major reader in feminist antimilitarism (and the one most oft cited) see McAllister, ed. (1982), a text that presents much of the theorizing and activist record to that year, including an excerpt from the Women's Pentagon Action Unity Statement, it still stands as a handbook and resource for movement activists. An interesting sidebar to this citation is that most of the feminist antimilitarist writing is published through the activist presses such as New Society. Much of the feminist antimilitarism is enacted and theorized in antimilitarist demonstrations and in action handbooks. It does not achieve status in academe except, notably, as it developed into academic "ecofeminism," a transition I will track later in the book.

4. Enloe does not say get rid of the military in her writings, yet her analyses of the workings of patriarchal militarism certainly create the sense that getting rid of the military would be the only just solution. My reading of her work is that there is some ambivalence about the question of militaries themselves, but no doubt she holds that masculinist militaries generate incredible harm; e.g., the epigraph (1990a, 1992, 1993a).

5. Haphazard, but exciting, connections were built from the pagan culture in which much of the direct action movement was sustained. See Starhawk (1974, 1978) for an account by one widely recognized as a spiritual/political spokesperson in the movement. See B. Epstein (1991) for a critical analysis of the movement's use of pagan spirituality, and Sturgeon (1995), for an analysis of the in-

tegration of movement culture and politics with its self-reflexive theorizing. See also Haraway (1985) for a discussion of the interconnections in the movement theorized in the figure of the cyborg goddess.

6. For accounts of the struggle for and pleas for the completion of a peace process in the region see the moving collection of essays in Hurwitz, ed. (1992); Falbel et al., eds. (1990); and Ferguson (1995).

7. For a fabulous account of the stages in coming to terms with, or at least raising the interesting questions about, the Persian Gulf War (including the build up) as it was developing, see Enloe (1993b: 161–200).

8. That they were men of color is, in itself, no great surprise to students of military demographics, as men of color have often been targeted for recruitment, especially during times of ground combat such as the Vietnam War.

9. Phyllis Schlafly in Huckshorn (1991).

10. Amongst the writings contributing to these analyses were several chapters in Darnovsky et al., eds. (1995); Fuentes (1991).

11. This control of the media during the Gulf War and the way that the war was in part fought in the media is discussed by Darnovsky et al., eds. (1995: 223–32). Also see Peters, ed. (1992).

12. A curious recent development, spinning off of the Kelly Flynn case, is the reconsideration of the military's adultery laws. I don't know of any other public institution that carries laws on the appropriate extramarital behavior of its members. Certainly, there is no civilian, secular law against adultery. In fact, the interesting twist to recent controversy over President Clinton's affair with Monica Lewinsky has been about his lying to the grand jury, not about the legality of the act itself. Of course, this belies the deeper issue of allegations of his pattern of sexual harassment, behavior that is in theory against the law.

13. Sturgeon uses this term to describe the movement's activist theoretical production. The concept of direct theory accounts for the direct action movements' "practices and structures as a form of theorizing through practice, a praxis I call 'direct theory,' a lived analysis of contemporary domination and resistance" (Sturgeon 1995: 36).

14. Ruddick (1983, 1984). Di Leonardo (1985) presents an insightful review of several books taking this stance.

15. I was well instructed by the work done in Bridenthal et al., eds. (1984) to recognize the terrible legacy of state power that is bolstered by women's fervent embrace of traditional and circumscribed roles as protectresses, of the children and thus of reproducers of the state, with these roles frequently fastened to increased militarization.

16. Di Leonardo (1985).

17. See Sturgeon (1997) for a discussion of this view of the "essentialism"

taint on feminist antimilitarism. I also watched part of this debate unfold at the spokescouncil meeting for the Mothers and Others Day Action at the Nevada Test Site, Mothers' Day 1987. A group of my friends from Santa Cruz, all members of a local coven, came all dressed as pregnant mothers—a phenomenon Sturgeon recounts—saying to me that the reason they did it was to express their desire, male and female alike, to embody the caring attributes of mothering in hopes of saving the planet from the death of nuclear war.

18. Some excellent accounts of this period are Evans (1980); Chafe (1980); Carson (1981); Breines (1982). For a detailed account of the development of feminist critiques of the sixties movements as they emerged from the movements see Evans (1980); Piercy in Morgan, ed. (1970); Langer (1973); anonymous position paper by women in SNCC (actually written by Mary King and Casey Hayden) 1964 conference (personal files), and response paper by Cynthia Washington (personal files). In addition see the unpublished manuscript of Feinman (1988), "Out of the Sandbox: SLATE and the Emergence of a New Left," which details a history of women's relationship to the left at the intersection of the old and new lefts, presents a discussion of the relationship of militance in the sixties movements to the increasing repression of women in those movements.

19. My understanding of the ways that the liberal state creates and sustains the gendered artifice of public and private spheres was first developed through teaching with Wendy Brown and then reinforced through reading her 1995 book, in which, especially in her chapter, "The Man in the State," she describes (as she taught) the ways that the state has taken up the role of the "father" as a diffused but nonetheless patriarchal power figure.

20. See especially Evans (1980) for the classic discussion of the dynamics inside the movements.

21. Anzaldúa (1987). And before Anzaldúa, Chela Sandoval, whose work on oppositional consciousness, while overcirculated and undercited, influenced a broad range of scholars in the Santa Cruz intellectual community of faculty and graduate students in thinking about situated oppositional politics of women of color as a model. See especially Chela Sandoval, "U.S. Third World Feminism: The Theory and Method of Oppositional Consciousness in the Postmodern World" *Genders* 10 (1991):1–24.

22. See for example, Smith, ed. (1983) and Moraga and Anzaldúa, eds. (1983) two edited volumes that began the extensive response of women of color to a feminism that was heretofore mainstreamed as white. It is important to note, that, although beyond the scope of this discussion, origin stories of feminism's history and major players are contested stories as evidenced in K. King (1994). See especially chapter 1 for a discussion of the multiple histories of U.S. women's

movements and the meanings embedded in telling those histories one way or another.

23. B. Epstein (1991). This is a fact that is often overlooked by theorists of the new social movements, yet is a critical piece of the legacy of the movements.

24. See Smith, ed. (1983) and Moraga and Anzaldúa, eds. (1983). Tragically, Kitchen Table Press has folded now and we are in danger of losing access to these critical texts for ourselves and our students.

25. Reprinted as the frontispiece of the nonviolent action handbook of the "Mother's and Others Day Action, Nevada Test Site, May 8, 1987."

26. See Reed (1992: 124–26); see Sturgeon (1997: 62–65). For several more in-depth accounts of the Women's Pentagon Actions see the following texts: Pines (1981); King in L. Jones, ed. (1983); and B. Epstein (1991).

27. Ruddick (1980).

28. From Cambridge Women's Peace Collective (1984: 7).

29. McAllister, ed. (1982); Deming (1984); Harris and King, eds. (1989); Cook and Kirk (1983); direct action handbooks in personal collection.

30. Abzug, who left us in March 1998, was a founding second-wave feminist and activist antimilitarist. She founded Women's Strike for Peace in the early 1960s, the National Women's Political Caucus in the 1970s, the Women's Foreign Policy Council, and WEDO, the Women's Environmental Development Organization. She coined the slogan "A woman's place is in the House," and on her first day in Congress introduced a resolution to end the Vietnam War. Of course, it did not pass. Abzug, writing in 1991 makes the following connections between women's antimilitarist activism and political change:

> It was thousands of women marching and demonstrating against dangerous Strontium 90 nuclear fallout who helped us win the ban on atmospheric nuclear tests and who have continued their struggle against the nuclear arms race and hazards in areas ranging from Greenham Common, Europe, and the U.S. to Africa and Asia. In the endangered islands of the South Pacific, women have organized to demand a Pacific nuclear free zone and the protest the plundering of their land and fragile ecosystems by foreign companies. Abzug (1991).

31. See Swerdlow (1993).

32. See Pierson (1988).

33. See White (1992). Also see Feinman (1998) for a discussion of the conflation of women antimilitarists' positions and women antifeminist militarists' positions.

34. Carol Cohn is doing some very intriguing research to this effect, finding that women in the military do love what they do! (personal communication).

35. See Sturgeon (1995).

36. Personal collection of direct action nonviolence preparation handbooks.

37. Barbara Omolade, "We Speak for the Planet," in Harris and King, eds. (1989: 171–89, quote from 172).

38. See Sturgeon (1997) for the first full historical treatment of the Woman-Earth Feminist Peace Institute, and a studied analysis of its problems in working toward racial parity, esp. 77–112.

39. Kirk and Okazawa-Rey (1996: 7).

40. Warnock in McAllister, ed. (1982: 29).

41. B. Epstein (1991).

42. Much of the street talk about the Bay Area response to the escalating confrontation between the Iraqi government and the United States government in the spring of 1998 was that activists were organized more quickly than ever by utilizing Internet-works of Bay area peace groups to coordinate meeting times and places for rapid response marches and protests.

43. For a very provocative history and mapping out of the sacred lands of the nuclear age see Kuletz (1998).

44. B. Epstein (1991).

45. For several more in-depth accounts of the Women's Pentagon Actions see the following texts: Pines (1981); Y. King (1983); B. Epstein (1991); and Reed (1992). Sturgeon (1995), is also important here for her work in describing the encampments as prefigurative communities. She demonstrates through her analyses of what she calls the movement's "direct theorizing" the ways that the movement was precisely about enacting an alternative constructive culture to destructive nuclear culture.

46. Sturgeon (1991: 285).

47. Sturgeon (1997: 149).

48. For early ecofeminist writings (at the juncture of feminist antimilitarism and ecological activism, see two anthologies of ecofeminism especially for their capture of two different moments in ecofeminist development: Plant, ed. (1989) which develops a collective and problematic voice of activists interpreting ecofeminism, and Diamond and Orenstein, eds. (1990) which is comprised of the proceedings from the first academic conference of ecofeminists and moves the terrain of ecofeminism significantly toward the academy. Although Sturgeon and I started the conversation together about the implications of this shift of ecofeminist writing to the academy, Sturgeon (1997) fully explores the many implications of this transition in her analysis of ecofeminism.

49. *Woman of Power* (1988).

50. For example, Caldecott and Leland (1983); Cambridge Women's Peace Collective (1984); L. Jones, ed. (1983); "Feminism and Ecology" (1981); "The

Great Goddess" (1982); Linton and Whitman (1982); Y. King (1983); Y. King (1981); and Y. King (1983)

51. See Mansbridge (1986).

52. NOW web site: www.now.org/publ. NOW has, over time, changed its position and engagement with women in the military, from its early refutations of the military (NOW National Conference 1971), to its argument that women in the military should be drafted the same as men (NOW National Board 1980), to its incorporation of women in the military as a focus section of its work and its inclusion of Lieutenant Colonel Karen Johnson (USAF) ret., in the early 1990s as National Secretary and now as Vice President, Membership.

53. Summers (1991: 90–91).

54. Hartsock in Stiehm, ed. (1982).

55. Schroeder in Summers (1991).

56. Holm (1982).

57. Barkalow with Raab (1990).

58. Moskos (1990).

59. Ibid.

60. Stiehm, ed. (1982); and Stiehm (1989). An interesting set of arguments run through Stiehm's publications. A strong feminist throughout, she nevertheless holds a position that recognizes the role of violence in certain situations. Her first book, on nonviolence, ends with an argument that valorous though it is, nonviolent response is reserved for particular situations. I don't think she would call herself an antimilitarist as such. Her subsequent work moves through discussions of the ways that the military's masculinist culture is, or is not, coping with the presence of women. It is a refreshing look at the way masculinism operates inside that culture, rather than at the ways women are inside it. She insists (*Arms and the Enlisted Woman*) that the women are quite ordinary, after all.

61. Katzenstein (1990: 53).

62. Stiehm (1982).

63. Stiehm (1989: 225).

64. NOW National Conference (1971).

65. NOW National Board (1980).

66. Becraft (1989).

67. K. Johnson (n.d.).

68. Holm (1982).

69. Ebbert and Hall (1993: preface).

70. Treadwell (1954); and Morden (1990).

71. For instance, B. Moore (1990; 1991: 364–84; 1995; and 1996). Other authors with this approach include Merriman (1998); Zimmerman (1995); De Pauw (1998).

72. For example, Barkalow with Raab (1990).

73. Several examples of this method are Schneider and Schneider (1988) and Weber (1993).

74. De Pauw (1998).

75. See Holm (1982); Ebbert and Hall (1993); Treadwell (1954); Morden (1990); Barkalow with Raab (1990); and Schneider and Schneider (1988) for straightforward progressive accounts of women's inclusion and their anticipated continued advancement. See Rogan (1981) for a studied account of the heterosexual integration of the forces, including the problems raised by dissolving the women only and (albeit disputed) lesbian friendly, if not dominated, environment of the pre-1976 period. See Weber (1993); Shilts (1994); Bérubé and D'Emilio (1984); and Bennecke and Dodge (1990) for accounts of the lesbian and gay soldiers already present in the forces.

76. This briefly surfaced, in the spring of 1996, on the *Minerva* Internet list regarding Johnnie Phelps's now legendary account of her tenure in the WAC headquarters with Eisenhower. She recounted, in Randy Shilts's book, that when Eisenhower asked her to list the lesbians under her command she told him that it would include most of her staff and that the list would be topped off with her name. This was also recounted in the film "After Stonewall." She estimated that 90 percent of the women in the WAC (Women's Army Corp) were lesbians. Other WACs have begun disputing her claim, and there are the beginnings of a research project of WACs' oral history to refute Phelps.

77. See Bennecke and Dodge (1990); Herbert (1997, 1998); and Fenner (1995).

78. For instance, in the summer of 1996, I attended an Air Show at Watsonville Airport, which had a booth and events displaying women's aviation history. A featured component was the WAVES (Women Aviators Volunteering for Emergency Service) of WWII. I gazed transfixed at the old photos trying to discern somehow the "truth" of lesbian histories in the Forces. The clothing styles of those women—largely to accommodate their work as pilots—made the signals difficult to read. None of the captions identified the women as straight or not, though several included "family photos." So, given the difference in the then and now regarding the politics of lesbian identity, it is a formidable task to ascertain the truth in such claims.

79. Fuentes (1991).

Notes to Chapter 2

1. We are, of course indebted to feminist thinking here in remembering the ways the culture is an interactive space engaging both public and private for-

mations of social, political, and economic relations where neither public nor private are actual spaces but rather constructed for the convenience of a liberalism that sought to distinguish legitimated and illegitimated relations of power. Antonio Gramsci's work clearly undergirds this notion of a cultural hegemony as one which is pervasive through the "layers" of society, and feminist work has taught us that the "layers" are a trope designed for the convenience of those in power.

2. Cock and Nathan (1989: 4–5). Thank you to Carol Cohn for pointing out this book to me as a result of our ongoing discussion of how to define militarism.

3. Lorde (1984). When I first read the phrase "The Master's Tools Will Never Dismantle the Master's House," I was struck by the sheer enormity of its implications if truly taken to heart. See also Brown (1995: 193).

4. K. King (1994) reminds us that the stories of feminism's origins vary with different effect in the telling; she brings forward Cellestine Ware and her book *Woman Power* to remind us that women of color were present in early radical feminist work and that they, particularly Ware, pioneered the method of conceptualizing interlocking identities. Other writers who have worked through and developed this method for activist scholarship include Anzaldúa (1987); Davis (1990); Deming (1981, 1984); Haraway (1985); Lorde (1984); Rich (1977); and Smith, ed. (1983).

5. Omi and Winant (1986) map an analysis of the socially and historically contingent construction of race, and insist on this kind of specificity as a way of accurately reflecting the politics of marking race and ethnicity, and particularly seeing the way that race is constructed in the service of the state.

6. See Ferguson (1984) regarding the construction of bureaucracy as an apparatus of masculinist power, and Brown (1995: 166–96) for a study of the man in the state.

7. See a series of articles in *Feminist Review*, by Barrett and McIntosh (1985); Ramazanoglu et al. (1986); and Bhavnani and Coulson (1986).

8. Bhavnani and Coulson (1986: 89).

9. See especially Zala Chandler, "Antiracism, Antisexism, and Peace (Sapphire's Perspective)"; Barbara Omolade, "We Speak for the Planet"; and Lourdes Benería and Rebecca Blank, "Women and the Economics of Military Spending"; all in Harris and King, eds. (1989). The term "double jeopardy," of course, comes from Frances Beale in "Double Jeopardy: To Be Black and Female," in Morgan, ed. (1970: 340–53).

10. Brown (1995: 193).

11. Stiehm (1989).

12. Enloe (1993b: 15).

13. Gray (1997).

14. See for example O'Connor (1973); Harrison and Bluestone (1988); Klare (1981); and Edsall (1984).

15. This included white men and men of color due to the influence of the antiwar movement generally discrediting United States foreign policy and the precise organizing against the draft in the Black communities against the war due to the over-recruitment of young Black men as draftees. Near his death, Martin Luther King, Jr., began to develop speeches about this topic and certainly Stokely Carmichael was vocal about it early on in SNCC (Student Nonviolent Coordinating Committee).

16. This space for women is highly contested as the positions of "feminist," "women of color," "womanist," and many partial combinations continue to be developed.

17. One of the more curious tie-ins to this story is a quote by Bush from the 1992 presidential debates in which he said (responding to Clinton's plan to bring home 50,000 of the 150,000 soldiers in Europe.): "If you throw another 50,000 kids on the street because of cutting recklessly in troop levels, you're going to put a lot more out of work." Bush's hint here is that there are a number of ways in which the military benefits the domestic economy and disguises the crisis in civilian employment opportunities.

18. Harvey (1989: 122).

19. Santoli (1995).

20. See B. Moore (1995).

21. Conversation with Enloe has brought this point to my attention.

22. Enloe (1992: 16).

23. Brown (1995: chapter 1).

24. See Gray (1997); and Addis et al., eds. (1994).

25. This term is Cohn's (1987). I borrow it here to highlight the ways that technological discourse and actual planning are also having an impact on the possibilities for women soldiers in the military and as much as Cohn teaches us that this discourse allows defense planners to think the unthinkable, it also, through its deployment, allows women access to technostrategic muscle power, thus confounding the very gendered construction from which it was birthed.

26. The power of the military and the power of the martial act shifts from soldiers to computers (bolstered by the hidden labor of their caregivers—the new camp followers: AI techies.) Can a woman warrior save us from this computerized militarist masculinity? It has certainly been speculated upon in science fiction: witness *Terminator 2* and Linda Hamilton's ecofeminist earth saving warrior; of course, she ends up needing the help of the good male cyborg to defeat the bad one (who, by the way, has a liquid, smaller, almost boyish—read effeminate—presence!)

27. Brown (1995: 174).

28. Ibid., 10.

29. Jameson (1984); Lash and Urry (1988); Harvey (1989).

30. Gramsci (1978). Furthermore, even where including women as crucial to the process of revolution, Marxism always answered the woman question through and only through economic class-based revolution. See Engels (1972); Lenin (1938); Luxemburg (1971) for early approaches to the issue.

31. See Marcuse (1964); Horkheimer (1947), Habermas (1974).

32. Some important theorists of this school are Aglietta (1979); and Lipietz (1987). One of the issues I have with this school is its tendency to create a mechanical view of the operations of capital without accounting for human agency in influencing the path capital takes. Thus their work, in some curious parallels to the neoconservatives, ends up with no room for political action. In the U.S. Social Structures of Accumulation School see Davis (1978); Weisskopf (1981); and Bowles et al. (1983).

33. The distinction between the two schools is that while the Regulation School mainly concerns itself with the internal logic of capitalism, arguing that the structures of accumulation and regulation are fixed, the U.S. theorists of the Social Structures School see these moments and processes in the crises as deeply impacted by socioeconomic struggles. In other words, for the U.S. Social Structures theorists, the adaptations made by capital are in response to worker pressures. These would go both ways, explaining labor-capital accords of the 1930s and the flight of capital in the postfordist period to areas where workers were not yet organized collectively.

34. I rely on Foucault for this insight, albeit loosely, through his analysis of power and resistance (1980a, 1980b).

35. Lash and Urry (1988).

36. Jameson (1984).

37. For a detailed analysis see Rubin in Reiter (1975); Hartmann (1976); and Eisenstein, ed. (1979). In addition, Sturgeon (1991) tells us that the new social movement theorists (and I would add the same about the post modern/post fordists) posit "that these economic changes are accompanied by the growing involvement of the state in previously autonomous or 'private' spheres of civil society as it attempts to manage the rupturing of social relations produced by changes in the forces of production" (252). This analysis is paralleled in feminist studies of the state and the welfare apparatus through the early 1990s with the arguments that the state has intervened where "traditional" family economies have broken down. However, as Sturgeon points out, this model erroneously assumes that at one time the private sphere was discrete from the state. Of course, by the middle 1990s this picture is contested by the Congress where an attempt

to disengage the federal government from the so-called private sphere is underway—looking more like a struggle over race and state's rights at its core. In this light, feminist arguments that the state is no less patriarchal than the man (its father) make total sense.

38. I will use this term to loosely describe the postfordist, late capitalist, and regulation school theorists, all of whom are connected to some version of left economics, while deferring to Epstein's (1991) map of their precise location in relation to one another for more specific analysis.

39. Agliettta (1979).

40. See Reed (1992).

41. Laclau and Mouffe (1987).

42. For a more detailed account of the transference of patriarchy to the state see Fraser (1989); and Ferguson (1984). Both authors develop accounts of the role of the welfare state in taking over what was once considered the privatized duty of the male breadwinner. Where they differ is in their versions of the usefulness of the welfare state as a site for feminist activism. Where Fraser tells us that a change in the focus towards "needs discourse" as an activist politics, Ferguson sees the state as regenerating the dependence on patriarchy and seeks its demise. Another major work on the welfare state which centers feminist analyses and overall, leans more toward the Fraser model, is Gordon, ed. (1990). See also MacKinnon (1989); for an overview of some of the contemporary debates about feminism, Marxism, and the State. Also see Brown (1995) for a precise discussion, though presenting little hope for activist interventions, of the ways that patriarchy adheres in the core of the state and the problems presented for freedom by asking the patriarchy for protection from itself, as it were.

43. See Darnovsky (1996), UCSC dissertation manuscript for an argument about the possibilities and limitations of the "green consumer-activist".

44. Piven and Cloward (1977); Mink (1995); Kirby (1980).

45. Mink (1986); Omi and Winant (1986); Gilroy (1987); and Hall (1988). These authors develop both nationally and internationally located accounts of the impact of racial politics on the development of national identity and the production of international relations. Omi and Winant, and Gwendolyn Mink offer specifics regarding the use of race in the formation of U.S. political process, which are quite informative to notions of nationalism and international economic practices.

46. Harvey (1989).

47. This concept was developed by Alain Lipietz of the Regulation School, and takes off from the global systems theorists' maps, which establish the notion of the periphery as indicative of the frontiers of international capitalist expansion—often synonymous with the so-called underdeveloped nations.

48. Harvey (1989: 147).
49. Ibid., 159.
50. Laclau and Mouffe (1985).
51. Harvey (1989: 155).
52. This argument has also been made in the case of Japanese patriarchal capitalism by Miyake (1991).
53. Harvey (1989: 302).
54. B. Epstein (1991).
55. Personal communication with Haraway, March 28, 1996.
56. Haraway (1988).
57. Mies (1986).
58. See for example Stallard et al. (1983); Fernández-Kelly (1983); Ong (1987); Enloe (1990a, 1993b).
59. Enloe (1990a); Fernández-Kelly (1983); Ong (1987).
60. Enloe (1990a); Fernández-Kelly (1983); Fuentes and Ehrenreich (1983); and Mitter (1986).
61. Fuentes and Ehrenreich (1983).
62. I mean this to represent both the notion of being left out of the "rewards" of capitalist accumulation and the location of women, in the global systems theory sense, as the key workers in the underdeveloped countries which constitute the periphery of capitalist internationalism. See Wallerstein (1974), although his description is a megasystems one and is not racialized or gendered in the ways I have modified it.
63. Fernández-Kelly (1983: 70).
64. Ong (1987).
65. U.S. Department of Commerce, Bureau of the Census; Stallard et al. (1983); Lefkowitz and Withhorn (1986); and Omolade (1986).
66. As recently as October 26, 1992 in the *San Jose Mercury News* studies were cited showing women's improved financial position in relation to men, listing women's earnings at 72 cents for every man's dollar.
67. Kuhn and Bluestone in Benería and Stimpson, eds. (1987).
68. Ibid., 9.
69. Amott and Matthaei (1996: 19).
70. These figures are from O'Connor, in Benería and Stimpson, eds. (1987).
71. Ong (1987: 97).
72. Enloe (1990a); Fernández-Kelly (1983).
73. See Fernández-Kelly (1983); Ong (1987); and Enloe (1990a).
74. Ong (1987: 148).
75. Fernández-Kelly (1983: 42).
76. Enloe (1990a: 159).

77. Fernández-Kelly (1983: 90).

78. Ong (1987: 156).

79. Report by the Bureau of Labor Statistics and the Bureau of the Census, Second Quarter, 1996.

80. Escobar (1989).

81. See H. White (1987); Jameson (1984); and Foucault (1980b).

82. Escobar (1989: 28).

83. B. Epstein (1991); Sturgeon (1991); and Sturgeon (1995).

84. Laclau and Mouffe (1985).

85. Goodwyn (1978). See Richard Hofstadter's *Age of Reform* (1995), in which he examines the Populist movement in the late nineteenth century United States with the conclusion that the Populists were a reactionary group seeking to overthrow the established democratic government. Also see Turner and Killian (1957); Parsons (1951); Kornhauser (1959); and Gurr (1970).

86. Some excellent accounts of this period are Evans (1980); Chafe (1980); Carson (1981); Breines (1982).

87. B. Epstein (1991). This is a fact that is often overlooked by theorists of the new social movements, yet is a critical piece of the legacy of the movements.

88. See for example Tilly (1978); McCarthy and Zald (1977); Gamson (1984); and most popularly Piven and Cloward (1977).

89. Piven and Cloward (1977).

90. I am indebted here to Noël Sturgeon for her insights regarding resource mobilization theory and the many enlightening conversations we have had and field studies we have done together regarding social movements and social movement theories more generally.

91. Useem (1975).

92. McAdam (1982).

93. For a detailed account of the development of a feminist critique of the sixties movements as it emerged from the movements see Evans (1980); Piercy in Morgan, ed. (1970); Langer (1973); anonymous position paper by women in SNCC (actually written by Mary King and Casey Hayden) 1964 conference, personal files; response paper by Cynthia Washington, personal files and reprinted in Mary King, *Freedom Song* (1987). In addition see Feinman's unpublished manuscript (1988), "Out of the Sandbox: SLATE and the Emergence of a New Left," which details a history of women's relationship to the left at the intersection of the old and new lefts and presents a discussion of the relationship of militance in the sixties movements to the increasing repression of women in those movements.

94. An example of this problem can be seen in the direct action which took place at United Technologies Corporation in Sunnyvale, October 1989. Here

the environmentally oriented Greens formed a coalition with the Alliance to Stop First Strike and the Bay Area Peace Test. They collectively developed statements which included both the environmental hazards of the plant and the nuclear arms issue by discussing the ways that each perpetuated the other. There was a great deal of tension in the coalition as each side expressed concern that its issue was taking a back seat to the other. These organizations did not go on in coalition after the action. However, over time we can see that each learned to make more of the connection in their independent actions. This serves as an example of the down side of temporary coalitions in that the groups did not work together over a long enough period of time, or with the organizational investment to work through the differences.

95. Touraine (1981).

96. Offe (1985).

97. Melucci (1985).

98. Melucci (1980).

99. Sturgeon (1991) and B. Epstein (1991) use this concept to describe the political agenda of the direct action movement. Breines (1982) was actually the first to use this concept to reflect on movement aims in a discussion of the prefigurative politics of the New Left "based on suspicion of hierarchy, leadership and the concentration of power," as a radical challenge to existing society.

100. In Laclau and Mouffe (1985), they describe the hegemonic formation resulting from a series of connections through what they call nodal points (constructed of precise political interests) which can then be used to generate a political position somewhat akin to the concept of a coalition.

101. Laclau and Mouffe (1985: 168).

102. B. Epstein (1991: 247–49).

103. For some examples see Piercy (1970); Evans (1980); and also see Morgan, ed. (1970), for a collection of early movement writings.

104. B. Epstein (1991).

105. For several more in depth accounts of the Women's Pentagon Actions see the following texts: Pines (1981); King in L. Jones, ed. (1983); and B. Epstein (1991).

106. B. Epstein (1991: 228).

107. Sturgeon (1991: 121).

108. Joreen (Jo Freeman) in Koedt et al., eds. (1973).

109. Sturgeon (1991: 285).

110. Her term to describe the movement's own theoretical action production. Sturgeon uses the concept of direct theory to account for the direct action movements' "practices and structures as a form of theorizing through practice,

a praxis I call 'direct theory,' a lived analysis of contemporary domination and resistance." Sturgeon in Darnovsky et al. (1995: 36).

111. Enloe (1983) and Cohn (1987).

112. See Herbert (1997) for a depth analysis of the ways that women in the military manage their gender in order to manage the effects of the delineation of proper gender performances for soldier women.

Notes to Chapter 3

The epigraph is Schlafly's response to the numbers of women deployed in the Gulf War.

1. Hartsock in Stiehm, ed. (1984: 149).

2. Kerber in Challinor and Beisner, eds. (1987: 1–21). Also see Kerber (1980) for a more detailed history of the relationship of women to the production of Revolutionary America.

3. Mink in Gordon, ed. (1990: 92–122); and Mink (1995).

4. See also Goodman (1979).

5. Kerber (1980).

6. My initial understandings of martial citizenship have come from Gwendolyn Mink in the process of teaching with her on the development of democratic practice in the history of the United States. I also first learned to think about the construction of the liberal state and the relationship of private to public spheres within it in precisely gendered form through teaching with Wendy Brown on the question of gender justice in liberal capitalism. Each of their exacting teaching methods inspired my research and deeply shaped my understandings of the politics of the gendered state. Though, of course, they may not recognize traces of their thoughts in mine!

7. Kerber (1987).

8. Ibid., 2.

9. For a discussion about the formative connections between republican mother citizens and white supremacy, see Mink in Gordon, ed. (1990: 92–122). For a provocative discovery of the ways in which the racialized component of the formation of the welfare state is often left out of the story, see these comparative quotes: Mink at 97 (Gordon, ed. 1990) and Paula Baker at 63 (Gordon, ed. 1990). Both authors discuss the motivations of the women reformers. Mink presents the statement of Rheta Childe Dorr as the women reformers' strategy to link uplift with racial purity, while by omitting race as a component of the quote Baker can suggest that it was merely about strategies of uplift through domesticity.

10. Quote from Benjamin Franklin, "Observations Concerning the Increase of Mankind," quoted in Takaki (1993: 79).

11. Mink (1990, 1995).

12. See Haraway (1989) for the way that this racialization of citizenship was constructed in the sciences, "naturalizing" the superiority of whites as evolved beings.

13. Mink (1995). Delany quoted in Takaki (1993: 131–32).

14. Kerber in Challinor and Beisner, eds. (1987: 1–21).

15. See John Butler (1980); and Butler in Dietz et al., eds. (1991); Foner (1974); and Takaki (1993).

16. Butler in Dietz et al., eds. (1991: 27–50).

17. After the Civil War, many newly enfranchised African Americans also perceived and acted on the link between citizenship and economic power by seeking land ownership to secure citizenship.

18. *The Color of Honor: The Japanese-American Soldier in WWII* (San Francisco, CA: Cross Current Media; National Asian American Telecommunications Association [distributor], 1987). Of course, several Japanese Americans sued the federal government for unequal protection due to being jailed in the internment camps. This led to the landmark civil rights ruling in *Korematsu*. One figure of this period, George Yamada, was first jailed in the conscientious objector camp in California and then removed—against great protest from his fellow COs—to the internment camp. See Goosen (1997).

19. Mink (1990).

20. Ibid., 92–95.

21. Ibid., 94.

22. For studies of the masculinist culture of the armed forces see Karst (1991).

23. Takaki (1993: 131, 152).

24. Mink (1995: 18–23).

25. John Butler (1980); Dietz et al., eds. (1991); Foner (1974), and B. Moore (1991).

26. See Wheelwright (1989); Burgess (1994); Blanton (1993); and figures such as the famous and differently documented "Molly Pitcher" of the American Revolution; and Deborah Samson, whose fictionalized autobiography, *The Female Review,* recounted her incognito martial service in the American Revolution (her husband collected a widower's pension based on her service) De Pauw (1998: 125–31).

27. Lafin (1967). Note also that women taking up arms in civil wars, women (mis)taken for men and impressed off the streets, and women caught in the crossfire are topics not covered in this project. See also R. Hall (1993).

28. Elshtain (1987).

29. Gluck (1987); Honey (1984); Wise and Wise (1994); and Summerfield (1989).

30. Morden (1990); Larson (1995); and Gruhitz-Hoyt (1995).

31. Ebbert and Hall (1993).

32. For documentation of women's long-standing support work see Bridenthal et al., eds. (1984); Enloe (1983, 1990a); Summerfield (1989); and Elshtain (1987).

33. Enloe (1990a); Sturdevant and Stoltzfus (1992); Fusco (1992); and Committee on Armed Services, Military Personnel and Compensation Subcommittee, House of Representatives (1988).

34. Bridenthal (1984); and Summerfield (1989).

35. For details on this history see Kessler-Harris (1982); Milkman (1985).

36. See Sturdevant and Stoltzfus (1992); Enloe (1990a, 1993b); Barry (1995); and Kirk and Okazawa-Rey (1998).

37. Holm (1982).

38. Merriman (1998).

39. The WAVES were later integrated to the Navy but women were still referred to as WAVES until well into the 1970s.

40. Jordan and Enloe (1985: 106).

41. This move to integrate the forces by race further eroded the 1857 Supreme Court ruling in *Dred Scott v. Sanford* (19 HOW, 393, 420) where one of the key proofs that African Americans were not citizens was that they were not, officially, allowed in combat.

42. Kirby (1980).

43. See Keppler papers collection, Resource Center for Nonviolence, Santa Cruz, California. For an instructive history of women's work against World War II in the CO camps, see Goosen (1997).

44. Karst (1991); Bennecke and Dodge (1990); Shilts (1994).

45. Holm (1982).

46. Binkin and Bach (1977). This story is covered in detail in Morden (1990). These first two women were Brigadier General Anna Mae Hays, Chief of the Army Nurse Corps, and Brigadier General Elizabeth P. Hoisington, Director of WAC (Women's Army Corp). The first was a medical specialist and the second an administrator. It would be a number of years yet for a woman to be made General based on her actual martial service.

47. B. Moore (1991).

48. Jordan and Enloe (1985); and Morden (1990: 347–50).

49. See B. Moore (1990, 1991, 1995).

50. Rogan (1981) gives an extended treatment of the culture of the base in

terms of gender relations. She does not discuss the race demonstrations which occurred at the base during this same time period.

51. Rogan (1981: 158).

52. Shilts (1994: 107–8).

53. Herbert (1997).

54. This argument is supported in Bennecke and Dodge (1990) and further supported by 1996 research in legal organizations analyzing the conditions for lesbians and gays in the forces since Clinton's "Don't Ask, Don't Tell, Don't Pursue" policy went into effect.

55. Statement culled from www.now.org/military/.

56. As quoted in Binkin and Bach (1977: 14).

57. Information in this section was culled from several sources including Geraci (1995); Holm (1982); Zimmerman (1995); Jordan and Enloe (1985); and Witherspoon (1988).

58. The Pentagon issued this directive in the year 1972 through the Central All-Volunteer Task Force, U.S. Department of Defense.

59. Klare (1981).

60. In the late 1970s President Carter issued an executive order for the development of a strategy called the Rapid Deployment Force. This strategy was implemented in the Reagan administration as a light mobile fighting wing that could be drawn from a variety of divisions custom tailored to the specific battle.

61. Binkin and Bach (1977).

62. The heroic stature of former chair of the Joint Chiefs of Staff General Colin Powell is testament to the changes that have developed in the racial hierarchy of the forces and of American politics more generally. First, in his role as the former chair he was the highest ranking African American male or female in the armed forces. Well respected by the mainstream of electoral politics and by the public, he was (and still is) a powerful political figure, or at least a glorified pawn in the electoral tokenism business. His invitation to a presidential bid in 1996 was further evidence of this perceived opening in racial relations and especially by virtue of the validation of his martial service. His sobering refusal to run for president, in part influenced by the fears that his presidential bid was particularly life threatening because he was African American, was in stark contradiction to how seemingly nonthreatening a political figure he cut.

63. 1981 Defense Manpower Data Center figures from Binken and Eitelberg et al. (1982); and Verduga and Grafton (1988).

64. Young (1982).

65. Holm (1982: 270).

66. Becraft (1991). Racial/ethnic categories are the armed forces'.

67. U.S. Department of Defense (1995).

68. Office of the Secretary of Defense (1996).

69. B. Moore (1991: 365).

70. Ibid.

71. See Carson (1981) and Chafe (1980); Isserman (1987); and McAdam (1982).

72. For some examples see Evans (1980); Breines (1982); Echols (1989); and D'Emilio (1983).

73. Fenner (1995: 580).

74. *Rostker v. Goldberg* (453 U.S. 57, 1981).

Notes to Chapter 4

1. Although, as Fenner (1995) has shown, it was not the first time the question of women's role in the forces was raised, I think that this was the first time the question was stabilized enough as a public issue to remain a salient question and to see its stakes deepened in debates over strategic approaches to its resolution.

2. Berry (1986: 56–59).

3. *Congressional Record* (1972).

4. For historical and political accounts of the ERA ratification struggles of the 1970s and early 1980s I am relying on Berry (1986); Boles (1979); Equal Rights Amendment Project (1976); Mansbridge (1986); and Stimpson, ed. (1972). For right wing accounts of the threat of the ERA see Schlafly (1977); and for analyses of the right wing attacks on ERA see Brady and Tedin (1976); Felsenthal (1981); Harding (1981); and Petchesky (1981). Sonia Alvarez first turned me on to the right wing women's writings. I am grateful to her for her reading lists and stimulating discussion on this material.

5. Mansbridge (1986).

6. Felsenthal (1981).

7. Equal Rights Amendment Project (1976).

8. Berry (1986); Ehrenreich (1981).

9. See especially Schlafly (1977).

10. Hunter (1981) used this term to describe a symbol laden with meaning and used as a political sign. The ERA came to represent for the New Right the sign of moral, political, and social deterioration.

11. Schlafly (1974).

12. Berry (1986: 65).

13. Boles (1979: 94).

14. Ibid.; Brady and Tedin (1976); Berry (1986); Ehrenreich (1981).

15. Flake (1984: 86).

16. Deutchman and Prince-Embry (1982).

17. Viguerie (1981).

18. Schlafly (1977: 76).

19. Hildebrand (1976).

20. Ibid.

21. 531 F. 2d 114, 2d Circuit, 1976. Prior to this case the issue was heard in the lower courts on several different occassions. *Struck v. Secretary of Defense* (460 F. 2d 1372, 9th Circuit, 1971) and *Guitierrez v. Laird* (346 F. Supp. 289) both found that discharging pregnant women was a military necessity on the grounds of rational basis for sex classification. By 1972, *Robinson v. Rand* (340 F. Supp. 37, D. Colo, 1972) found that discharging pregnant service women violated their due process rights.

22. Holm (1982: 301–2). Jeanne Holm, Major General, USAF (ret), is one of the pioneering women in the Armed Forces. She fought for women's access to the Forces, and maintained a stellar record and a series of firsts for herself. She has written a book cited above, which is by far the most thorough and accurate account of the history of women in the Forces that I have encountered. Her work is impressive by all accounts.

23. Parr (1983: 240–41).

24. 455 Supp. 291, D.D.C., 1978.

25. "Testimony of General Fred C. Weyand," *H.R. 9832 to Eliminate Discrimination Based on Sex with Respect to the Appointment and Admission of Persons to the Service Academies* (Washington, DC: Government Printing Office, 1975: 166), as quoted in Binkin and Bach (1977: 43).

26. Zimmerman (1995).

27. Quotes from Zimmerman (1995: 236–37). The article referred to in the *New Republic* by Burke (1992) was "Dames at Sea." Burke (1993) presents a more extended treatment of the topic in "Inside the Clubhouse."

28. See front page of the *San Jose Mercury News,* January 13, 1994, which paired a picture and story of Shannon Faulkner with a story on Les Aspin lifting the Risk Rule and thus allowing women access to more combat-related jobs. Also Faludi (1994).

29. This debate has caught my attention on the listserve for Minerva Center, H-MINERVA@msu.edu, during the month of April 1996. In it, proponents of women's military careers vilify or vindicate Faulkner because of her symbolic stature

30. Faludi (1994).

31. Eisenstein (1981).

32. U.S. National Commission on the Observance of International Women's Year (1978: 42).

33. Ibid., 51.

34. "Opposing Views" (1975).

35. U.S. National Commission on the Observance of International Women's Year (1978: 89).

36. Schlafly (1977); Gilder (1975).

37. Schlafly (1977: 98).

38. Quoted in Rowes (1979).

39. See Conover and Gray (1983) for a discussion from a social movement theoretical perspective on how the STOP ERA campaign was so successful. See also Felsenthal (1981) on how Schlafly became the leader of the anti-ERA campaigns by the late 1970s, in charge of all the anti-ERA campaigns in the unratified states.

40. Binkin and Bach (1977).

41. Ibid., 1–2.

42. Ibid., 98–101.

43. Ibid., 109–10.

Notes to Chapter 5

1. Chapkis and Wings (1981: 18).

2. *San Francisco Chronicle*, March 3, 1980: A 12.

3. Senate Manpower and Personnel Subcommittee (1980).

4. As quoted in Holm (1982: 359).

5. NOW National Board (1980).

6. Mansbridge (1986: 86).

7. *United States v. O'Brien* (391 U.S. 367, 377, 1968); *United States v. Follon* (407 F. 2d 621, 7th Circuit, 1969); *United States v. Cook* (311 F. Supp. 618, WD Pa., 1970); *Gilligan v. Morgan* (413 U.S. 1, 10, 1973); *Schlesinger v. Ballard* (419 U.S. 498, 510, 1975); and *United States v. Reiser* (532 F. 2d 673, 9th Circuit, 1976).

8. *U.S. v. St. Clair* (291 F. Supp. 122, 1968).

9. Rhode (1989: 99).

10. NOW *amicus curiae*, as quoted in Tiffany in Chapkis, ed. (1981: 38).

11. Ibid.

12. *Rostker v. Goldberg* (453 U.S. 57, 1981).

13. W. Williams (1982).

14. Enloe is instructive here in the work she does to uncover women's participation in militarism. See Enloe (1983, 1990a); Stiehm's analysis (1982) demonstrates for us the ways that women's and men's non-resistance to martial

enactments is the equivalent of consent because of the benefits reaped from being protected.

15. K. Jones in Elshtain and Tobias, eds. (1990: 127).

16. Ibid., 128.

17. Elshtain, in Elshtain and Tobias, eds. (1990: 265).

18. U.S. Department of Defense (1988b).

19. Holm (1982).

20. Shilts (1994: 379–80).

21. Holm (1982).

22. Jordan and Enloe (1985).

23. B. Moore (1991).

24. Jordan and Enloe (1985); see Francine D'Amico in Weinstein and White, eds. (1997).

25. House Armed Services Committee (1995).

26. Karst (1991); Shilts (1994: 376–79, 532).

27. Bennecke and Dodge (1990); Shilts (1994); Karst (1991); and Blacksmith, ed. (1992).

28. Shilts (1994: 561).

29. Office of the Secretary of Defense (1988).

30. B. Moore (1991: 370).

31. U.S. Department of Defense (1988a).

32. Ibid., ii.

33. Ibid., v; Judith Merkinson of GABRIELA paper presented at the International Sociologists Association conference, University of California, Santa Cruz, May 19, 1996.

34. See Sturdevant and Stoltzfus (1992); and Enloe (1990b).

35. See Dworkin (1987); MacKinnon (1987); and Rubin (1975).

36. U.S. Department of Defense (1988a: v).

37. Ibid., 10.

38. Ibid., 22.

39. Testimony of Judith Gibson, Committee on Armed Services, Military Personnel and Compensation Subcommittee, House of Representatives (1988: 24).

40. Testimony of Mrs. Sydney Hickey (ibid., 41).

41. Sturdevant and Stoltzfus (1992). For a discussion of the development of controls on male soldiers for venereal disease and the medical surveillance of brothels by military police certifying "clean prostitutes" see Brandt (1985); and for a discussion of the situation of prostitutes during the Vietnam War in parts of the Pacific Rim see Brownmiller (1975), especially regarding the creation of

R&R areas and the certification of Vietnamese prostitutes by Army medics. Bringing these issues up to date and generating a new international feminist antimilitarist activism on the issues is the organization East Asia-U.S. Women's Network Against U.S. Militarism. See Kirk and Okazawa-Rey in Lorentzen and Turpin, eds. (1998).

42. See Enloe (1990); Sturdevant and Stoltzfus (1993); Fusco (1992: 20); Kirk and Okazawa-Rey (1998).

43. Testimony by Carolyn Becraft, Committee on Armed Services, Military Personnel and Compensation Subcommittee, House of Representatives (1988: 63).

44. See Harris and King, eds. (1989); and the nonviolent direct action handbooks for Seabrook, Diablo Canyon, Mothers and Others Day Actions, and Lockheed: Stop First Strike, all in personal files.

45. This issue about both sexes coming together ignores and denies the sexual activity already well established, if underground, among lesbian soldiers and among gay soldiers, especially in the period where the troops were totally sex-segregated (recalling my earlier account of lesbians in the Women's Army Corp).

Notes to Chapter 6

The epigraph is a summary of the argument in Haraway (1985: 65–107).

1. See Fenner (1995: 596).

2. Bray in De Pauw (1991b).

3. Ibid.

4. Ibid.

5. Committee on Armed Services, Military Personnel and Compensation Subcommittee, House of Representatives, (1990).

6. Jehn statement (ibid., 23).

7. Cahill statement, (ibid., 78).

8. Sergeant Justice statement (ibid.).

9. Major Kucharczyk statement (ibid., 88).

10. Captain Conley statement (ibid., 88–89). This statement is tragically highlighted by the suicide of Admiral Boorda in May 1996.

11. Women's Research and Education Institute (1990). Note the racial categories are the Department of Defense's.

12. This is the story where a young girl came before the committee hearings on whether to go to war against Iraq and testified that she had seen Iraqi soldiers raid a Kuwaiti hospital and overturn scores of incubators with Kuwaiti babies in them. She was emotional and effective in spurring the congressmen on to a just

war. It was later revealed that she was the daughter of a high ranking Kuwaiti official and that the story was fabricated.

13. U.S. Department of Defense (1992).

14. Randolph (1991).

15. An earlier version of this chapter was published within an article titled "Reweaving the New World Order: An Ecofeminist Analysis," in Darnovsky et al. (1995).

16. De Pauw (1991c).

17. Reinhold (1991).

18. During the summer of 1992, stories emerged in the press about women soldiers being raped both as prisoners of war and by fellow male soldiers, providing fuel for the argument that women need to be protected from the battlefield. The women's positions were that they expected to be treated poorly as prisoners of war and saw no need for special dispensation. A story about a male soldier who claims to have been raped got very short shrift in the media and by Congress.

19. M. Thompson (1993).

20. Russell (1989); Cohn (1987); Cohn (1990); nonviolence preparation handbooks: "Lockheed: Stop First Strike," "Mother's and Others Day," "Diablo," in personal files; Feinman in Darnovsky et al., eds. (1995).

21. In 1980, 8 women were targeted as suspected lesbians aboard the *USS Norton Sound*. In 1988, 70 suspected lesbians were targeted for investigation at Parris Island, and 30 suspected lesbians were targeted on the *USS Yellowstone*. See Bennecke and Dodge (1990); and Weber (1993), an anthology of anonymous, first hand, lesbian accounts of life in the forces.

22. See "Armed Forces Target Lesbians" (1993), includes chart from General Accounting Office figures. For broader discussion see Bennecke and Dodge (1990); and Shilts (1994).

23. Shilts (1994: 719).

24. Quotes from Tucker (1993).

25. See Herbert (1998) for an extended account of the ways in which women manage their gender to further their military careers.

26. Phyllis Schlafly, President Eagle Forum, in debate with Patricia Ireland, President NOW, at Stanford University, May 4, 1993.

27. Zimmerman (1995). Another recent book on the Navy which presents, from the point of view of servicemembers, a more encouraged and forward looking account of the Navy and the Tailhook scandal is Ebbert and Hall (1993).

28. These were culled from her reading of Mack and Connell (1980). For a more contemporary analysis of these "folk traditions" as she wryly names them see Burke (1993), and "Pernicious Cohesion" in Stiehm, ed. (1996: 205–19).

29. Committee on Armed Services, Military Personnel and Compensation Subcommittee, House of Representatives, Defense Policy Panel (1992b). Another major hearing was held in 1994 to follow up on the implimentation of earlier policy changes addressing each of the services: Committee on Armed Services, House of Representatives, (1994).

30. Ruddick (1982).

31. Note that several of the members of the Presidential Commission were members of the Heritage Foundation, and of Concerned Women of America.

32. Tuten in Goldman, ed. (1982); Gilder (1979); Horowitz (1992); Schlafly (1977); Donnelly (1992); Cropsey (1980); Yarbrough (1985); and Mitchell (1989).

33. John Butler (1991); and Foner (1974).

34. Note that the 104th Congress fought to pull the U.S. out of the collective peacekeeping efforts and retain military autonomy in those actions. It is also a coincidence worth further study that women are given broader access at the moment when the forces are downsizing, and preoccupied with base closures and base clean-ups.

35. Enloe (1992, 1993b).

36. See Zimmerman (1995) for the most thorough account of the Tailhook event, hearings, and repercussions.

37. Francke (1997); and S. White (1992).

38. House Armed Services Committee draft of Defense Appropriations Act Fiscal 1993.

39. De Pauw (1991a).

40. Hereinafter referred to as PCR.

41. In November 1995, for instance, women soldiers in Israel petitioned for access to combat roles which, contrary to popular understanding in the states, have been off limits to Israeli women soldiers.

42. Ebbert and Hall (1993).

Notes to Chapter 7

1. In 1995, the Army had completed a report indicating that women soldiers, when trained extensively were able to develop the appropriate upper body strength for participation in hand to hand combat. Women soldiers are still restricted from ground combat.

2. This refers to the Cleaver family in the sit-com "Leave it to Beaver," that, along with a number of other family shows in its time (1950s and early 1960s) presented a model of the nuclear family as heterosexual, white, and extremely nuclear. These families were also characterized by strictly divided gender roles:

mom at home with the children, and dad off to work 9 to 5. The resilience of the myth of this model can be seen in the right wing and fundamentalist, as well as mainstream, fervent longing for and hearkening toward a renewal of the good old days where nuclear families solved all social—and economic—problems. Coontz (1992) carefully evaluates the fallacy of this myth by demonstrating the multitudinous ways in which nuclear families were neither independent, nor ideal. Meyerowitz, ed. (1994) likewise edited a collection of essays that delivers the same message about the economic, social, and political realities for women in that most longed after period.

3. For example, see Karst (1991); Enloe (1990a, 1993b).

4. It is important to note that the National Archives holds all the records from the reports in Record Group 220, which were generated under the Commission's auspices. I choose not to compare the Record Groups to this official report because I am interested in figuring out the import of this public representation of the debate over women's roles and the material represented in the official report is the material agreed on by the commission members of majority in each recommendation vote.

5. For accounts of this period in American history see especially Kutler (1982); and Mitford (1956).

6. Mathews (1992). This story is also recounted in Zimmerman (1995: 138).

7. See Public Law 102-190, Government Printing Office, 1991.

8. See for example Donnelly in Blacksmith, ed. (1992).

9. Finch (1994).

10. PCR, 98–99.

11. Coco Fusco, interview with Ninotchka Rosca of GABRIELA (the international Filipina women's rights organization) in "Army Rules," *Village Voice*, August 11, 1991, 20.

12. Women have been training in and training others in Air Force and Naval fighter aircraft since the mid 1970s especially and in Armed Forces supply aircraft since the World Wars.

13. PCR, 97.

14. Addis (1994) and Gray (1997).

15. PCR, 19.

16. The Supreme Court resolved questions of discrimination against workers who are pregnant or potentially pregnant in its decision on *U.A.W. v. Johnson Controls, Inc.* (111 Supr. Ct. 1196, 1991). Here the court specifically stated that Title VII as amended through the Pregnancy Disabilities Act, expressly prohibited job discrimination on the basis of pregnancy, this included—as was specific for this case—the question of job exclusion to protect a fetus, or its potential presence.

17. PCR, 42.

18. Ibid., 43.

19. Ibid., 49.

20. Testimony before the commission, September 11, 1992 (PCR, 84).

21. PCR, 46.

22. Ibid., 46.

23. See especially Horowitz (1992).

24. PCR, 59–60.

25. Zimmerman (1995: 195–215) also remarks upon this silence as no consideration inside the commission was given to the forms of discrimination faced by the women soldiers. Schlafly makes a public comment about the incapacity of women to soldier if they weren't able to defend themselves at Tailhook.

26. "Combat Roles for Women a Step Closer" (1993).

27. Representative William Dannemeyer (R-CA) quoted in the *Philadelphia Inquirer*, December 10, 1992.

28. For background archival material on lesbians in the forces since the 1950s see Bérubé and D'Emilio (1984); and Humphrey (1990). For first-hand accounts of lesbians in the forces (with pseudonyms of course) see Weber (1993).

29. Quoted in M. Thompson (1992).

30. Shilts (1994: 743–4).

31. RAND (1993) (MR-323-OSD).

32. Memorandum from the Secretary of Defense, Les Aspin, January 13, 1994.

33. Santoli (1995). The Defense Authorization Act FY2000 includes provisions for extended access to food stamps on bases.

Notes to Chapter 8

1. B. Moore (1996).

2. Addis (1994: 18).

3. See ibid.

4. Firestone (1970).

5. See Haraway (1997); and although not particularly feminist, the important work on the impact of technology on war and soldiering in Gray (1997) in which he discusses the development and deployment of new versions of weaponry unreliant on gendered bodies, but rather simply useable bodies.

6. See Barasch (1983).

7. See especially Cohn (1987: 687–718); Hartsock in Stiehm, ed. (1983).

8. Satchell as quoted in Gray (1997).

9. Ibid., 202.

10. See Cohn (1990).

11. See her autobiographical essay "An Officer and a Feminist" in D'Amico and Weinstein, eds. (1999).

12. It is interesting, I think, to note here that in most accounts of the war it is referred to not as a war but as Operation Desert Storm. An image that conveys the relief of rain to a parched area? At least it does not mark the experience with the ravages of real wars. In fact, control of the press in the war contributed to this image most directly.

13. U.S. Department of Defense (1992).

14. A study released by the Army Research Institute of Environmental Medicine indicated that women can be trained to perform with the upper body strength required for ground combat duty, and is beginning to cause a ruckus about breaking down the last barrier to combat roles for women. *Santa Cruz Sentinel,* January 30, 1996, A-1,12.

15. Stiehm in Stiehm, ed. (1996: 292). As a side note, this book in its paperback form presents on the cover the first African American woman Naval Flight Officer. This is the first general book on women in the military that I am aware of showcasing a woman of color on the cover.

16. Conversation with Ferguson at the "Frontline Feminisms: Women, War, and Resistance" Conference (January 1996) in response to my paper where I first explored these film images.

17. Thanks to Maia Feinman Welcher for reminding me of her name.

18. Herbert (1998).

19. While this is being dealt with, if unevenly, at the legal level in the forces it remains a problem forces wide.

20. Kirk Childress, Esq., Staff Attorney, Service Members Legal Defense Network, http://www.sldn.org.

BIBLIOGRAPHY

Abramovitz, Mimi. *Regulating the Lives of Women: Social Welfare Policy.* Boston: South End, 1988.

Abzug, Bella. "Women and the Fate of the Earth: The World Women's Congress for a Healthy Planet." *Woman of Power* 20 (spring 1991): 26–27.

Abzug, Bella, and Mim Kelber. *Gender Gap.* Boston: Houghton Mifflin, 1984.

Adams, Judith Porter. *Peacework: Oral Histories of Women Peace Activists.* Boston: Twayne, 1990.

Addis, Elisabetta. "Women and the Consequences of Being a Soldier." In Addis et al., eds., *Women Soldiers,* 1994.

Addis, Elisabetta, Valeria Russo, and Lorenza Sebesta, eds. *Women Soldiers: Images and Realities.* New York: St. Martin's, 1994.

Aglietta, Michel. "Phases of U.S. Capitalist Expansion." *New Left Review* 110 (1978): 17.

———. *A Theory of Capitalist Regulation: The U.S. Experience.* London: Verso, 1979.

Albert, Michael, and David Dellinger. *Beyond Survival: New Directions for the Disarmament Movement.* Boston: South End, 1979.

Albrecht-Heide, Astrid. "The Peaceful Sex." In Chapkis, ed., *Loaded Questions,* 1981.

Alcoff, Linda. "Cultural Feminism versus Post-Structuralism: The Identity Crisis in Feminist Theory." *Signs* 13 (1988): 405–36.

Allport, Catherine G. *We Are the Web: The Women's Encampment for a Future of Peace and Justice.* New York: Artemis Project, 1984.

Ambrose, Stephen E. *Rise to Globalism: American Foreign Policy Since 1938.* New York: Penguin Books, 1971, 1985.

Amott, Teresa, and Julie Matthaei. *Race, Gender, and Work: A Multi-cultural Economic History of Women in the United States.* Boston: South End, 1996.

Amsden, Alice. "Third World Industrialization: 'Global Fordism' or a New Model?" *New Left Review* 182 (July–August 1990): 3–31.

Anderson, Benedict. *Imagined Communities.* London: Verso, 1983.

Angus, Ian, and Sut Jhally, eds. *Cultural Politics in Contemporary America.* New York: Routledge, 1989.

Anzaldúa, Gloria. *Borderlands/La Frontera: The New Mestiza.* San Francisco: Spinsters/Aunt Lute, 1987.

Arendt, Hannah. *Eichmann in Jerusalem.* New York: Viking, 1963a.

———. *On Revolution.* New York: Viking, 1963b.

"Armed Forces Target Lesbians." *San Jose Mercury News,* February 14, 1993, A1, A30.

Asch, Beth J. (National Defense Research Institute). *Designing Military Pay: Contributions and Implications of the Economics Literature.* Santa Monica, CA: RAND, 1993.

Asch, Beth, and John T. Warner. (National Defense Research Institute). *A Theory of Military Compensation and Personnel Policy.* Santa Monica, CA: RAND, 1994.

Attebury, Lieutenant Colonel Mary Ann (USAFR). "Women and Their Wartime Roles." *Minerva: Quarterly Report on Women and the Military* 8, no. 1 (spring 1990): 11–28.

Barasch, Marc Ian. *The Little Black Book of Atomic War.* New York: Dell, 1983.

Barkalow, Carol. "Women Have What It Takes." *Newsweek,* August 5, 1991, 30.

Barkalow, Carol, with Andrea Raab. *In the Men's House: An Inside Account of Life in the Army by One of West Point's First Female Graduates.* New York: Poseidon, 1990.

Barrett, Michèle, and Mary McIntosh. "Ethnocentrism and Socialist-Feminist Theory." *Feminist Review* 20 (1985): 23–47.

Barry, Kathleen. *The Prostitution of Sexuality: The Global Exploitation of Women.* New York: New York University Press, 1995.

Barry, U. "Women and the Military System." *Women's Studies International Forum* 13, no. 3 (1990): 281.

Bartky, Sandra Lee. "Foucault, Femininity, and the Modernization of Patriarchal Power." In Diamond and Quinby, eds., *Feminism and Foucault,* 1988.

———. *Femininity and Domination.* New York: Routledge, 1990.

Becker, Susan. *The Origins of the Equal Rights Amendment: American Feminism between the Wars.* Westport, CT: Greenwood, 1981.

Becraft, Carolyn. "Women in the Military: Bureaucratic Policies and Politics." *Bureaucrat* 18, no. 3 (fall 1989): 33–36.

———. "Women in the Military, 1980–1990." Washington, DC: Women's Research and Education Institute, June 1990.

———. *Women in the Armed Services: The War in the Persian Gulf.* Washington, DC: Women's Research and Education Institute, 1991.

Bell, Bruce D., and Robert B. Iadeluca. "The Origins of Volunteer Support for Army Family Programs." *Minerva: Quarterly Report on Women and the Military* (fall 1988): 26–43.

Bell, Daniel. *The Coming of Post-Industrial Society: A Venture in Social Forecasting*. New York: Basic Books, 1973.

Benería, Lourdes, and Catharine R. Stimpson, eds. *Women, Households, and the Economy*. New Brunswick, NJ: Rutgers University Press, 1987.

Bennecke, Michelle, and Kirstin Dodge. "Military Women in Nontraditional Job Fields: Casualties in the Armed Forces War on Homosexuals." *Harvard Women's Law Journal* 13 (spring 1990): 215–50.

Berry, Mary Frances. *Why ERA Failed: Politics, Women's Rights and the Amending Process of the Constitution*. Bloomington: Indiana University Press, 1986.

Berry, Mary Frances, and John Blassingame. *Long Memory: The Black Experience in America*. New York: Oxford University Press, 1982.

Bérubé, Allan, and John D'Emilio. "The Military and Lesbians during the McCarthy Years." *Signs* 9, no. 4 (summer 1984): 759–75.

Bhavnani, Kum Kum, and Margaret Coulson. "Transforming Socialist Feminism: The Challenge of Racism." Special issue: *Socialist Feminism: Out of the Blue* in *Feminist Review* 23 (summer 1986): 81–92.

Biehl, Janet. "What Is Social Ecofeminism?" *Green Perspectives* 11 (October 1988): 1–8.

———. *Rethinking Ecofeminist Politics*. Boston: South End, 1990.

Binkin, Martin, and Shirley J. Bach. *Women and the Military*. Washington, DC: Brookings Institute, 1977.

Binkin, Martin, Mark Eitelberg, et al. *Blacks in the Military*. Washington, DC: Brookings Institute, 1982.

Bird, Elizabeth Ann R. "The Social Construction of Nature: Theoretical Approaches to the History of Environmental Problems." *Environmental Review* 11, no. 4 (winter 1987): 255–64.

Blacksmith, E. A., ed. *Women in the Military*. New York: H. W. Wilson Co., 1992.

Blanton, DeAnne. "Women Soldiers in the Civil War." *Prologue* 25 (spring 1993): 27–33.

Block, Fred. *Revising State Theory: Essays in Politics and Postindustrialism*. Philadelphia: Temple University Press, 1987.

Boggs, Carl. *Social Movements and Political Power*. Philadelphia: Temple University Press, 1986.

Boles, Janet K. *The Politics of the Equal Rights Amendment*. New York: Longman, 1979.

Bondurant, Joan V. *Conquest of Violence: The Gandhian Philosophy of Conflict*. Berkeley: University of California Press, 1965.

Bookchin, Murray. *Post-Scarcity Anarchism*. San Francisco: Ramparts, 1971.

Bookman, Ann, and Sandra Morgen, eds. *Women and the Politics of Empowerment.* Philadelphia: Temple University Press, 1988.

Boris, Eileen, and Peter Bardaglio. "The Transformation of Patriarchy: The Historic Role of the State." In Diamond, ed., *Families, Politics, and Public Policy,* 1983.

Bowles, Samuel, David M. Gordon, and Thomas Weisskopf. *Beyond the Wasteland: A Democratic Alternative to Economic Decline.* New York: Anchor, 1983.

Brady, David W., and Kenneth Tedin. "Ladies in Pink: Religion and the Anti-ERA Movement." *Social Science Quarterly* 56, no. 4 (March 1976): 564.

Brandt, Alan M. *No Magic Bullet: A Social History of Venereal Disease in the United States since 1880.* New York: Oxford University Press, 1985.

Breines, Winifred. *Community Organization in the New Left, 1962–1968: The Great Refusal.* New York: Praeger Publishers, CBS Inc., 1982.

Brenner, Joanna. "Beyond Essentialism: Feminist Theory and Strategy in the Peace Movement." In Davis and Sprinker, eds., *Reshaping the U.S. Left,* 1988.

Brenner, Robert, and Mark Glick. "The Regulation Approach—Theory and History." *New Left Review* 188 (July–August 1991): 45–119.

Bridenthal, Renata, Atina Grossman, and Marion Kaplan, eds. *When Biology Became Destiny: Women in Weimar and Nazi Germany.* New York: Monthly Review Press, 1984.

Bridenthal, Renata, and Claudia Koontz, eds. *Becoming Visible: Women in European History.* Boston: Houghton Mifflin, 1977.

Brooks-Higgenbotham, Evelyn. "The Problem of Race in Women's History." In Weed, ed., *Coming to Terms,* 1989.

Brown, Wendy. *States of Injury: Power and Freedom in Late Modernity.* Princeton, NJ: Princeton University Press, 1995.

Brownmiller, Susan. *Against Our Will: Men, Women, and Rape.* New York: Simon and Schuster, 1975.

Buckingham, William A., Jr., ed. *Defense Planning for the 1990s.* 10th National Security Affairs Conference. Washington, DC: National Defense University Press, 1984.

Buffalo Symposium. "Feminist Discourse, Moral Values and the Law—A Conversation." *Buffalo Law Review* 34 (1985): 11–87.

Bunch, Charlotte. *Feminism in the 1980s: Facing Down the Right.* Denver, CO: Charlotte Bunch, 1981.

Burgess, Lauren Cook, ed. *An Uncommon Soldier: The Civil War Letters of Sarah Rosetta Wakeman.* Pasadena, MD: The Minerva Center, 1994.

Burke, Carol. "Dames at Sea: Life in the Naval Academy." *New Republic,* August 17, 1992, 16.

————. "Inside the Clubhouse." *The Women's Review of Books* 10, no. 5 (February 1993): 20–21.

————. "Pernicious Cohesion." In Stiehm, ed., *Its Our Military Too!* 1996.

Butler, John S. *Inequality in the Military: The Black Experience*. Saratoga, CA: Century 21 Publishing, 1980.

————. "The Military as a Vehicle for Social Integration: The Afro-Amercian Experience as Data." In Dietz et al., eds., *Ethnicity, Integration, and the Military*, 1991.

Butler, Judith. *Gender Trouble: Feminism and the Subversion of Identity*. New York: Routledge, 1990.

Cagan, Leslie. "Women and the Anti-Draft Movement." *Radical America* 14, no. 5 (September–October 1980): 9–19.

Caldecott, Leonie, and Stephanie Leland. *Reclaim the Earth: Women Speak Out for Life on Earth*. London: Women's Press, 1983.

Cambridge Women's Peace Collective. *My Country Is the Whole World: An Anthology of Women's Work on Peace and War*. London: Pandora, 1984.

Campbell, D'Ann. "Combating the Gender Gulf." *Minerva: Quarterly Report on Women in the Armed Forces* 10, no. 3–4 (fall–winter 1992): 13–41.

Cantarow, Ellen. *Moving the Mountain: Women Working for Social Change*. Old Westbury, NY: Feminist Press, 1980.

Carson, Clayborn. *In Struggle: SNCC and the Black Awakening of the 1960s*. Boston: Harvard University Press, 1981.

Chafe, William H. *Civilities and Civil Rights*. New York: Oxford University Press, 1980.

Challinor, Joan R., and Robert L. Beisner, eds. *Arms at Rest*. New York: Greenwood, 1987.

Chapkis, Wendy, ed. *Loaded Questions: Women in the Military*. Amsterdam: Transnational Institute, 1981.

Chapkis, Wendy, and Mary Wings. "The Private Benjamin Syndrome." In Chapkis, ed., *Loaded Questions*, 1981.

Chuchryk, Patricia. "Subversive Mothers: The Women's Opposition to the Military Regime in Chile: 1973–1983." Paper presented at the XIII International Congress of Latin American Studies Association, Boston, October 1986.

Cock, Jacklyn. "Women and the Military: Implications for Demilitarization in the 1990s in South Africa." *Gender and Society* 8, no. 2 (June 1994): 152–69.

Cock, Jacklyn, and Laurie Nathan. *War and Society: The Militarisation of South Africa*. Capetown: David and Phillip, 1989.

Cohen, Jean. "Between Crisis Management and Social Movements." *Telos* 12 (1982): 21–40.

———. "Rethinking Social Movements." *Berkeley Journal of Sociology* 28 (1983): 97.

———. "Strategy or Identity: New Theoretical Paradigms and Contemporary Social Movements." *Social Research* 52 (1985): 663–716.

Cohn, Carol. "Sex and Death in the Rational World of Defense Intellectuals." *Signs* 12 (summer 1987): 687–718.

———. "Clean Bombs and Clean Language." In Elshtain and Tobias, eds., *Women, Militarism, and War,* 1990.

Collins, Patricia Hill. "The Social Construction of Black Feminist Thought." *Signs* 14, no. 4 (1989): 745–73.

Combahee River Collective. "A Black Feminist Statement." In Hull et al., eds., *All the Women Are White, All the Blacks Are Men, But Some of Us Are Brave,* 1982.

"Combat Roles for Women a Step Closer." *Congressional Quarterly Almanac,* 1993, 463.

Committee on Armed Services, House of Representatives. *Hearings on the National Defense Authorization Act for Fiscal Years 1992 and 1993—HR 2100.* HASC 102–11. Hearings, March 13, 20, April 17, and July 31, 1991. Washington, DC: U.S. Government Printing Office, 1991.

———. *Sexual Harassment of Military Women and Improving the Military Complaint System.* 103d Congress, 2d session. March 9, 1994. HASC 103–44. Washington, DC: U.S. Government Printing Office, 1994.

———. *Assignment of Army and Marine Corps Women under the New Definition of Ground Combat.* 103d Congress, 2d session. October 6, 1994. Washington, DC: U.S. Government Printing Office, 1995a.

———. *An Assessment of Racial Discrimination in the Military: A Global Perspective.* 103d Congress, 2d session. Committee print no. 8. December 30, 1994. Washington, DC: U.S. Government Printing Office, 1995b.

Committee on Armed Services, Military Personnel and Compensation Subcommittee, House of Representatives. *Women in the Military.* 100th Congress, 1st and 2d sessions. October 1 and November 19, 1987, and February 4, 1988. Washington DC: U.S. Government Printing Office, 1988.

———. *Women in the Military: Hearings.* 101st Congress, 1st session. March 20, 1990. HASC 101–63. Washington, DC: U.S. Government Printing Office, 1990.

———. *Parenting Issues of Operation Desert Storm.* 102d Congress, 1st session. Hearing, February 19, 1991. Washington, DC: U.S. Government Printing Office, 1991.

———. *Implementation of the Repeal of the Combat Exclusion on Female Aviators.* 102d Congress, 2d session. January 29, 1992. Washington, DC: U.S. Government Printing Office, 1992a.

———, Defense Policy Panel. *Women in the Military: The Tailhook Affair and the Problem of Sexual Harassment.* 102d Congress, 2d session. September 14, 1992. Washington, DC: U.S. Government Printing Office, 1992b.

———, Military Forces and Personnel Subcommittee. *Women in Combat.* Hearing, May 12, 1993. HASC 103–20. 103d Congress, 2d Session. Washington, DC: U.S. Government Printing Office, 1994.

Congressional Record. Vol. 18, pt. 7 (1972): 9337.

Conover, Pamela Johnston, and Virginia Gray. *Feminism and the New Right.* New York: Praeger Publishers, 1983.

Cook, Alice, and Gwyn Kirk. *Greenham Women Everywhere.* London: Pluto, 1983.

Cooke, Miriam, and Angela Woollacott, eds. *Gendering War Talk.* Princeton, NJ: Princeton University Press, 1993.

Cooney, Robert, and Helen Michalowski. *The Power of the People.* Culver City, CA: Peace Press, 1977.

Coontz, Stephanie. *The Way We Never Were.* New York: Basic Books, Harper-Collins, 1992.

Cropsey, Seth. "Women in Combat?" *Public Interest* 61 (fall 1980): 58–73.

Dallmayr, Fred R. "Hegemony and Democracy: On Laclau and Mouffe." *Strategies* (fall 1988): 29–49.

Daly, Mary. *Gyn/Ecology.* Boston: Beacon, 1978.

D'Amico, Francine. "Women at Arms: The Combat Controversy." *Minerva: Quarterly Report on Women in the Armed Forces* 8, no. 2 (summer 1990): 1–19.

———. "Tailhook: Deinstitutionalizing the Military's 'Woman Problem.'" In Weinstein and White, eds., *Wives and Warriors,* 1997.

D'Amico, Francine, and Laurie Weinstein, eds. *Gender Camouflage: Women and the U.S. Military.* New York: New York University Press, 1999.

Darnovsky, Marcy. "The Green Challenge to Consumer Culture." Ph.D. diss., University of California, 1996.

Darnovsky, Marcy, Barbara Epstein, and Richard Flacks, eds. *Cultural Politics and Social Movements.* Philadelphia: Temple University Press, 1995.

David, Miriam. "Moral and Maternal: The Family in the Right." In Ruth Levitas, ed., *The Ideology of the New Right.* Cambridge: Polity, 1986.

Davis, Angela. "Reflections on the Black Woman's Role in the Community of Slaves." *Black Scholar* 12, no. 6 (1981): 2–15.

———. *Women, Culture, and Politics.* New York: Vintage, 1990.

Davis, Mike. "Fordism in Crisis: A Review of Michel Aglietta's 'Regulation et crisis: L'experience des Etats-Unis.'" *Review* 2 (1978).

———. *Prisoners of the American Dream*. London: Verso, 1986.

Davis, Mike, and Michael Sprinker, eds. *Reshaping the U.S. Left: Popular Struggles in the 1980s*. New York: Verso, 1988.

D'Eaubonne, Françoise. "Feminism or Death." In Elaine Marks and Isabelle de Courtivron, eds. *New French Feminisms: An Anthology*. Amherst: University of Massachusetts Press, 1980.

de Lauretis, Teresa, ed. *Feminist Studies/Critical Studies*. Bloomington: Indiana University Press, 1986.

———. "The Essence of the Triangle." *Differences* 1 (summer 1989): 3–37.

Delsman, Mary A. *Everything You Need to Know about ERA*. Riverside, CA: Maranza, 1975.

D'Emilio, John. *Sexual Politics, Sexual Communities*. Chicago: University of Chicago Press, 1983.

Deming, Barbara. *Remembering Who We Are*. Tallahassee: Pagoda Publishing, 1981.

———. *We Are All Part of One Another: A Barbara Deming Reader*. Ed. Jane Meyerding. Philadelphia: New Society Publishers, 1984.

De Pauw, Linda Grant. "Congress Repeals Restrictions on Women Flying Combat Aircraft." *Minerva Bulletin Board* 4, no. 2 (summer 1991a): 3–4.

———. "Combat Controversy Destroyed Her Career Says Linda Bray." *Minerva Bulletin Board* 4, no. 2 (summer 1991b): 4.

———. "Media Study finds Gender Bias in Gulf War Coverage." *Minerva Bulletin Board* 4, no. 2 (summer 1991c): 8–9.

———. *Battlecries and Lullabies: Women in War from Prehistory to the Present*. Norman: University of Oklahoma Press, 1998.

De Santes, Marie. "The Middle East Crisis: A Dilemma for Women." *Off Our Backs* 20, no. 8 (October 1990): 10.

Deutchman, Iva E., and Sandra Prince-Embry. "Political Ideology of Pro- and Anti-ERA Women." *Women and Politics* 2, nos. 1, 2 (spring-summer 1982): 39–55.

Devilbiss, M. C. "Women in Combat: A Quick Summary of the Arguments on Both Sides." *Minerva: Quarterly Report on Women and the Military* 8, no. 1 (spring 1990): 29–30.

Diamond, Irene, ed. *Families, Politics, and Public Policy: A Feminist Dialogue on Women and the State*. New York: Longman, 1983.

Diamond, Irene, and Lee Quinby, eds. *Feminism and Foucault*. Boston: Northeastern University Press, 1988.

Diamond, Irene, and Gloria Orenstein. "Ecofeminism: Weaving the Worlds Together." *Feminist Studies* 14 (summer 1988): 368–70.

———, eds. *Reweaving the World: The Emergence of Ecofeminism*. San Francisco, CA: Sierra Club Books, 1990.

Dickey, Jim. "Gays Sent to Gulf Face Added Isolation." *San Jose Mercury News,* February 24, 1991, A15.

Dienstfrey, Stephen. "Women Veterans Exposure to Combat." *Armed Forces and Society* 4, no. 4 (summer 1988): 549–88.

Dietz, Henry, Jerrold Elkin, and Maurice Roumani, eds. *Ethnicity, Integration, and the Military*. IUS Special Editions on Armed Force and Society, no. 3. Boulder, CO: Westview, 1991.

di Leonardo, Micaela. "Morals, Mothers, and Militarism." *Feminist Studies* 11, no.3 (fall 1985): 599–617.

Dill, Bonnie Thornton. "Race, Class, and Gender: Prospects for an All-Inclusive Sisterhood." *Feminist Studies* 9, no. 1 (spring 1983): 131.

Donnelly, Elaine. "Mommy, What Did You Do in the War?" In Blacksmith, ed., *Women in the Military,* 1992.

Dorsen, Norman, ed. *The Rights of Groups*. New York: ACLU, 1984.

Dunivin, Karen O. "Military Culture: Change and Continuity." *Armed Forces and Society* 20, no. 4 (summer 1994): 531–47.

Dworkin, Andrea. *Right Wing Women*. New York: Perigee Books, 1978.

———. *Intercourse*. New York: Free Press, 1987.

Dyer, Kate, ed. *Gays in Uniform*. Boston: Alyson Publishing, 1990.

Ebbert, Jean, and Marie Beth Hall. *Crossed Currents: Navy Women from WWI to Tailhook*. Washington, DC: Brassey's, 1993.

Echols, Alice. "The New Feminism of Yin and Yang." In Ann Snitow, Christine Stansell, and Sharon Thompson, eds., *Power of Desire: The Politics of Sexuality*. New York: Monthly Review Press, 1983.

———. *Daring to Be Bad: Radical Feminism in America, 1967–1975*. Minneapolis: University of Minnesota Press, 1989.

Eder, Klaus. "The 'New Social Movements': Moral Crusades, Political Pressure, or Social Movements." *Social Research* 52, no. 4 (winter 1985): 869.

Edsall, Thomas Byrne. *The New Politics of Inequality*. New York: Norton, 1984.

Ehrenreich, Barbara. "The Women's Movement: Feminist and Anti-Feminist." *Radical America* 15, nos. 1, 2 (spring 1981): 93–101.

———. *The Hearts of Men: American Dreams and the Flight from Commitment*. Garden City, NJ: Anchor/Doubleday, 1984.

———. *Blood Rites: Origins and the History of the Passions of War*. New York: Metropolitan Books, 1997.

Eisenstein, Zillah. "Anti-Feminism in the Politics and the Election of 1980." *Feminist Studies* 7, no. 2 (summer 1981): 187–205.

———. "The Sexual Politics of the New Right." In Keohane et al., eds., *Feminist Theory*, 1982.

———. "The State, the Patriarchal Family, and Working Mothers." In Diamond, ed., *Families, Politics, and Public Policy*, 1983.

———. *Feminism and Sexual Equality.* New York: Monthly Review Press, 1984.

———. *The Female Body and the Law.* Berkeley: University of California Press, 1988.

———, ed. *Capitalist Patriarchy and the Case for Socialist Feminism.* New York: Monthly Review Press, 1979.

Elshtain, Jean Bethke. "Antigone's Daughters: Reflections on Female Identity and the State." In Diamond, ed., *Families, Politics, and Public Policy*, 1983.

———. *Women and War.* New York: Basic Books, 1987.

Elshtain, Jean Bethke, and Sheila Tobias, eds. *Women, Militarism, and War: Essays in History, Politics, and Social Theory.* Savage, MD: Rowman and Littlefield, 1990.

Emberley, Julia, and Donna Landry. "Coverage of Greenham and Greenham as 'Coverage.'" *Feminist Studies* 15, no. 3 (fall 1989): 485–99.

Engels, Frederick. "Origin of the Family, Private Property, and the State." In *The Marx and Engels Reader.* Ed. Robert C. Tucker. New York: Norton, 1972.

English, Deirdre, Barbara Epstein, Barbara Haber, and Judy Maclean. "The Impasse of Socialist Feminism: A Conversation." *Socialist Review* 15, no. 1 (1985): 93–110.

Enloe, Cynthia. *Ethnic Soldiers.* Athens: University of Georgia Press, 1980.

———. "The Military Model." In Chapkis, ed., *Loaded Questions*, 1981a.

———. "NATO's Interest in Women: The Lesson Machine." In Chapkis, ed., *Loaded Questions*, 1981b.

———. *Does Khaki Become You? The Militarization of Women's Lives.* Boston: South End, 1983.

———. "United States Country Report: Women and Militarization in the Late 80s." *Minerva: Quarterly Report on Women and the Military* 6, no. 2 (spring 1988): 72–92.

———. *Bananas, Beaches, and Bases: Making Feminist Sense of International Politics.* Berkeley: University of California Press, 1990a.

———. "Bananas, Beaches, and Patriarchy." In Elshtain and Tobias, eds., *Women, Militarism, and War*, 1990b.

———. "The Politics of Constructing the American Woman Soldier as a Professionalized 'First Class Citizen': Some Lessons from the Gulf War." *Minerva: Quarterly Report on Women and the Military* 10, no. 1 (spring 1992): 14–31.

———. "The Right to Fight: Feminist Catch-22." *Ms.* 4, no. 1 (July–August 1993a): 87.

———. *The Morning After: Sexual Politics at the End of the Cold War.* Berkeley: University of California Press, 1993b.

Epstein, Barbara (Easton). "Feminism and the Contemporary Family." *Socialist Review* 8, no. 3 (May–June 1978): 11–37.

———. "The Culture of Direct Action: Livermore Action Group and the Peace Movement." *Socialist Review* 15, no. 4–5 (1985): 31–61.

———. "The Politics of Prefigurative Community: The Non-violent Direct Action Movement." In Davis and Sprinker, eds., *Reshaping the U.S. Left,* 1988.

———. "Rethinking Social Movement Theory." *Socialist Review* 20, no. 1 (1990): 35–66.

———. *Political Protest and Cultural Revolution.* Berkeley: University of California Press, 1991.

Epstein, Barbara (Easton), and Kate Ellis. "The Pro-Family Left in the United States: Two Comments." *Feminist Review* 14 (June 1983): 35–49.

Epstein, Cynthia Fuchs. *Women in Law.* New York: Basic Books, 1982.

Equal Rights Amendment Project. *Impact ERA.* Millbrae, CA: Les Femmes Publishing, 1976.

Escobar, Arturo. "Social Science Discourse and New Social Movements Research in Latin America: Trends and Debates." Paper presented at the Latin American Studies Association 15th International Conference, San Juan, Puerto Rico, September 21–23, 1989.

Estrich, Susan, and Virginia Kerr. "Sexual Justice." In Dorsen, ed., *The Rights of Groups,* 1984.

Evans, Sara. *Personal Politics: The Roots of Women's Liberation in the Civil Rights Movement and the New Left.* New York: Vintage, 1980.

Falbel, Rita, Irena Klepfitz, and Donna Nevel, eds. *Jewish Women's Call for Peace.* Ithaca, NY: Firebrand Books, 1990.

Faludi, Susan. *Backlash.* New York: Crown Publishers, 1991.

———. "The Naked Citadel." *New Yorker,* September 5, 1994, 62.

Farrow, Lynn, ed. *Anarchism and Feminism.* Brisbane: Brickburner Press, 1981.

Feinman, Ilene Rose. "Reweaving the New World Order: An Ecofeminist Analysis." In Darnovsky et al., eds., *Cultural Politics and Social Movements,* 1995.

———. "Women Warriors/Women Peacemakers: Will the Real Feminists Please Stand Up!" In Lorentzen and Turpin, eds., *The Women and War Reader,* 1998.

Felsenthal, Carol. *The Sweetheart of the Silent Majority.* New York: Doubleday, 1981.

"Feminism and Ecology." Special issue: *Heresies* 4, no. 1, issue 13 (fall 1981).

Fenner, Lorry Marie. "Ideology and Amnesia: The Public Debate on Women in the American Military, 1940–1973." Ph.D. diss., University of Michigan, 1995.

Ferguson, Kathy E. *The Feminist Case against Bureacracy.* Philadelphia: Temple University Press, 1984.

———. *Kibbutz Journal: Reflections on Gender, Race and Militarism in Israel.* Pasadena, CA: Trilogy Books, 1995.

Fernández-Kelly, María Patricia. *For We Are Sold, I and My People: Women and Industry in Mexico's Frontier.* Albany: SUNY Press, 1983.

Ferree, Myrna Marx, and Beth H. Hess. *Controversy and Coalition: The New Feminist Movement.* Boston: Twayne, 1985.

Finch, Capt. Mary. "Women in Combat: One Commissioner Reports." *Minerva: Quarterly Report on Women and the Military* 12, no. 1 (spring 1994).

Fineman, Martha Albertson, and Nancy Sweet Thomadsen. *At the Boundaries of Law: Feminism and Legal Theory.* New York: Routledge, 1991.

Finley, Lucinda M. "Transcending Equality Theory." *Columbia Law Review* (1986): 1118–82.

Firestone, Shulamith. *The Dialectic of Sex.* New York: Bantam Books, 1970.

Flacks, Richard. *Making History.* New York: Columbia University Press, 1988.

Flake, Carol. *Redemptorama: Culture, Politics, and the New Evangelicalism.* Garden City, NJ: Anchor, 1984.

Flanders, Laura. "Mothers Fight on Many Fronts." *New Directions for Women* 20, no. 20 (March–April 1991): 1.

Flax, Jane. "Postmodernism and Gender Relations Theory." *Signs* 12 (1987): 621–24.

Foner, Jack. *Blacks and the Military in American History: A New Perspective.* New York: Praeger, 1974.

Foucault, Michel. *Discipline and Punish: The Birth of the Prison.* Trans. Alan Sheridan. New York: Vintage Books, 1979.

———. *The History of Sexuality, Vol. 1: An Introduction.* Trans. Robert Hurley. New York: Random House/Vintage, 1980a.

———. *Power/Knowledge: Selected Interviews and Other Writings 1972–1977.* Trans. and ed. Colin Gordon. New York: Pantheon Books, 1980b.

Francke, Linda Bird. *Ground Zero: The Gender Wars in the Military.* New York: Simon and Schuster, 1997.

Frank, Andre Gunder, and Martha Fuentes. "Nine Theses on Social Movements." *Economic and Political Weekly,* August 29, 1987, 1503–10.

Frank, Dana. "Housewives, Socialists, and the Politics of Food: The 1917 New York Cost-of-Living Protests." *Feminist Studies* 11, no. 2 (1985): 255–85.

Fraser, Nancy. *Unruly Practices: Power, Discourse and Gender in Contemporary Social Theory.* Minneapolis: University of Minnesota Press, 1989.

———. "Struggle over Needs: An Outline of a Socialist Feminist Critical Theory of Late-Capitalist Political Culture." In Gordon, ed., *Women, the State, and Welfare,* 1990.

Freeman, Jo. "The Tyranny of Structurelessness." In Koedt et al., eds., *Radical Feminism,* 1973.

———. *The Politics of Women's Liberation.* New York: Longman, 1975.

———, ed. *Social Movements of the Sixties and Seventies.* New York: Longman, 1983.

Fuentes, Annette. "Women Warriors? Equality, Yes—Militarism, No." *Nation,* October 28, 1991, 516.

Fuentes, Annette, and Barbara Ehrenreich. *Women in the Global Factory.* New York: Institute for New Communications, 1983.

Fusco, Coco. "Army Rules." *Village Voice,* August 11, 1992, 20.

Fuss, Diana. *Essentially Speaking.* New York: Routledge, 1989.

Gamson, William A. "Organizing the Poor: A Review Essay on Piven and Cloward's *Poor People's Movements.*" *Theory and Society* 13 (1984): 567–85.

Garson, Barbara. *The Electronic Sweatshop.* New York: Penguin Books, 1988.

Gemmette, Elizabeth Villiers. "Armed Combat: The Women's Movement Mobilizes Troops in Readiness for the Inevitable Constitutional Attack." *Women's Rights Law Reporter* 12, no. 2 (summer 1990): 89–101.

Geraci, Karen Sellers. "Women in Combat." *Minerva: Quarterly Report* 12, no. 1 (spring 1995): 19–35.

Geras, Norman. "Post-Marxism?" *New Left Review* 163 (May/June 1987): 40–82.

———. "Ex-Marxism without Substance: Being a Real Reply to Laclau and Mouffe." *New Left Review* 169 (May–June 1988): 34–61.

Giddings, Paula. *When and Where I Enter.* New York: William Morrow, 1984.

Gilder, George F. *Sexual Suicide.* New York: Bantam Books, 1975.

———. "The Case against Women in Combat." *New York Times Magazine,* January 28, 1979, 29–31, 44, 46.

Gill, Sandra K. "Attitudes toward the ERA." *Social Perspectives* 28 (1986): 441.

Gilroy, Paul. *Ain't No Black in the Union Jack.* London: Hutchinson Press, 1987.

———. "Cultural Studies and Ethnic Absolutism." In Lawrence Grossberg, Paula A. Treichler, and Cary Nelson, eds., *Cultural Studies.* New York: Routledge, 1992.

Gitlin, Todd. *The Whole World Is Watching: The Media in the Making and Unmaking of the New Left.* Berkeley: University of California Press, 1980.

———. *The Sixties: Years of Hope, Days of Rage.* New York: Bantam, 1987.

Gluck, Sherna Berger. *Rosie the Riveter Revisited: Women, the War, and Social Change.* Boston: G. K. Hall, 1987.

Goldman, Nancy Loring, ed. *Female Soldiers—Combatants or Noncombatants? Historical and Contemporary Perspectives.* Westport, CT: Greenwood, 1982.

Goldstein, Leslie Friedman. *The Constitutional Rights of Women: Cases in Law and Social Change.* Madison: University of Wisconsin Press, 1988.

Goodman, Jill Laurie. "Women, War and Equality: An Examination of Sex Discrimination in the Military." *Women's Rights Law Reporter* 4 (summer 1979): 175–90.

Goodwyn, Lawrence. *The Populist Moment.* New York: Oxford University Press, 1978.

Goosen, Rachel Waltner. *Women against the Good War: Conscientious Objection and Gender on the American Homefront, 1941–1947.* Chapel Hill: University of North Carolina Press, 1997.

Gordon, Linda, ed. *Women, the State, and Welfare.* Madison: University of Wisconsin Press, 1990.

Graham, Julie. "Fordism/Post-Fordism, Marxism/Post-Marxism: The Second Cultural Divide?" *Rethinking Marxism* 4 (spring 1991): 39–58.

Gramsci, Antonio. *Selections from the Prison Notebooks.* Trans. and ed. Quinton Hoare and Geoffrey Nowell Smith. New York: International Publishers, 1978.

Gray, Chris (Crystal) Hables. *Computers as Weapons and Metaphors: The U.S. Military 1940–90.* Ph.D. diss., University of California, Santa Cruz, 1991.

———. *Postmodern War: The New Politics of Conflict.* New York: Guilford, 1997.

"The Great Goddess." Special issue: *Heresies* 2, no. 1, issue 5 (fall 1982).

Green Letter. *War and Resistance.* San Francisco: *Green Letter* 6, no. 4 (spring 1991).

Greens' Committees of Correspondence SPAKA Conference Proceedings, 1989. Personal files.

Griffin, Susan. *Woman and Nature: The Roaring inside Her.* New York: Harper & Row, 1978.

———. *A Chorus of Stones: The Private Life of War.* New York: Doubleday, 1992.

Gruhitz-Hoyt, Olga. *They Also Served: American Women in World War II.* Secaucus, NJ: Carol Publishing Group, 1995.

Gruner, Elliot. "Women as POWs: Forgetting the Rhonda Cornum Story." *Minerva: Quarterly Report on Women and the Military* 13, no. 1 (spring 1996): 1–14.

Gurr, Ted. *Why Men Rebel.* Princeton, NJ: Princeton University Press, 1970.

Gyorgy, Anna, and friends. *No Nukes: Everyone's Guide to Nuclear Power.* Boston: South End, 1979.

Habermas, Jürgen. *Theory and Practice.* London: Heineman Press, 1974.

Hackworth, Colonel David H. "War and the Second Sex." *Newsweek,* August 5, 1991, 24–29.

———. "How to Make a Real Warrior." *Newsweek,* September 4, 1995, 28.

Hale, Mariclaire, and Leo Kanowitz. "Women and the Draft: A Response to Critiques of the Equal Rights Amendment." *Hastings Law Journal* 23 (1971): 199.

Hall, Richard. *Patriots in Disguise: Women Warriors of the Civil War.* New York: Marlowe and Co., 1993.

Hall, Stuart. "Gramsci's Relevance for the Study of Race and Ethnicity." *Journal of Communication Inquiry* 10, no. 2 (1986): 5–27.

———. *Hard Road to Renewal: Thatcherism and the Left.* London: Verso, 1988.

Hall, Stuart, and Martin Jacques, eds. *New Times: The Changing Face of Politics in the 1990s.* London: Lawrence and Wishart, 1989.

Halliday, Fred. *The Making of the Second Cold War.* London: Verso, 1983.

Hansen, Karen V., and Ilene J. Phillipson, eds. *Women, Class and the Feminist Imagination: A Socialist Feminist Reader.* Philadelphia: Temple University Press, 1990.

Haraway, Donna. "A Manifesto for Cyborgs: Science, Technology and Socialist Feminism in the 1980s." *Socialist Review* 15, no. 2 (1985): 65–108.

———. "Situated Knowledges: The Science Question in Feminism and the Privilege of Partial Perspective." *Feminist Studies* 14, no. 3 (1988): 575–99.

———. *Primate Visions: Gender, Race, and Nature in the World of Modern Science.* New York: Routledge, 1989.

———. "Gender for a Marxist Dictionary: The Sexual Politics of a Word." In *Simians, Cyborgs and Women.* New York: Routledge, 1991.

———. *Modest_Witness@Second_Millenium.FemaleMan©_Meets_Oncomouse[a]: Feminism and Technoscience.* New York: Routledge, 1997.

Harding, Susan. "Family Reform Movements: Recent Feminism and Its Opposition." *Feminist Studies* 7, no. 1 (spring 1981): 51.

Harford, Barbara, and Sarah Hopkins, eds. *Greenham Common: Women at the Wire.* London: Women's Press, 1984.

Harris, Adrienne, and Ynestra King, eds. *Rocking the Ship of State.* Boulder, CO: Westview, 1989.

Harris, Louis, et al. *Survey of Female Veterans: A Study of the Needs, Attitudes, and Experiences of Women Veterans.* Veterans Administration, Washington, DC, 1985.

Harrison, Bennett, and Barry Bluestone. *The Great U-Turn: Corporate Restructuring and the Polarization of America.* New York: Basic Books, 1988.

Hartmann, Heidi. "Capitalism, Patriarchy and Job Segregation by Sex." *Signs* 1, no. 2 (1976): 137–69.

———. "The Family as Locus of Gender, Class and Poltical Struggle: The Example of Housework." *Signs* 6, no. 3 (1981): 366–94.

Hartsock, Nancy. "The Barracks Community in Western Political Thought: Prologomena to a Feminist Critique of War and Politics." In Stiehm, ed., *Women and Men's Wars,* 1982.

———. *Money, Sex and Power: Toward a Feminist Historical Materialism.* New York: Longman, 1983.

———. "Prologue to a Feminist Critique of War and Politics." In Steihm, ed., *Women's Views of the Political World of Men,* 1984.

Harvey, David. *The Condition of Postmodernity.* Cambridge, MA: Basil Blackwell, 1989.

Hatch, Orrin. "Women's Initiative." Congressional Record, United States Senate. 98th Congress, 1st Session. November 18, 1983.

Hayes, Lois. "Separatism and Disobedience: the Seneca Women's Peace Encampment." *Radical America* 17, no. 4 (July–August 1983): 55–64.

Haynes, Karima. "Sisters in Arms." *Ebony* 49, no. 5 (March 1994): 118.

Hegel, Georg Wilhelm Friedrich. *Reason in History.* Trans. Robert S. Hartman. Indianapolis: Bobbs-Merrill, 1953.

———. *Philosophy of Right.* Trans. T. M. Knox. New York: Oxford University Press, 1976.

Herbert, Melissa. "Guarding the Nation, Guarding Ourselves: The Management of Hetero/Homo/Sexuality among Women in the Military." *Minerva: Quarterly Report on Women and the Military* 15, no. 2 (summer 1997): 60–76.

———. *Camouflage Isn't Only for Combat: Gender, Sexuality, and Women in the Military.* New York: New York University Press, 1998.

Hershey, Lieutenant General Lewis B., Director Selective Service System. *Legal Aspects of Selective Service.* Washington, DC: U.S. Government Printing Office, 1969.

Hewlett, Sylvia Ann. *A Lesser Life: The Myth of Women's Liberation in America.* New York: William Morrow, 1986.

Hildebrand, Ginny, "How to Answer the Right Wing: Behind the Campaign to Stop the ERA." *Militant* 40, no. 9 (March 5, 1976): 9.

Hirsch, Joachim. "The Crisis of Fordism, Transformations of the 'Keynesian' Security State, and New Social Movements." *Research in Social Movements, Conflicts and Change* 10 (1988): 43–55.

Hoff, Joan. *Law, Gender, and Injustice: A Legal History of U.S. Women.* New York: New York University Press, 1991.

Hofstadter, Richard. *Age of Reform: From Bryan to F.D.R.* New York: Knopf, 1955.

Holland-Cunz, Barbara. "Women as Nature's Self-Awareness: Prospects of the Ecofeminist Movement." Paper presented at UCSC Social Movements and Cultural Politics Conference, Santa Cruz, CA, March 1991.

Holm, Maj. Gen. Jeanne, USAF (Ret). *Women in the Military: An Unfinished Revolution.* Novato: Presidio, 1982.

Honey, Maureen. *Creating Rosie the Riveter: Class, Gender, and Propaganda.* Amherst: University of Massachusetts Press, 1984.

hooks, bell. *Ain't I a Woman? Black Women and Feminism.* Boston: South End, 1981.

———. *Feminist Theory: From Margin to Center.* Boston: South End, 1982.

———. *Yearning.* Boston: South End, 1990.

Horkheimer, Max. *Eclipse of Reason.* New York: Oxford University Press, 1947.

Horowitz, David. "The Feminist Assault on the Military." Studio City, CA: The Center for the Study of Popular Culture, n.d. Reprinted in *National Review* 44, no. 19 (October 5, 1992): 46.

Hosek, James R., Christine E. Peterson, and Joanna Zorn Heilbrunnet. *Military Pay Gaps and Caps.* National Defense Research Institute. Santa Monica, CA: RAND, 1994.

House Armed Services Committee. 103d Congress, 2d session. December 30, 1994. Washington, DC: U.S. Government Printing Office, 1995.

House of Representatives. *National Defense Authorization Act for Fiscal Year 1994: Conference Report to Accompany HR 2401.* 103d Congress, 1st session. November 10, 1993. Report 103–35. Washington, DC: U.S. Government Printing Office, 1993.

"House Panel Votes to Let Women Fly Combat Missions." *San Jose Mercury News,* May 9, 1991, A1.

Howes, Ruth H., and Michael R. Stevenson. *Women and the Use of Military Force.* Boulder, CO: Lynn Riener Publishing, 1993.

Huckshorn, Kristin. "War May Curb Women's Role in Military." *San Jose Mercury News,* February 24, 1991, 15A.

Hull, Gloria, Patricia Bell Scott, and Barbara Smith, eds. *All the Women Are White, All the Blacks Are Men, But Some of Us Are Brave: Black Women's Studies.* Old Westbury, CT: Feminist Press, 1982.

Humphrey, Mary Ann. *My Country, My Right to Serve: Experiences of Gay Men and Women in the Military: World War II to the Present.* New York: Harper-Collins, 1990.

Hunter, Allen. "In the Wings: New Right Ideology and Organization." *Radical America* 15, nos. 1, 2 (spring 1981): 113–38.

Huntington, Samuel P. "The United States: Decline or Renewal?" *Foreign Affairs* 67, no. 2 (winter 1988–89): 76–97.

Hurwitz, Deena, ed. *Walking the Red Line: Israelis in Search of Justice for Palestine.* Philadelphia: New Society, 1992.

Isserman, Maurice. *If I Had a Hammer: The Death of the Old Left and the Birth of the New.* New York: Basic Books, 1987.

Jameson, Fredric. "Postmodernism, or the Cultural Logic of Late Capitalism." *New Left Review* 146 (July–August 1984): 53–93.

Jenson, Jane. "Rebel Sons: The Regulation School; An Interview with Alain Lipietz." *French Politics and Society* (September 1987): 17–26.

Jessop, Bob. "Regulation Theory, Post-Fordism, and the State." *Capital and Class* 34 (spring 1988): 147.

Jessop, Bob, Kevin Bonnett, Simon Bromley, and Tom Ling. *Thatcherism: A Tale of Two Nations.* New York: Basil Blackwell, 1989.

Johnson, Barbara. *A World of Difference.* Baltimore: Johns Hopkins University Press, 1987.

Johnson, Karen. "Viewpoint: Soldiers Who Work Together Should Train Together." n.d. www.now.org.

Johnson, Lynn. "Weaving a Web of Life: Women's Pentagon Action, 1981." *WIN,* January 15, 1982.

Jones, Kathleen. "Dividing the Ranks: Women and the Draft." *Women and Politics* 4, no. 4 (winter 1984): 75–87.

Jones, Lynne, ed. *Keeping the Peace.* London: Women's Press, 1983.

Jordan, Harold, and Cynthia Enloe. "Black Women and the Military." *Minerva: Quarterly Report on Women and the Military* 3, no. 1 (winter 1985): 105–16.

Jordan, June. "Requiem for Sara: War's Working Class." *Progressive* 55 (February 1991): 18.

Kairys, D. *The Politics of Law: A Progressive Critique.* New York: Pantheon, 1982.

Kaledin, Euginia. *Mothers and More: American Women in the 1950s.* Boston: Twayne, 1984.

Kaminsky, Amy. "Gender, Race, Raza." *Feminist Studies* 20, no. 1 (spring 1994): 7–31.

Kantrowitz, Barbara, et al. "The Right to Fight." *Newsweek,* August 5, 1991, 22–23.

Kaplan, Temma. "Female Consciousness and Collective Action: The Case of Barcelona: 1910–1918." *Signs* 7 (1982): 545–66.

Karst, Kenneth. "The Pursuit of Manhood and the Desegregation of the Armed Forces." *UCLA Law Review* 38, no. 3 (1991): 499–581.

Katzenstein, Mary Fainsod. "Feminism within American Institutions: Unobtrusive Mobilization in the 1980s." *Signs* 16, no. 1 (autumn 1990): 27–54.

———. "The Spectacle as Political Resistance: Feminist and Gay/Lesbian Politics in the Military." *Minerva: Quarterly Report on Women and the Military* 11, no. 1 (spring 1993): 1–16.

———. *Faithful and Fearless: Moving Feminist Protest inside the Church and Military.* Princeton, NJ: Princeton University Press, 1998.

Keohane, Nannerl O., Michelle Rosaldo, and Barbara Gelpi, eds. *Feminist Theory: A Critique of Ideology.* Chicago: University of Chicago Press, 1982.

Keppler, Roy. Papers. Collection at the Resource Center for Nonviolence, Santa Cruz, CA.

Kerber, Linda K. *Women of the Republic: Intellect and Ideology in Revolutionary America.* Chapel Hill: University of North Carolina, 1980.

———. "'May All Our Citizens Be Soldiers, and All Our Soldiers Citizens': The Ambiguities of Female Citizenship in the New Nation." In Challinor and Beisner, eds., *Arms at Rest,* 1987.

Kessler-Harris, Alice. *Out to Work.* New York: Oxford University Press, 1982.

King, Deborah. "Multiple Jeopardy, Multiple Consciousness: The Context of a Black Feminist Ideology." In Micheline Malson et al., eds., *Feminist Theory in Practice and Process.* Chicago: University of Chicago Press, 1986.

King, Katie. *Theory in Its Feminist Travels.* Bloomington: University of Indiana Press, 1994.

King, Mary. *Freedom Song: A Personal Story of the 1960s Civil Rights Movement.* New York: Morrow, 1987.

King, Ynestra. "Feminism and the Revolt of Nature." *Heresies* 13 (1981): 12–16.

———. "All Is Connectedness: Scenes from the Women's Pentagon Action." In L. Jones, ed., *Keeping the Peace,* 1983.

———. "Towards an Ecological Feminism and a Feminist Ecology." In Rothschild, ed., *Machina ex Dea,* 1983.

———. "What Is Ecofeminism?" *Nation,* December 1987, 730–31.

Kirby, John. *Black Americans in the Roosevelt Era: Liberalism and Race.* Knoxville: University of Tennessee Press, 1980.

Kirk, Gwyn, and Margo Okazawa-Rey. "Military Security: Confronting the Oxymoron." *Crossroads* 60 (April–May 1996): 4–7.

———. "Making Connections: Building an East Asia–U.S. Women's Network against U.S. Militarism." In Lorentzen and Turpin, eds., *The Women and War Reader,* 1998.

Kirkwood, R. Cortland. *Exerpts from Hearings: Presidential Commission on the Assignment of Women in the Armed Forces*. Washington, DC: Department of Communications and Congressional Affairs, 1992.

Klare, Michael T. *Beyond the Vietnam Syndrome: U.S. Interventionism in the 1980s*. Washington, DC: Institute for Policy Studies, 1981.

———. "Policing the Gulf—and the World." *Nation*, October 15, 1990a, 401.

———. "The New World War." *Progressive* 54, no. 11 (November 1990b): 14–17.

Koedt, Anne, Ellen Levine, and Anita Rapone, eds. *Radical Feminism*. New York: Quadrangle, 1973.

Kornblum, Lori S. "Women Warriors in a Man's World: The Combat Exclusion." *Law and Inequality: A Journal of Theory and Practice* 2 (1984): 351.

Kornegger, Peggy. "Anarchism: The Feminist Connection." In Farrow, ed. *Anarchism and Feminism*, 1981.

Kornhauser, William. *The Politics of Mass Society*. New York: Free Press, 1959.

Kotz, David M. "Long Waves and Social Structures of Accumulation: A Critique and Reinterpretation." Unpublished paper, Department of Economics, University of Massachusettes at Amherst. June 1988.

Kuletz, Valerie L. *The Tainted Desert: Environmental Ruin in the American West*. New York: Routledge, 1998.

Kurin, Kytha. "Anarcha-Feminism: Why the Hyphen?" In Farrow, ed., *Anarchism and Feminism*, 1981.

Kutler, Stanley I. *The American Inquisition: Justice and Injustice in the Cold War*. New York: Hill and Wang, 1982.

Laclau, Ernesto. "Building a New Left: An Interview with Ernesto Laclau." *Strategies* 1 (fall 1988): 10–29.

Laclau, Ernesto, and Chantal Mouffe. *Hegemony and Socialist Strategy*. London: Verso, 1985.

———. "Post-Marxism without Apologies." *New Left Review* 166 (November–December 1987): 161.

Lafin, John. *Women in Battle*. London: Abelard-Schuman, 1967.

LaHaye, Beverly. *The Restless Woman*. Grand Rapids, MI: Zondervan, 1984.

Landers, Robert K. "Should Women Be Allowed in Combat?" *Congressional Quarterly's Editorial Research Reports* 2, no. 14 (October 13, 1989): 570.

Langer, Elinor. "Notes for Next Time." *Working Papers* (fall 1973): 48–83.

Larson, C. Kay. *'Til I Come Marching Home: A Brief History of Women in World War II*. Pasadena, MD: Minerva Center, 1995.

Lash, Scott, and John Urry. *The End of Organized Capitalism*. Madison: University of Wisconsin Press, 1988.

Lefkowitz, Rochelle, and Ann Withorn, eds. *For Crying Out Loud: Women and Poverty in the United States.* New York: Pilgrim, 1986.

Lenin, V. I. *Women and Society.* New York: International Publishers, 1938.

Lilie, Joyce R., Roger Handberg, Jr., and Wanda Lowry. "Women State Legislators and the ERA: Dimensions of Support and Opposition." *Women and Politics* 2, nos. 1, 2 (spring–summer 1982): 23–38.

Lindgren, J. Ralph, and Nadine Taub. *The Law of Sex Discrimination.* St. Paul, MN: West, 1988.

Linton, Rhoda, and Michelle Whitman. "With Mourning, Rage, Empowerment and Defiance: The 1981 Women's Pentagon Action." *Socialist Review* 12, nos. 63, 64 (May–August 1982): 11–36.

Lipietz, Alain. "New Tendencies in the International Division of Labor: Regimes of Accumulation and Modes of Regulation." In Allen J. Scott and Michael Storper, eds., *Production, Work, Territory: The Geographical Anatomy of Industrial Capitalism.* Boston: Allen Unwin, 1986.

———. *Mirages and Miracles.* London: Verso, 1987.

Littleton, Christine. "Reconstructing Sexual Equality." *California Law Review* 75 (July 1987): 1279–1337.

Lorde, Audre. "The Master's Tools Will Never Dismantle the Master's House." In *Sister/Outsider.* Trumansberg, NY: Crossing, 1984.

Lorentzen, Lois, and Julie Turpin, eds. *The Women and War Reader.* New York: New York University Press, 1998.

Lowe, Marian, and Ruth Hubbard, eds. *Woman's Nature: Rationalizations of Inequality.* New York: Pergamon, 1983.

Lugones, Maria C., and Elizabeth Spellman. "Have We Got a Theory for You! Feminist Theory, Cultural Imperialism, and the Demand for 'the Woman's Voice.'" *Women's Studies International Forum* 6 (1983): 573–81.

Luker, Kristin. *Abortion and the Politics of Motherhood.* Berkeley: University of California Press, 1984.

Luxemburg, Rosa. *Selected Political Writings of Rosa Luxemburg.* Ed. Dick Howard. New York: Monthly Review Press, 1971.

MacDonald, Sharon, Pat Holden, and Shirley Ardener, eds. *Images of Women in Peace and War: Cross-Cultural and Historical Perspectives.* Madison: University of Wisconsin Press, 1988.

MacEwan, Arthur. "International Economic Crisis and the Limits of Macropolicy." *Socialist Review* 9, no. 11 (November–December 1981): 13–138.

———. "What's 'New' about the 'New International Economy'?" *Socialist Review* 21, no. 3–4 (July–December 1991): 111.

Mack, Vice Admiral William (ret.), and Lieutenant Commander Royal W.

Connell. *Naval Ceremonies, Customs, and Traditions.* Annapolis, MD: Naval Institute Press, 1980.

MacKinnon, Catharine. "Feminism, Marxism, and the State: An Agenda for Theory." *Signs* 7 (1982): 227–56.

———. *Feminism Unmodified: Discourses on Life and Law.* Cambridge: Harvard University Press, 1987.

———. *Toward a Feminist Theory of the State.* Cambridge: Harvard University Press, 1989.

———. "Reflections on Sex Equality under the Law." *Yale Law Journal* 100, no. 5 (March 1991): 1281–1328.

Mainardi, Pat. "The Politics of Housework." In Morgan, ed., *Sisterhood Is Powerful,* 1970.

Mall, Janice. "Military as a Ticket to the Mainstream." *Los Angeles Times,* September 15, 1985, 4.

Mandel, Ernest. *Late Capitalism.* London: New Left Books, 1975.

Mann, Herman. *The Female Review: Life of Deborah Sampson.* New York: AMS Press, 1982.

Mansbridge, Jane. *Why We Lost the ERA.* Chicago: University of Chicago Press, 1986.

Marcuse, Herbert. *One Dimensional Man.* Boston: Beacon, 1964.

———. *Counterrevolution and Revolt.* London: Allen Lane, 1972.

Margolis, Maxine. *Mothers and Such: Views of American Women and Why They Changed.* Berkeley: University of California Press, 1984.

Martin, Emily. *The Woman in the Body: A Cultural Analysis of Reproduction.* Boston: Beacon, 1987.

Marx, Karl. "Theses on Feuerbach." *The Marx-Engels Reader.* Ed. Robert C. Tucker. New York: Norton, 1972.

———. *Capital, Vol. 1.* Trans. Ben Fowkes. New York: Vintage, 1977.

Mathews, William. "Don't Expect Sweeping Changes for Women." *Navy Times,* November 2, 1992.

Mayer, Margit. "U.S. and European Theoretical Approaches to Social Movements: From the Sixties to the Eighties." Paper presented at the ASA Conference, Toronto, Canada. November 2–5, 1989.

———, ed. *New Social Movements in Western Europe and the United States.* London: Hutchinson, 1989.

McAdam, Doug. *Political Process and the Development of the Black Insurgency, 1930–1970.* Chicago: University of Chicago Press, 1982.

———. *Freedom Summer.* New York: Oxford University Press, 1988.

McAllister, Pam, ed. *Reweaving the Web of Life: Feminism and Nonviolence.* Philadelphia: New Society, 1982.

———. *You Can't Kill the Spirit*. Philadelphia: New Society, 1988.

McCarthy, John, and Mayer Zald. "Resource Mobilization and Social Movements." *American Journal of Sociology* 82, no. 6 (1977): 100.

McCoy, Melanie. "Combat in the Courts: Gender Equity in the Military: An Analysis of Supreme Court Voting Behavior." *Minerva: Quarterly Report on Women and the Miltiary* 13, nos. 3, 4 (1995): 69–95.

McCullough, Mary B. "Company Commander Reports from Panama." *Minerva Bulletin Board* 3, no. 1 (spring 1990): 1–2.

Melucci, Alberto. "The New Social Movements: A Theoretical Approach." *Social Science Information* 19, no. 12 (1980): 199.

———. "An End to Social Movements? Introductory Paper to the Section on 'New Movements and Change in Organizational Forms.'" *Social Science Information* 23, nos. 4, 5 (1984): 819.

———. "The Symbolic Challenge of Contemporary Movements." *Social Research* 52, no. 4 (1985): 789–816.

———. *Nomads of the Present*. London: Century Hutchinson, 1989.

Merchant, Carolyn. *The Death of Nature*. New York: Harper & Row, 1980.

———. "The Theoretical Structure of Ecological Revolutions." *Environmental Review* 11, no. 4 (winter 1987): 265–74.

Merriman, Molly. *Clipped Wings: The Rise and Fall of the Women Air Force Service Pilots (WASPs) of World War II*. New York: New York University Press, 1998.

Merton, Andrew H. *Enemies of Choice: The Right to Life Movement and Its Threat to Abortion*. Boston: Beacon, 1981.

Meyerowitz, Joanne, ed. *Not June Cleaver: Women and Gender in Postwar America, 1945–1960*. Philadelphia: Temple University Press, 1994.

Mies, Maria. *Patriarchy and Accumulation on a World Scale: Women in the International Division of Labor*. London: Zed Press, 1986.

"Military Manpower Recruiting and Enlistment Results for the Active Component—First Half of Fiscal Year 1990." Washington, DC: U.S. Government Printing Office, 1990.

Milkman, Ruth. *Women, Work, and Protest*. Boston: Routledge & Keegan Paul, 1985.

Miller, James. *Democracy Is in the Streets*. New York: Simon and Schuster, 1987.

Mink, Gwendolyn. *Old Labor and New Immigrants in American Political Development*. Ithaca, NY: Cornell University Press, 1986.

———. "The Lady and the Tramp: Gender, Race, and the Origins of the American Welfare State." In Gordon, ed., *Women, the State, and Welfare*, 1990.

———. *The Wages of Motherhood: Inequality in the Welfare State, 1917–1942*. Ithaca, NY: Cornell University Press, 1995.

Minnow, Martha. *Making All the Difference: Inclusion, Exclusion and American Law*. Ithaca, NY: Cornell University Press, 1990.

Mitchell, Brian. *Weak Link: the Feminization of the American Military*. Washington, DC: Regnery Gateway, 1989.

Mitford, Jessica. *A Fine Old Conflict*. New York: Vintage, 1956.

Mitter, Swasti. *Common Fate, Common Bond: Women in the Global Economy*. New York: Pluto, 1986.

Miyake, Yoshiko. "Women, Work, Family, and the State in Japan, 1868–1990." Ph.D. diss., University of California, 1991.

Moore, Brenda L. "Black, Female, and in Uniform: An African-American Woman in the United States Army, 1973–1979." *Minerva: Quarterly Report on Women and the Military* 8, no. 2 (summer 1990): 62–66.

———. "African-American Women in the U.S. Military." *Armed Forces and Society* 17, no. 3 (1991): 363–84.

———. "Changing Laws and Women of Color in the U.S. Military." *Minerva: Quarterly Report on Women and the Military* 13, nos. 3, 4 (fall–winter 1995): 15–24.

———. *To Serve My Country, to Serve My Race: The Story of the Only African American WACs Stationed Overseas during World War II*. New York: New York University Press, 1996.

Moore, Molly. "Pentagon Renting Cruise Ships for R&R in Gulf." *Washington Post*, December 14, 1990, A1.

Moraga, Cherríe, and Gloria Anzaldúa, eds. *This Bridge Called My Back: Writings by Women of Color*, 2d ed. New York: Kitchen Table, 1983.

Morden, Betty J. *The Women's Army Corp: 1948–1978*. Washington, DC: U.S. Government Printing Office, 1990.

Morgan, Robin, ed. *Sisterhood Is Powerful*. New York: Vintage, 1970.

Moskos, Charles. "Army Women." *Atlantic Monthly* (August 1990): 70–74.

Mouffe, Chantal. "Hegemony and New Political Subjects: Toward a New Concept of Democracy." In Nelson and Grossberg, eds., *Marxism and the Interpretation of Culture*, 1988a.

———. "American Liberalism and Its Critics: Rawls, Taylor, Sandel, and Walzer." *Praxis International* 8, no. 2 (July 1988b): 193–206.

———. "Radical Democracy: Modern or Postmodern?" In Ross, ed., *Universal Abandon?* 1988c.

Mouzelis, Nicos. "Marxism or Post-Marxism." *New Left Review* 167 (January–February 1988): 107.

Murray, Robin. "Fordism and Post-Fordism." In Hall and Jacques, eds., *New Times*, 1989.

Nash, June, and María Patricia Fernández-Kelly, eds. *Women, Men, and the International Division of Labor.* Albany: SUNY Press, 1983.

Nation. Patriotism: Special Issue 253, no. 3 (July 15–22, 1990).

National Commission in the Observance of International Women's Year. *The Spirit of Houston.* Washington, DC: U.S. Government Printing Office, 1978.

Nelson, Cary, and Lawrence Grossberg, eds. *Marxism and the Interpretation of Culture.* Champaign: University of Illinois Press, 1988.

Nordheimer, Jon. "Women's Role in Combat: The War Resumes." *New York Times,* May 26, 1991, A1, A14.

Norman, Elizabeth M. *Women at War: The Story of 50 Military Nurses Who Served in Vietnam.* Philadelphia: University of Pennsylvania Press, 1990.

Northrup, Terrell. "Personal Security, Political Security: The Relationship among Conceptions of Gender, War and Peace." *Research in Social Movements, Conflicts and Change* 12 (1990): 267–99.

NOW National Board. "Opposition to Draft and Registration." January 1980. www.now.org.

NOW National Conference. "Women and War." 1971. www.now.org.

O'Connor, James. *Fiscal Crisis of the State.* New York: St. Martin's, 1973.

Offe, Claus. "New Social Movements: Challenging the Boundaries of Institutional Politics." *Social Research* 52, no. 4 (1985): 817–68.

Office of the Secretary of Defense. *Military Women in the Department of Defense.* Washington DC: U.S. Government Printing Office, 1988.

———. *Defense 95 Almanac.* Issue 5. Washington, DC: U.S. Government Printing Office, 1996.

Omi, Michael, and Howard Winant. *Racial Formation in the United States: From the 1960s to the 1980s.* New York: Routledge & Keegan Paul, 1986.

Omolade, Barbara. *It's a Family Affair: The Real Lives of Black Single Mothers.* New York: Kitchen Table, Woman of Color, 1986.

Ong, Aihwa. *Spirits of Resistance and Capitalist Discipline: Factory Workers in Malaysia.* Albany: SUNY Press, 1987.

"Opposing Views: Is Equal Rights Movement Dead? Interview with Phyllis Schlafly." *U.S. News and World Report,* December 1, 1975, 39–40.

Ortner, Sherry. "Is Female to Male as Nature Is to Culture?" In Michelle Z. Rosaldo and Louise Lamphere, *Woman, Culture, and Society.* Stanford, CA: Stanford University Press, 1974.

Parr, Carol C. "Women in the Military." In Tinker, ed., *Women in Washington,* 1983.

Parsons, Talcott. *The Social System.* New York: Free Press, 1951.

Pateman, Carole. *Participation and Democratic Theory.* Cambridge: Cambridge University Press, 1970.

———. *The Problem of Political Obligation: A Critique of Liberal Theory.* Berkeley: University of California Press, 1985.

———. *The Sexual Contract.* Stanford, CA: Stanford University Press, 1988.

Penley, Constance, and Andrew Ross, eds. *Technoculture.* Minneapolis: University of Minnesota Press, 1991.

People. Special Issue: Mom Goes to War. September 10, 1990.

Petchesky, Rosalind. "Anti-Abortion, Anti-Feminism, and the Rise of the New Right." *Feminist Studies* 7, no. 2 (summer 1981): 206–46.

———. *Abortion and Woman's Choice: The State, Sexuality, and Reproductive Freedom.* Boston: Northeastern University Press, 1984.

Peters, Nancy J., ed. *City Lights Review 5: War after War.* San Francisco: City Lights Books, 1992.

Piercy, Marge. "The Grand Coolie Damn." In Morgan, ed., *Sisterhood Is Powerful,* 1970.

Pierson, Ruth Roach. "'Did Your Mother Wear Army Boots?' Feminist Theory and Women's Relation to War, Peace and Revolution." In MacDonald et al., eds., *Images of Women in Peace and War,* 1988.

Pines, Susan. "Women's Pentagon Action." *WRL NEWS* (January–February 1981): 1.

Piven, Frances Fox, and Richard A. Cloward. *Poor People's Movements.* New York: Vintage, 1977.

Plant, Judith, ed. *Healing the Wounds: The Promise of Ecofeminism.* Philadelphia: New Society, 1989.

Pohl, Frances K. "Tailhook 91: Women, Violence, and the U.S. Navy." *Z Magazine* 7, no. 6 (June 1994): 40.

Presidential Commission on the Assignment of Women to the Armed Forces. *Report to the President.* November 15, 1992. Washington, DC: U.S. Government Printing Office, 1992.

President's Commission on an All Volunteer Armed Force. *The Report of the President's Commission on an All Volunteer Force.* Washington, DC: U.S. Government Printing Office, 1970.

Puget Sound Women's Peace Camp. *We Are Ordinary Women: A Chronicle of the Puget Sound Women's Peace Camp.* Seattle, WA: Seal, 1985.

Ramazanoglu, Caroline, Hamida Kazi, Sue Lees, and Heidi Safia Mirza. "Feedback: Feminism and Racism—Responses to Michèle Barrett and Mary McIntosh." *Signs* 11, no. 22 (1986): 83–105.

RAND National Defense Research Institute. *Sexual Orientation and U.S. Military Personnel Policy: Options and Assessment.* Santa Monica, CA: RAND, 1993.

Randolph, Laura. "The Untold Story of Black Women in the Gulf War." *Ebony* 46, no. 11 (September 1991): 100–107.

Reagon, Bernice Johnson. "Coalition Politics: Turning the Century." In Smith, ed., *Home Girls*, 1983.

Reed, Thomas Vernon. *Fifteen Jugglers, Five Believers: Literary Politics and the Poetics of American Social Movements*. Berkeley: University of California Press, 1992.

Reinhold, Robert. (*New York Times*). "Pin-up: Troops in Persian Gulf Fall for Utah Undercover Cop." *Sacramento Bee*, February 17, 1991, A11.

Reiter, Ranya Rapp, ed. *Toward an Anthropology of Women*. New York: Monthly Review Press, 1975.

Report of the Subcommittee on Manpower and Personnel of the Senate Armed Services Committee. 126th Congress. Record no. 13880 and record 6530–6550. June 10, 1980.

Rhode, Deborah L. *Justice and Gender: Sex Discrimination and the Law*. Cambridge: Harvard University Press, 1989.

Rich, Adrienne. *Of Woman Born: Motherhood as Experience and Institution*. New York: Bantam, 1977.

Riley, Denise. *Am I That Name? Feminism and the Category of Women in History*. Minneapolis: University of Minnesota Press, 1988.

Rogan, Helen. *Mixed Company: Women in the Modern Army*. New York: Putnam, 1981.

Rogin, Michael. *Ronald Reagan, the Movie, and Other Episodes in Political Demonology*. Berkeley: University of California Press, 1987.

Ross, Andrew, ed. *Universal Abandon? The Politics of Postmodernism*. Minneapolis: University of Minnesota Press, 1988.

Roth, Roland. "Fordism and the New Social Movements." In Mayer, ed., *New Social Movements in Western Europe and the United States*, 1989.

Rothschild, Jane. *Machina ex Dea: Feminist Perspectives on Technology*. New York: Pergamon, 1983.

Roush, Paul E. "Combat Exclusion: Military Necessity or Another Name for Bigotry." *Minerva: Quarterly Report on Women and the Military* 8, no. 3 (fall 1990): 1–15.

Rowbotham, Sheila. *Woman's Consciousness, Man's World*. Harmondsworth, England: Penguin, 1973.

Rowes, Barbara. *The Book of Quotes*. New York: Dutton, 1979.

Rubin, Gayle. "The Traffic in Women: Notes on the Political Economy of Sex." In Reiter, ed., *Toward an Anthropology of Women*, 1975.

Ruddick, Sara. "Maternal Thinking." *Feminist Studies* 6, no. 2 (summer 1980): 342–67.

Ruddick, Sara. "Drafting Women: Pieces of a Puzzle." College Park, MD: Center for Philosophy and Public Policy, University of Maryland, 1982.

———. "Pacifying the Forces: Drafting Women in the Interests of Peace." *Signs* 8, no. 3 (1983): 471–89.

———. "Women in the Military." Report from the Center for Philosophy and Public Policy, no. 4. College Park, MD, 1984.

Rupp, Leila J. *Mobilizing Women for War: German and American Propoganda, 1939–45.* Princeton, NJ: Princeton University Press, 1978.

Russell, Diana E. H., ed. *Exposing Nuclear Phallacies.* New York: Pergamon, 1989.

Rustin, Michael. "The Politics of Post-Fordism: Or, the Trouble with 'New Times.'" *New Left Review* 175 (May–June 1989): 54–77.

Salleh, Ariel K. "Epistemology and the Metaphors of Production: An Eco-feminist Reading of Critical Theory." *Studies in the Humanities* 15, no. 2 (December 1988): 130–39.

Santoli, Al. "When It's Tougher Here Than Over There: They're Fighting to Stay above the Poverty Line." *Parade Magazine, San Jose Mercury News,* March 28, 1995, 4–6.

Satchell, Michael. The New U.S. Military: Pride, Brains, and Brawn. *San Francisco Chronicle,* April 20, 1985, 2.

Sayers, Sohnya, et al., eds. *The Sixties, without Apology.* Minneapolis: University of Minnesota Press, 1984.

Schaar, John H. *Legitimacy in the Modern State.* New Brunswick, NJ: Transaction Books, 1981.

Schlafly, Phyllis. *Phyllis Schlafly Report 8.* Vol. 5 (December 1974).

———. *The Power of the Positive Woman.* New Rochelle, NY: Arlington House, 1977.

Schneider, Dorothy, and Carl Schneider. *Sound Off.* New York: Dutton, 1988.

Sciolino, Elaine. "Battle Lines Are Shifting on Women and War." *New York Times,* January 25, 1990, A1.

Scott, Joan W. "Gender: A Useful Category of Historical Analysis." In Weed, ed., *Coming to Terms,* 1989a.

———. "Commentary: Cyborgian Socialist?" In Weed, ed., *Coming to Terms,* 1989b.

Sedwick, Cathy, and Reba Williams. "Black Women and the ERA." *Black Scholar* 7 (July–August 1976): 24.

Segal, Mady Weschler, and David R. Segal. "Social Change and the Participation of Women in the American Military." *Research in Social Movements, Conflicts and Change* 5 (1983): 235–58.

Senate Committee on the Judiciary. *Equal Rights for Men and Women.* Senate Report no. 689, 92d Congress, 2d Session, 1972.

———, Subcommittee on Constitutional Amendments. 91st Congress, 2d session. Equal Rights Amendment Hearings. Senate Joint Resolution 61, 1970.

Senate Manpower and Personnel Subcommittee of the Senate Armed Services Committee. *Women and the Draft.* Senate Report 96–826. Washington, DC: U.S. Government Printing Office, 1980.

Sherman, Janann. "They Either Need These Women or They Do Not: Margaret Chase Smith and the Fight for Regular Status for Women in the Military." *Journal of Military History* 54, no. 1 (January 1990): 47–58.

Shields, Patricia M. "Women Pilots in Combat: Attitudes of Male and Female Pilots." *Minerva: Quarterly Report on Women and the Military* 8, no. 2 (summer 1990): 21–35.

Shilts, Randy. *Conduct Unbecoming: Gays and Lesbians in the U.S. Military.* New York: Fawcett Columbine, 1994.

Slavin, Sarah. "The Equal Rights Amendment." *Women and Politics* 2, nos. 1, 2 (1982): 30.

Smelser, Neil. *The Theory of Collective Behavior.* New York: Free Press, 1951.

Smith, Barbara, ed. *Home Girls: A Black Feminist Anthology.* New York: Kitchen Table, 1983.

Smith-Rosenberg, Carol. "The Body Politic." In Weed, ed., *Coming to Terms,* 1989.

Snitow, Ann. "A Gender Diary." In Harris and King, eds., *Rocking the Ship of State,* 1989.

Sofia, Zoë. "Exterminating Fetuses: Abortion, Disarmament and the Sexo-Semiotics of Extraterrestrialism." *Diacritics* 14, no. 2 (1984): 47–59.

Spivak, Gayatri Chakravorty. *In Other Worlds: Essays in Cultural Politics.* New York: Routledge, 1988.

Spretnak, Charlene, ed. *The Politics of Women's Spirituality.* New York: Anchor, 1982.

Stacey, Judith. "The New Conservative Feminism." *Feminist Studies* 9, no. 3 (fall 1983): 559–84.

Stallard, Karin, Barbara Ehrenreich, and Holly Sklar. *Poverty in the American Dream: Women and Children First.* Boston: South End, 1983.

Starhawk. *Spiral Dance.* San Francisco: Harper and Row, 1974.

———. *Dreaming the Dark.* San Francisco: Harper and Row, 1978.

———. *Truth or Dare: Encounters with Power, Authority and Mystery.* San Francisco: Harper and Row, 1990.

Stiehm, Judith. *Bring Me Men and Women: Mandated Change at the US Air Force Academy.* Berkeley: University of California Press, 1981.

——. "The Protected, the Protector, the Defender." *Women's Studies International Forum* 5, no. 3–4 (1982): 367–76.

——. *Arms and the Enlisted Woman.* Philadelphia: Temple University Press, 1989.

——. "Women and the Combat Exemption." *Parameters: Journal of the US Army War College* 10, no. 2 (n.d.).

——, ed. *Women and Men's Wars.* Oxford: Pergamon, 1982.

——, ed. *Women's Views of the Political World of Men.* Dobbs Ferry, NY: Transnational Publishers, 1984.

——, ed. *It's Our Military Too! Women and the U.S. Military.* Philadelphia: Temple University Press, 1996.

Stimpson, Catharine, ed. *Women and the Equal Rights Amendment: Senate Subcommittee Hearings on the Constitutional Amendment, 91st Congress.* New York: Bowker, 1972.

Stone, Anne. *Women in the Military: International Perspectives.* Washington, DC: Women's Research and Education Institute, 1994.

Sturdevant, Saundra Pollock, and Brenda Stoltzfus. *Let the Good Times Roll: Prostitution and the U.S. Military in Asia.* New York: New Press, 1992.

Sturgeon, Noël. "Positional Feminism, Ecofeminism, and Radical Feminism Revisited." *American Philosophical Newsletter of Feminism and Philosophy* 93, no. 1 (1989): 41–47.

——. "Direct Theory and Political Action: The Political Theory of the U.S. Nonviolent Direct Action Movement." Ph.D. diss., University of California, 1991.

——. "Theorizing Movements: Direct Action and Direct Theory." In Darnovsky et al., eds., *Cultural Politics and Social Movements,* 1995.

——. *Ecofeminist Natures.* New York: Routledge, 1997.

Summerfield, Penny. *Women Workers in the Second World War: Production and Patriarchy in Conflict.* London: Routledge, 1989.

Summers, Anne. "Pat Schroeder: Fighting for Military Moms." *Ms.* (May–June 1991): 90–92.

Swerdlow, Amy. *Women Strike for Peace.* Chicago: University of Chicago Press, 1993.

Takaki, Ronald. *A Different Mirror: A Multicultural History of America.* Boston: Back Bay Books, 1993.

Taub, Nadine, and Wendy Williams. "Will Equality Require More Than Assimilation . . ." *Rutgers Law Review* 37, no. 4 (summer 1985): 825–44.

Thompson, Janna. "Women and War." *Women's Studies International Forum* 14, no. 1–2 (1991): 63–75.

Thompson, Mark. "Critics See Disaster If Gays Join Military." *San Jose Mercury News,* December 10, 1992, C3.

———. "Lesbians Harder Hit by the Military's Ban: They Were Dismissed at a Higher Rate." *Philadelphia Inquirer,* February 14, 1993, A1.

Tiffany, Jennifer. "The Equal Opportunity Trap." In Chapkis, ed., *Loaded Questions,* 1981.

Tilly, Charles. *From Mobilization to Revolution.* Reading, MA: Addison Wesley, 1978.

———. "Models and Realities of Popular Collective Action." *Social Research* 52, 4 (winter 1985): 717–48.

Tinker, Irene, ed. *Women in Washington: Advocates for Public Policy.* Beverly Hills: Sage, 1983.

Touraine, Alain. *The Post-Industrial Society: Tomorrow's Social History: Classes, Conflicts and Culture in the Programmed Society.* New York: Random House, 1971.

———. *The Voice and the Eye: An Analysis of Social Movements.* Cambridge: Cambridge University Press, 1981.

———. "An Introduction to the Study of Social Movements." *Social Research* 52, no. 4 (1985) 749–88.

Treadwell, Mattie B. *The Women's Army Corp.* Washington, DC: U.S. Government Printing Office, 1954.

Trinh, T. Minh-ha. *Woman, Native, Other: Writing Postcoloniality and Feminism.* Bloomington: Indiana University Press, 1989.

Truman, President Harry S. "Executive Order 10240. April 27, 1951: Regulations Governing the Separation from the Service of Certain Women Serving in the Regular Army, Navy, Marine Corps, or Air Force." Washington, DC: U.S. Government Printing Office, 1951.

Tsing, Anna Lowenhaupt. *In the Realm of the Diamond Queen: Marginality in an Out of the Way Place.* Princeton, NJ: Princeton University Press, 1993.

Tucker, Scott. "Panic in the Pentagon: Will Queers Demoralize the Military?" *Z Magazine,* June 1993, 46–48.

Turner, R. H., and L. M. Killian. *Collective Behavior.* Englewood Cliffs, NJ: Prentice-Hall, 1957.

Tuten, Jeff. "The Argument against Female Combatants." In Goldman, ed., *Female Soldiers,* 1982.

United States Code, 1980. *Congressional and Administrative News.* 2612, 2649.

United States Government. "Military Manpower Recruiting and Enlistment Results for the Active Component—First Half of Fiscal Year 1990." Washington, DC: U.S. Government Printing Office, July 1990.

U.S. Department of Defense. *Going Strong! Women in Defense.* Washington, DC: U.S. Government Printing Office, 1984.

———. *Report: Task Force on Women in the Military.* Washington, DC: Defense Department, January 1988a.

———. *Military Women in the Department of Defense,* vol. 6, July 1988. Washington, DC: U.S. Government Printing Office, 1988b.

———. "Task Force Report on Women in the Military, 1989." Washington, DC: U.S. Government Printing Office, 1989.

———. Office of the Secretary of Defense. *Military Women in the Department of Defense.* Vol. 8, July 1990.

———. *Conduct of the Persian Gulf War: Final Report to Congress.* Title V Report, April 1992. Washington, DC: U.S. Government Printing Office, 1992.

———. Inspector General. *Tailhook 91: Part 2: Events at the 35th Annual Tailhook Symposium.* Washington, DC: U.S. Government Printing Office, February 1993.

———. "Distribution of Active Duty Forces by Service, Rank, Sex, and Ethnic Group." September 30, 1995. DMDC-3035.

U.S. National Commission on the Observance of International Women's Year. *The Spirit of Houston: The First National Women's Conference.* Report to the President, March 1978.

Useem, Michael. *Protest Movements in America.* Indianapolis: Bobbs Merrill, 1975.

Verduga, Naomi, and Frances C. Grafton. "An Overview of Hispanics in the Active Enlisted Army: 1980–86." Virginia: Manpower and Personnel Research Laboratory, U.S. Army Research Institute for the Behavioral and Social Sciences. July 1988, Army Project no. 2Q263731A792.

Viguerie, Richard A. *The New Right: We're Ready to Lead.* Falls Church, VA: Viguerie, 1981.

Walker, Richard. "Is There a Service Economy? The Changing Capitalist Division of Labor." *Science and Society* 49.1 (1985): 42–83.

Wallerstein, Immanuel Maurice. *The Modern World-System.* New York: Academic Press, 1974.

Ware, Cellestine. *Woman Power: The Movement for Women's Liberation.* New York: Tower Publications, 1970.

Warren, Karen. "The Power and Promise of Ecological Feminism." *Environmental Ethics* 12, no. 2 (summer 1990): 125–47.

———, ed. *Ecological Feminism.* Special issue: *Hypatia* 6, no. 1 (1991).

Weber, Wini S. *Lesbians in the Military Speak Out*. Northboro, MA: Madwoman Press, 1993.

Weed, Elizabeth, ed. *Coming to Terms: Feminism, Theory, Politics*. New York: Routledge, 1989.

Weinbaum, Batya. *The Curious Courtship of Women's Liberation and Socialism*. Boston: South End, 1978.

Weinstein, Laurie, and Christie C. White, eds. *Wives and Warriors: Women and the Military in the United States and Canada*. Westport, CT: Bergin & Garvey, 1997.

Weisskopf, Thomas. "The Current Economic Crisis in Historical Perspective." *Socialist Review* 9, no. 11 (May–June 1981): 9–53.

Wheelwright, Julie. *Amazons and Military Maids: Women Who Dressed as Men in Pursuit of Life, Liberty, and Happiness*. London: Pandora, 1989.

White, Hayden. "The Value of Narrativity in the Representation of Reality." *Critical Inquiry* 11, no. 1 (1980): 5–30.

———. *The Content of the Form: Narrative Discourse and Historical Representation*. Baltimore: Johns Hopkins University Press, 1987.

White, Sarah. *Report to the President*. Presidential Commission on Women in the Armed Forces, November 15, 1992, 121.

Williams, Patricia. "Alchemical Notes: Reconstructing Ideals from Deconstructed Rights." *Harvard Civil Rights–Civil Liberties Law Review* 22 (1987): 401–33.

Williams, Wendy. "The Equality Crisis: Some Reflections on Culture, Courts, and Feminism." *Women's Rights Law Reporter* 7 (1982): 175–90.

Willis, Ellen. "Radical Feminism and Feminist Radicalism." In Sayers et al., eds., *The Sixties, without Apology*, 1984.

———. "Sexual Politics." In Ian Angus and Sut Jhally, eds., *Cultural Politics in Contemporary America*. New York: Routledge, 1989.

Wilson, Heather. "Women in Combat." *National Interest* 32 (summer 1993): 75.

Wise, Nancy B., and Christy Wise. *A Mouthful of Rivets: Women and Work in World War II*. San Francisco: Jossey Bass, 1994.

Witherspoon, Ralph. "Female Soldiers in Combat." *Minerva Quarterly Report on Women and the Military* 6, no. 1 (spring 1988): 1–28.

Woman of Power. Special issue (spring 1988).

Women's Equity Action League. *Women and the Military*. Washington, DC: WEAL Education and Legal Defense Fund, 1980.

Women's Research and Education Institute. "Women in the Military: 1980–90." Pamphlet by Women's Research and Education Institute. Washington, DC, 1990.

Yarbrough, Jean. "The Feminist Mistake: Sexual Equality and the Decline of the American Military." *Policy Review* 33 (1985): 48–52.

Young, Iris Marion. *Justice and the Politics of Difference*. Princeton, NJ: Princeton University Press, 1990.

Young, Warren L. *Minorities in the Military: A Cross-National Study in World Perspective*. Westport, CT: Greenwood, 1982.

Yural-Davis, Nira. "Front and Rear: The Sexual Division of Labor in the Israeli Army." In Chapkis, ed., *Loaded Questions,* 1981.

Zaretsky, Eli. *Capitalism, the Family, and Personal Life*. New York: Harper and Row, 1976.

Zimmerman, Jean. *Tailspin: Women at War in the Wake of Tailhook*. New York: Doubleday, 1995.

Zumwaldt, Admiral Elmo. *Z-Gram 116*. Internal memo, Navy, August 7, 1972.

INDEX

Jones, Kathleen, on approach of NOW to women in military, 139
Jordan, Harold, and Cynthia Enloe, on racial demonstrations at Fort McLellan, Alabama, 99

Karst, Kenneth: lesbians in military, 230n. 44; masculinist citizenship, 229n. 22
Katzenstein, Mary Fainsod, 33, 40
Kennedy-Roth amendment, repeals restrictions on women flyers, 171
Kerber, Linda, 88
King, Ynestra, 21, 216n. 22
Kirk, Gwyn, and Margo Okazawa-Rey: "East Asia-U.S. Women's Network against U.S. Militarism," 26
Kitchen Table Press, 21
Klare, Michael, and Vietnam Syndrome, 103

Labor laws, child labor and protection, 113
Laclau, Ernesto, and Chantel Mouffe, and chain of equivalence, 62
Lesbian and gay: base culture, 95; discharge rates following Persian Gulf War, 165–66; and "don't ask, don't tell" policy, 106; and Sam Nunn, 195; Service Members Legal Defense Network, 212. *See also* Karst, Kenneth; Shilts, Randy
Lesbians: and discharge rates for homosexuality, 165; "don't ask, don't tell," 38; Kenneth Karst, 230n. 44; military witch hunts, 100; sexual orientation in women's forces, 39, 100; as soldiers, 143, 165
Liberal: feminists, 137, 205; patriarchal state, 46; republicanism, 90
Lockheed Corporation, 15, 23, 64–65
Lorde, Audre, 44
Low Intensity Conflicts (LIC), 103

Male citizens refuse draft, 50. See also *Rostker v. Goldberg* (1981)
Mandel, Ernest, and late capitalism, 58
Mansbridge, Jane, 31
Marine Corps: and discharge from service, 121; women Marines, 97
Martial citizenship, 10, 38, 88; and conscientious objectors, 199; and feminist antimilitarists, 199; martial service, 42;

martial valor, masculine martial citizen, 88, 93; ungendered, 154; and women, 199
Masculine martial citizenship and Presidential Commission Report, 182; masculinist culture and NOW, 101; and non-masculine soldiers, 184
Masculinism of state, 63
Masculinity, racialized, 21
Maternal thinking, 22, 24. *See also* Ruddick, Sara
McAdam, Doug, 76
Melucci, Alberto, 79
Mestiza, border consciousness, 20
Mexico, 70
Militarism: and citizenship, 137; as cultural hegemony, 45; and feminist critiques of, 139–40; as gendered, 45; and prerogative governmental power, 45. *See also* Feminist antimilitarism; Feminist egalitarian militarism; Masculine martial citizenship
Military: and adultery laws, 215n. 12; and democracy, 207; downsizing of ranks, 51; and first-class citizenship, 92; and gendered, 91–93; intervention, 84; masculinist institution, 19; as profession, 72; and racialized citizenship, 89; recruiters, 73; as social institution, 45 and women's citizenship, 89. *See also* Feminist Antimilitarism; Militarism; Military Occupational Specialties
Military academies, 72; women admitted, 50
Military bases, 95; and downsizing, 51; and poverty, 196–97
Military Occupational Specialties (MOSs), 1, 36
MINERVA listserv, 96. *See also* H-MINERVA
Mink, Gwendolyn, 61, 88, 228nn. 3, 6, 9. *See also* Citizen-mothers
Misogyny, and marching cadences, 123
Moore, Brenda, 99, 105; and effects of personnel cutbacks on African American women, 157; and racial inequity, 200
Moral Majority, 116
Morden, Bettie J., 37, 99
Moskos, Charles, 33
Mothering, symbolic importance of, 20–21, 29

ABOUT THE AUTHOR

Ilene Rose Feinman teaches U.S. politics, women's studies, and multicultural studies at the converted Fort Ord Army base, California State University, Monterey Bay. Feinman has been a feminist and peace activist/organizer in the Santa Cruz community for many years. In 1997, she received her Ph.D. in the History of Consciousness Board at the University of California, Santa Cruz. Feinman has also written on feminist antimilitarists and feminist soldiers for *The Women and War Reader* (also published by New York University Press).